PRAISE FOR
THE PRINCE OF LOS COCUYOS

"*The Prince of los Cocuyos* had me laughing time and again with its warm, sweetly self-deprecating portrait of an immigrant family attempting to straddle Cuban traditions and American trends."

—Andrew Solomon, author of *Far from the Tree*

"Walking into Blanco's memoir is as familiar as walking into my own home. Who knew it would be so familiar? Are we related? Do we have the same crazy relatives? Maybe the lives of all artists are like this, and just maybe when we recognize our colleagues as ourselves, we have come home, finally, to our spiritual family. Thank you, Richard, for this revelation and homecoming."

—Sandra Cisneros, author of *The House on Mango Street*

"Richard Blanco takes us on a thought-provoking, often hilarious ride in . . . his coming-of-age memoir. The Cuban and Spanish intellectual, who was the first Latino, openly gay man and immigrant to be commissioned a presidential inaugural poet, illustrates the story of his childhood in the 1970s." —*Latina* magazine

"A warm, emotionally intimate memoir." —*Kirkus Reviews*

"In Richard Blanco's Miami, memories linger outside coffee windows and in Cuban grocery store aisles. . . . In a series of loosely intertwined stories, Blanco describes a childhood marked by loss, humor and hints of an exotic land called America."

—Associated Press

"Blanco has a natural, unforced style that allows his characters' vibrancy and humor to shine through."

—*Publishers Weekly* (starred review)

"A work that is incredibly poignant at one moment, yet hysterically funny with the turn of the page." —Huffington Post

"Filled with colorful characters, often poignant and sometimes melancholy, Blanco's episodic memoir is a meditation on belonging, on self-acceptance, and on his family's almost mystical connection to Cuba."   —*Booklist*

"Blanco's touching reminiscence has a deep emotional truth. . . . [An] alternately hilarious and moving new memoir."   —*Bookpage*

"This memoir is an exceptional introduction to the writer and his capabilities. *The Prince of los Cocuyos* embodies the best of his poetic style, in particular his eye for detail and ability to put the reader right in the place where he is."   —*Orlando Weekly*

"[A] sensual new memoir. . . . Blanco's ear for poetry comes to light in the memoir's full-bodied language and knack for description . . . [evoking] the flavors, fabrics and smells of rundown South Beach hotels, all-night pig roasts, disco-era Quinces debuts."
                                        —*Atlanta Journal-Constitution*

"Funny and poignant, Richard Blanco's *The Prince of los Cocuyos* follows the author and his Cuban-American family in Miami. The details of this very American, yet immigrant experience make all the difference."   —*Los Angeles Campus Circle*

"Like many a great bildungsroman, *The Prince of los Cocuyos* . . . portrays a character who feels torn between several different worlds . . . His search for identity, belonging, and home is one that any reader, regardless of sexual orientation or ancestry, can identify with."
                                                        —*The Advocate*

"His eloquent and poetic writing has the ability to induce laughter, tears, and anger, sometimes on the same page. . . . Highly recommended, Richard Blanco's coming-of-age story is told with humor and humility and is a pleasure to read."   —Edge Media Network

"I adored every minute spent with young 'Riqui' and his endearing extended family. And at the end—an ending so beautiful and throat-catching—I felt wonderfully drenched in love."
                          —Monica Wood, author of *When We Were the Kennedys*

Dear Member of the Class of 2021,

Each year, a group of students, faculty, and staff selects a book for you, our newest students, to read for your first shared Duke intellectual experience. I am very pleased with their choice of Richard Blanco's memoir, "The Prince of Los Cocuyos: A Miami Childhood." As the nation's youngest Presidential Inaugural Poet, as well as the first Latinx and openly gay person to hold that position, Mr. Blanco writes both humorously and poignantly of growing up in an exiled Cuban family that moved to the United States in 1968. This selection provides timely insight into the experiences of an immigrant and first-generation college student who is navigating a series of life transitions, while simultaneously balancing their own identity and family influences. As such, the book also provides a window for reflecting on the creation of our own narratives. As a signature highlight of our summer reading program, Mr. Blanco will visit Duke to speak with you during orientation week, so come ready to ask questions.

Until then, enjoy your summer!

Steve Nowicki
Dean and Vice Provost for Undergraduate Education
Bass Fellow and Professor of Biology, Psychology, and Neurobiology

DUKE UNIVERSITY HONOR COUNCIL

CLASS OF 2021 SUMMER ESSAY CONTEST

Essay Prompt:

In The Prince of Los Cocuyos, Richard Blanco struggles to define his personal identity and reconcile conflicting cultural norms and expectations. In diverse settings—whether on Miami's beaches or here at Duke—how should individuals respond to community-imposed pressures to conform? Essays should be between 500-700 words, and may draw upon the book, historical examples, or personal experiences.

Details:

• **Deadline:** Sunday, August 13, at 11:59PM

• **Submission:** Please send entries to honorcouncilduke@gmail.com

• **Recognition:** Winners will receive a $500 cash prize, will be recognized during O-Week, be featured on the Honor Council website, and have their essay published in The Chronicle

Also by Richard Blanco

ecco

An Imprint of HarperCollins*Publishers*

The Prince of LOS COCUYOS

A Miami Childhood

RICHARD BLANCO

HarperCollins books may be purchased for educational, business, or sales promotional use. For information please e-mail the Special Markets Department at SPsales@harpercollins.com.

A hardcover edition of this book was published in 2014 by Ecco, an imprint of HarperCollins Publishers.

FIRST ECCO PAPERBACK EDITION PUBLISHED 2015.

Designed by Janet M. Evans

Library of Congress Cataloging-in-Publication Data has been applied for.

ISBN 978-0-06-279148-1

17 18 19 20 LSC/C 10 9 8 7 6 5 4 3 2 1

For Carlos "Caco" Blanco, El Guayo:
my confidant, babysitter, cohort,
superhero, ally, friend, and brother,
who has been and will be with me always

You need a village, if only for the pleasure of leaving it. Your own village means that you're not alone, that you know there's something of you in the people and the plants and the soil, that even when you are not there it waits to welcome you.

—CESARE PAVESE

CONTENTS

ACKNOWLEDGMENTS

*T*he act of becoming is one of two fundamental human acts, the other being loving. And we can't love without becoming, or become without loving. I have loved and I have become thanks to *mi familia*. My mother, Geysa, the woman with the prettiest name and one of the saddest and most beautiful stories in the world. My father, Carlos, who died before I could love him as much as I wanted to love him or thank him for naming me after Richard Nixon. My only brother, Carlos, a fixed star in my life who means more to me than I can express in these pages. My *abuelo*, Carlos (yes, all three of them were named Carlos!), who suffered through every one of my strikeouts at bat and yet kept cheering me on. And my *abuela*, Otmara: these pages have let me hate her, understand her, forgive her, and thank her for her failed attempts at "making me *un hombre*," which indirectly made me a writer. *Te quiero, Abuela.*

Beyond them, all my *tíos* and *tías*, especially Miriam, Toti, Emiliano, Magdalena, Olga, Armando, Pedro, and Elsa. Without them—their stories, their longing, and their memories—this book of my memories would not exist. My thanks also to all my *primos* and *primas*, especially Helen, Brenda, Mirita, Normi, Gilbert, and Bernie. I am who I am because you are who you are. And beyond them, my neighbors, *bodegueros*, teachers (especially Miss De Vos), buddies (Angel and Alex), girlfriends (especially Anabelle), and boyfriends (Darden, Michael, and Carlos). In other words: my entire village, *mi pueblo entero.*

Fast-forward to the days when I first desired to translate my experiences from poetry into prose and discover what my life would read like without line breaks. My thanks to Stuart Bernstein and Ruth Behar, who ushered me into the genre of memoir, and to Bill Clegg, who helped me think about these pages differently. I am indebted to Frank Cimler, who found a perfect home for this book at Ecco. And so, my thanks to Dan Halpern for believing in this story and agreeing to publish it.

Fast, fast-forward to the days of shaping my raw words into this book with my editor Libby Edelson at Ecco. We began to finish each other's sentences; she understood this book better than me, and at times, she understood me better than I understood myself. It was a literary love affair, still going strong. And later, Hilary Redmon, also at Ecco, who shed more light on these pages. In the final round, Leonard Nash, who scrutinized this book with an incredibly keen eye and tied up many loose ends that made a huge difference.

And there were others, as always, who helped me write and believe, believe and write. Among these, Alison Granucci, my literary fairy godmother, who continues to be a guiding light; Felicitas Thorne, who gave me much-needed time and space to finish part of this book; and, of course, my husband, Mark, who inspires me every day—not just to write, but to live and love.

AUTHOR'S NOTE

My childhood continues to amaze me as a constant reference point for who I've been, who I am, and who I will be. It feels concrete and accessible but, on some level, also elusive and fractured. As such, these pages are emotionally true, though not necessarily or entirely factual. Certainly, I've compressed events; changed the names of people, places, and things; and imagined dialogue. At times I have collaged two (or three) people into one, embroidered memories, or borrowed them. I've bent time and space in the way that the art of memory demands. My poet's soul believes that the emotional truth of these pages trumps everything. Read as you would read my poems, trusting that what is here is real, beyond what is real—that truer truth which we come to call a life.

THE PRINCE *of*
LOS COCUYOS ¬

ONE

THE FIRST REAL SAN GIVING DAY

*A*ccording to my *abuela*, once the revolution took hold in the midsixties, "*No había nada.* Castro rationed everything. Two eggs a week, *una libra* of rice every month, and two cups of *frijoles negros*, if there were any. There wasn't even any *azúcar*. Imagine Cuba without sugar!" she'd complain in her crackly voice. "*Gracias a Dios*, your *abuelo* worked at the sugar mill in Hormiguero." Every week, Abuela made sure he took home double or triple his sugar quota. With the extra pounds, she cooked up vats of *dulce de leche* and guava marmalade. She also traded with the town baker—a few cups of sugar for a few stale loaves she'd use to bake her homemade *pudín de pan*. She sold her confections on the black market, and in two years made enough money to buy visas and plane tickets to get the whole family out of Cuba.

A few months after we arrived in New York City, Abuela started her own business, sort of. Once a week she took the bus downtown to the discount stores and bought girdles, scented soaps, cigarette lighters, chocolate-covered cherries, alarm clocks, gold-plated earrings—anything of "quality" that she could mark up and resell door-to-door to the *puertoriqueñas* in our apartment building. "Those *muchachas* buy any *mierda* you bring to their door. They're too lazy to find the good prices," she would say. Abuela also worked at a purse factory, sewing the linings of the bags. Far shy of five feet tall and stocky, she wasn't exactly a bombshell, but that didn't stop her from using her broken English to sweet-talk her *americano* foreman into letting her buy the scuffed-up purses wholesale. She would then cover up the scratches with her eyebrow pencil and sell them at full price, good as new.

When we moved to Miami, Abuela became a bookie for *La bolita,* an illegal numbers racket run by Cuban *mafiosos.* She took bets all day long, recording them on a yellow legal pad and calling them in every night to Joaquín, the big boss. She also sold Puerto Rican lotto tickets, which she marked up twenty cents. Every month Graciela, her contact in San Juan, would send a stack of tickets; in exchange, Abuela split the profits with her: 25 percent for Graciela, 75 percent for herself. On Saturday nights, I'd help Abuela with her bookkeeping for the week. We'd set up at the kitchen table, her disproportionately large bust jutting out and over the tabletop and her short legs that didn't reach the floor swinging back and forth underneath the chair. "Make sure all the *pesos* are facing up—and all the same way," she instructed every time we'd begin sorting the various denominations into neat stacks.

As we handled the bills I tried teaching her about the father of our country, the Gettysburg Address, the Civil War, and the other bits of American history I was learning in school. *Who's this? What did he do?* I'd quiz her, pointing at the portrait of Jackson, his wavy hairdo and bushy eyebrows, on a twenty; or at Lincoln's narrow nose and deep-set eyes on a five. But it was useless: "*Ay, mi'jo,* they're all *americanos feos.* I don't care who they are, only what they can buy," she'd quip, thumbing through the bills, her fingernails always self-manicured but never painted. Without losing count, she'd quiz me on *la charada*—a traditional system of numbers paired with symbols used for divination and placing bets. She'd call out a number at random, and I'd answer with the corresponding symbol she had me memorize: *número 36—bodega; número 8—tigre; número 46—chino* (which I always forgot); *número 17—luna* (my favorite one)*; número 93—revolución,* the reason why I was born in *número 44—España* instead of in *número 92—Cuba.* Everything in the world seemed to have a number, even me: *número 13—niño.*

In a composition book with penciled-in rows and columns, she'd tally her profits, down to the nickels and dimes I helped her wrap into paper rolls. Sometimes—if I begged long enough—she let me keep the leftover coins that weren't enough to complete a new roll. It seemed like a fortune to me at age nine, enough to buy all the Bazooka bubble gum I wanted from the ice cream man once a week; even enough to buy TV time from my older brother, Caco, so I could watch old TV shows like *The Brady Bunch* instead of football. But every now and then I'd go broke paying him not to squeal on me, like the time he caught me coloring my fingernails with crayons. Eventually I'd earn the money back by making him sandwiches, cleaning up his side of our room, or getting paid off for not telling on him, like the time I found cuss words scribbled all over his history textbook—in ink! Still, it wasn't much money for him; he constantly bragged that he made more on a Saturday mowing lawns than I did in a whole month "playing around" with Abuela. He didn't need any of her "stupid" money, he claimed.

Once Abuela and I were done with our accounting, I followed her through the house as she stashed the money in her *guaquitas,* her code name for the hiding places she shared with only me. Ones, fives, and tens went into a manila envelope taped behind the toilet tank; twenties and fifties underneath a corner of the wall-to-wall carpeting in her bedroom. The coin rolls we hid in the pantry, buried in empty canisters of sugar and coffee. "In Cuba I had to hide my *pesos* from *la milicia*—those *hijos de puta*! That's when I started making *guaquitas*. I even had to hide my underwear from them," she'd claim. The pennies she tossed into an empty margarine tub she kept at the foot of her blessed San Lázaro statuette in her bedroom. Every Sunday morning she emptied the tub into a paper bag, and dropped the pennies into the poor box at St. Brendan's before mass. "You have to give a little to get a little, that's how it works, *mi'jo*," she'd profess, making the sign of the cross.

But somehow Abuela always seemed to get a whole lot more than she gave. She was just *dichosa*—lucky, she alleged, though she helped her luck along most of the time. When my parents had wanted to move from New York City down to Miami, she "gave" them ten thousand dollars for a down payment on a new house with a terracotta roof and a lush lawn. The same house where we now lived, located in a Miami suburb named Westchester, pronounced *Güecheste* by the working-class exiles like us who had begun to settle there once they got on their feet. Abuela had also agreed she'd take care of my brother and me while my father and mother worked full-time at my *tío* Pipo's bodega, named El Cocuyito—*The Little Firefly*. All Abuela wanted in exchange was for her and my *abuelo* to live with us rent-free—for life! My parents had agreed to the deal, and Abuela was sure to remind her daughter-in-law every time they got into a squabble over money matters: "*Gracias* to me and San Lázaro we have this *casita* and we don't live frozen in that horrible *Nueva York* anymore."

AFTER HAVING LIVED WITH ABUELA'S JABS FOR SEVERAL
years, Mamá grew tired of them and demanded that Abuela do most
of the cooking and pay for all the groceries every week. Abuela refused, pointing out all she had done—and was doing—for the family
already. Papá eventually had to intervene and negotiate between his
mother and his wife, until Abuela compromised, agreeing to help pay
for *some* of the groceries. After that, she became more frugal than
ever, complaining that her only income was her cut as a bookie and
Abuelo's measly retirement check from the few years he had worked
in New York City.

Every day, after she and Abuelo picked me up from school, she'd
chase after specials on name brands and daily staples at one of three
Cuban bodegas she frequented. Abuelo would pull his lawn chair
from the trunk and camp under a palm tree in the bodega parking lot,
smoking a cigar and reading a Spanish translation of a dime-store
Western in the shade while he waited. Abuela would tuck her beaded
coin purse in her brassiere—a tip she had picked up from the New
York *puertoriqueñas* who had taught her how to guard her cash against
would-be muggers. She'd march into the store du jour, bouncing in
her crepe-soled orthopedic shoes, with me in tow.

Some days we went to La Sorpresita—*The Little Surprise*—the
smallest of the three bodegas, with only one cash register and four
narrow aisles. The linoleum tiles were dingy, the metal shelves
were streaked with rusty scratches, and the store reeked of grease
from the *chicharrones* frying in the back room. But that didn't keep
Abuela away from the specials on Café Bustelo and El Cochinito-
brand lard that La Sorpresita ran every week. She was also friends
with Juanito the butcher, whose ghostly white face glowed pink

5

under the fluorescent lights. He was a cousin of Abuela's former neighbor Carmela, who was still in Cuba and with whom Abuela continued to correspond. Abuela would update Juanito on Carmela's latest news about the terrible *"situación"* in Cuba, speaking in whispers as if she were still back on the island being watched by the neighborhood defense committees. The conversation always ended with Juanito asking, *"Hasta cuándo*—until when?" and Abuela asking Juanito for a few cents off her *palomilla* steak or pork *pernil*. "See how we *cubanos* help each other—that's our way," she would say to me, following it with a variation on her motto: "We give a little, we get a little."

Some days we went to El Gallo de Oro—*The Golden Cock*— where the Cuban bread was ten cents cheaper than anyplace else, because it was made right in the store. The scent of loaves baking in the back-room ovens permeated the shop, mixing with the aroma of the Cuban coffee they brewed in their in-house *cafetería*. While chatting over shots of *café* (which she often "forgot" to pay for), Abuela became friendly with the owner's wife, Xiomara. They talked about the usual things: children, the terrible humidity, their hairdos, and how much longer *la Revolución* would last. Xiomara mostly listened and nodded her head while Abuela blabbered. *"Qué boba*—what a dummy she is," Abuela told me the day Xiomara agreed to let her buy day-old *pastelito* pastries for twenty cents. *"Ahora* I sell these for forty cents." Abuela started taking more and more advantage of her "friendship" with Xiomara—riffling through the shelves for dented canned goods, then asking for a discount, which Xiomara always gave her; same with the crushed boxes of laundry detergent, and eggs near their expiration date. But when Abuela showed up at the register asking for twenty-five cents off a bruised avocado, Xiomara had had enough. She squeezed the overripe avocado in her fist until it burst open and then threw it in the bag. "There's your discount, *tacaña*—you cheapskate," she said sternly, wiping her hand as she rang up the rest of Abuela's groceries. "Anything else?"

After the incident with Xiomara, we went mostly to La Caridad, named after the patroness of Cuba, Our Lady of Charity. The neon virgin with a flashing halo above the canopy was so lifelike that Abuela would insist I make the sign of the cross with her before going inside. It was the biggest of the three bodegas; they had shopping carts (not just baskets) and brand-new cash registers. At the end of each of the seven aisles there was always a pyramid of something or other tagged with ESPECIAL placards neatly written out in red Magic Marker. La Caridad was Abuela's favorite store, even though she believed all the cashiers were crooked. She'd check her change and receipt every time before leaving the register. The only cashier Abuela trusted was Consuelo, who had been consistently honest. But one day Consuelo charged Abuela $9.90 instead of $0.99 for a bag of plantain chips. Abuela caught the mistake; she made Consuelo void the entire purchase, start all over again, and call out the price on each item as she rang it up. "A crook—like the rest of them, *una sin-vergüenza*," Abuela told me, within earshot of Consuelo, as we grabbed our bags and headed toward the door.

Every once in a while we went to El Cocuyito, but mostly just to visit. Abuela always complained that *tío* Pipo, her own son, never gave her a big enough discount. But somehow she always managed to come away with a free handful of bruised mangos or a few loaves of day-old Cuban bread. I didn't care which bodega we shopped at; they all stocked the same Cuban food I ate every day: guava marmalade, chorizos, canned black beans, frozen tamales. They didn't carry many of the American foods like Pop-Tarts, Ritz Crackers, and Cool Whip, which I got to eat with Jimmy Dawson—one of only a handful of gringos in my class—whenever I went over to his house. You could only get those treats at the gigantic Winn-Dixie on Coral Way, right in the center of Güecheste, where a still plentiful but shrinking number of *americanos* shopped.

Every week I'd beg Abuela to go to the Winn-Dixie instead, but she refused to set foot in the place. "There's none of *our* food at *el Winn Deezee*. Only *los americanos* shop there," Abuela sneered. "It's too expensive anyway," she'd complain, dismissing my pleas, until the day she spotted a Winn-Dixie circular in the mail advertising a special too tempting for Abuela to ignore: a whole roasted chicken, its drumsticks crowned with fancy paper hats, and a banner beneath trumpeting its not-so-fancy price: *Whole Fryers 29¢ per lb.*

"What does *Whole Fryer* mean?" Abuela asked me. "*Pollo entero,*" I translated. "*¿De verdad?*" she said incredulously, "At La Caridad I pay thirty-four *centavos*—on *especial*." I played on her piqued curiosity, "*Sí, sí*, Abuela. It's a great price for chicken. *¡Increíble!* You could sure save a lot of money." She agreed, "Yes, good *precio*," and left the circular on the kitchen counter instead of tossing it out with the rest of the junk mail that came in English.

Few things intimidated Abuela; among these were black magic Santería and *americanos*. As for Santería, she once discovered *tía* Irma kept an Eleguá deity with snail shells for eyes behind her bathroom door. We never set foot in her house again. "She's not your real *tía*, anyway," she said. As for *americanos*, Abuela wouldn't go anywhere she perceived to be wholly American, at least not alone. This included the Social Security office downtown, any restaurant with English-only menus (even Kim's Chinese Palace on Ninety-seventh Avenue), fancy department stores like Burdines, and most definitely Winn-Dixie. But she also couldn't resist a bargain. "*Mira* how cheap *los pollos*," she told Mamá when she came

8

home from work that day. "Why don't we go to *el Winn Deezee?*" she asked, fishing for a partner. Mamá responded unenthusiastically: *"Bueno,* you go *si tú quieres.* You're doing all the groceries." What did Mamá care where our food came from or how much it cost, as long as there was enough to eat?

Dejected, Abuela tossed the Winn-Dixie flyer in the trash. But the following week the chicken appeared in the mail at twenty-six cents per pound, three cents cheaper than the week before; and then twenty-four cents the week after that. The fryers haunted Abuela. Her stinginess slowly overcame her fear of *americanos* until finally, she broke. *"Mi'jo,* will you go with me shopping *en el Winn Deezee mañana?"* she half asked, half commanded. "Of course, Abuela. *No te preocupes.* I'll go with you." It was the first time Abuela had ever needed me. Or rather, the first time we needed each other. She wouldn't dare go to Winn-Dixie without me. *Give a little, get a little,* I thought. Soon our pantry would be stocked with Crunch Berries cereal and Oreo cookies; our freezer stuffed with Swanson TV Dinners and Eskimo Pies; our fridge filled with Hawaiian Punch and American cheese.

The next day after school Abuela instructed Abuelo to drive to *el Winn Deezee* instead of La Caridad. *"¿Estás loca?* You're going there?" he asked, surprised. Abuela hesitated, so I answered for her, "We're going to buy *pollos*—they're really cheap." I didn't want Abuela to lose her nerve. *"Bueno,* I'll stay out here," Abuelo said, turning into the parking lot. A gigantic red neon sign marked its entrance, the letters spelling out WINN-DIXIE THE BEEF PEOPLE seeming to glow even in daylight. "What does *The Beef People* mean?" Abuela questioned me. I struggled for a translation that would make sense, but none did. *"La Gente de Carne,"* I finally offered. *"¿Cómo?* How can that be?" Abuela said, perplexed by the thought of *people made of meat*, which is what my literal translation meant in Spanish. "Why not *The Chicken People?* Or *The* Carne Puerco *People?*" she amused herself.

Abuela tore the advertisement for the fryer from the flyer and stuffed it into her coin purse, which she then stuffed in her bra, and kissed Abuelo good-bye as if she might not return. "*Dios nos ampare*—God be with us," she muttered. She said nothing until we reached the store entrance: "Now take me straight to *los pollos* and no talking to no one. We don't belong here." The electric doors yawned open. I reached for a shopping cart, twice as big as the ones at La Caridad, but Abuela tugged me back, saying *Don't you dare* with her wide-open eyes, too anxious to speak. I could barely speak myself, not from fear but from pure awe. I was finally in Winn-Dixie. The air-conditioned air smelled as crisp and clean as Lysol; each of the ten checkout lines was numbered with an illuminated sign, and the cashiers all wore polyester uniforms. Instead of warped squares of linoleum, polished terrazzo floors gleamed, and soft violin music rained from the speakers in the ceiling. I was finally in America.

Suddenly Abuela froze: "*¿Qué pasó?* What's that?" she whispered, startled by a price check announced over the PA system. "*Nada*, Abuela, *nada*," I assured her as we stepped into the produce section. It was full of fruits and vegetables I had never eaten or even heard of: *Brussels sprouts, squash, tangelos, apricots*—I kept pronouncing them in my mind, trying to imagine the taste from the sound of their names. Pretending I was looking for the chicken, I deliberately wove us through every aisle, taking it all in: the cartoon faces on the cereal boxes I'd seen only on TV—Toucan Sam, Cap'n Crunch, the Lucky Charms leprechaun; the frost like snow on the freezer cases; flavors of Jell-O I never knew existed: raspberry, black cherry, lime. Soup made from cheddar cheese? From potatoes? Broccoli? I wanted to buy and taste everything I saw.

But of all the things I had tried at Jimmy Dawson's house, my absolute favorite was Easy Cheese: we'd squirt cheese smiley faces, cheese stars, and cheese rainbows onto Ritz Crackers. And there, in the snack aisle, I saw it. "Can you buy me this, Abuela?" I asked, grabbing a can off the shelf. "What's that?" she asked. "It's *queso*, Abuela. *Queso americano.* Please, it's my favorite," I begged. "What? *¿Queso en una lata?*" she questioned, unable to fathom the idea of cheese in a can. But I could tell from the tone of her voice that she was intrigued. "Look," I said, spraying a dab on my finger and licking it off, "you don't even have to put it in the 'fridgerator."

She looked at me, at my finger, at the can, at my finger, at the can, and then back at me. "*Qué cosa. Cómo inventan los americanos,*" she marveled at the ingenuity of Americans. "Let me taste," she asked, holding out her index finger. "*Ay, qué rico . . .*" She paused and then questioned, "*Pero* how much it is?," taking the can from my hand to look at the price. "*Un peso* thirty-five! *Bueno,* okay, but only if you promise to eat it all. I don't want to be wasting food. But let's get a fresh one, *mi'jo,*" she said, putting the can back on the shelf and taking a new one.

Out of her element, Abuela had become strangely vulnerable, hardly putting up an argument like she usually did whenever I asked her to buy me something. Things were going even better than I'd hoped, but I didn't want to press my luck. The Ritz Crackers would have to wait until the next trip to Winn-Dixie. "*Bueno, vamos.* Where are *los pollos*? Take me there now, *ándale,*" Abuela ordered. In the back of the supermarket we found the refrigerated cases, a wall of meats with names that sounded like the nicknames of outlaw cowboys: *Ground Chuck, Rib Eye, Flank Steak.* As we walked the aisle, white-gloved hands seemed to magically appear from behind the sliding mirrored doors at the backs of the cases. The hands placed packages of meat already wrapped, priced, and labeled—clean and neat, unlike at La Sorpresita, where Juanito cut slabs of cow into steaks right in front of us, his blood-smeared apron like something from a horror movie.

"Al fin," Abuela declared with relief when we reached the chickens, each one resting on a Styrofoam tray and neatly wrapped in cellophane. Picking one up, Abuela praised its healthy-rosy skin and the size of its drumsticks, *"¡Qué lindo! En Cuba* we never had *pollos* this big." She checked the label, confirming the price was twenty-four cents per pound, and then rummaged through the chickens, inspecting each one with the same scrutiny she used to pick out fruit. Some were too big or too small; others too yellow or too pale; some too bony or too plump; others just right. "Okay, this one . . . this one . . . *y* these two . . . and . . . ," she said, handing me five chickens, then picking out another five she would carry. We made our way to the checkout, barely able to see over the fryers in our arms. "How they can sell *pollos* this cheap—I don't know. Next week we're coming to get more," she said, so delighted by the bargain that she began whistling "Guantanamera" as we stood at the checkout, forgetting she was surrounded by *americanos* and that we didn't belong in *el Winn Deezee.*

We plopped down the chickens and my Easy Cheese, not on a rubber conveyor belt but on a round, shiny steel turntable like some space-age contraption from *The Jetsons* that automatically spun the items around to the cashier. I'd never seen anything like it. The lady in front of us set down a plastic divider, separating her groceries from ours, and smiled politely. "How you doin'?" she asked. We nodded. *"Esa es americana, ¿verdad?"* Abuela asked me in a whisper, and I nodded, confirming that the lady was indeed American, after a quick glance at the freckles on her arms, her yellow hair, and her bright orange jumpsuit. The woman opened her carton of eggs and inspected each one. "You always gotta check 'em," she said, making small talk with us. But Abuela heard *chicken* instead of *check 'em*: "Yes, yes, always have chicken," she agreed, so enraptured that she dared speak her broken English to *la americana*, who looked at us uneasily and then scribbled out a check before darting away with her groceries. Maybe Abuela was right: *We don't belong here.*

The cashier was polite and American too, no doubt, judging from her name tag: *Beatrice,* not the Spanish *Beatriz.* "Good afternoon. How are you?" she asked. "Good. Good," Abuela replied buoyantly. After ringing up two chickens Beatrice paused, "I'm sorry, are you together?" she asked. "Yes," I answered. "Well, you can only take two chickens on special per customer. I'm sorry."

Knowing something had gone wrong, Abuela got panicky; she reached into her brassiere and pulled out the flyer from her coin purse. "Chicken. Chicken. Twenty-four cents. Chicken . . ." she began rambling before I had a chance to translate the matter. "Chicken. Chicken . . ." she continued, pointing at the photo of the fryer. Beatrice showed her the fine print that read *Limit 2 per customer.* But Abuela didn't care: "Chicken. Twenty-four cents for chicken. *Especial,*" she repeated, too frantic to understand what Beatrice was saying in English. "Abuela. Abuela—" I tried to interrupt, but she wouldn't listen.

Growing impatient, Beatrice reached for the public address mic and paged the manager: "Mr. Quigley to register five. Mr. Quigley, register five, please." By then everyone in line and at the adjacent registers was staring at us as if we were children throwing a tantrum in public. I was mortified. Finally becoming aware of the scene she was making, Abuela piped down and I was able to explain the situation. "*Qué cabrones. Qué barbaridad,*" she complained, looking sadly at the eight chickens left on the conveyor. "*Bueno,* okay. We take this one . . . and this one," she said. "What about this?" Beatrice asked, holding up the can of Easy Cheese. "Yes," I said. But Abuela barked, "I not buying nothing else here!" She paid with exact change when Mr. Quigley arrived. "Is okay. No *problema*. No *problema*." Abuela dismissed him and we whisked ourselves away with our two chickens. "*Esos americanos de mierda* and their rules, trying to trick me. This is worse than Cuba," she grumbled all the way back to the car, slamming the door. "*¿Qué pasó?*" Abuelo asked. "*Nada, nada.* Let's go to La Caridad. I'm never coming here again. *Pa' la mierda* with these Beefy People!" she shouted as Abuelo drove away.

Now what? I knew Abuela would never go back to Winn-Dixie after that fiasco. She was cheap, but she had her pride. We returned to our routine shopping at the bodegas: more plantains and chorizo; more yuca and black beans. No Easy Cheese. Abuela was as stubborn as she was cheap; however, she read the Winn-Dixie circulars every week, tracking the price of the chicken, trying to figure out how she could get her hands on more somehow. She asked my mother to go for her; our neighbor Teresa; our mechanic's wife, Loraine, who was half-Italian. But they all refused, claiming Winn-Dixie was no place for people like us. *How stupid* . . . I thought, . . . *so afraid of Americans.* Cubans were the weirdos in my eyes, always talking so loud and all at the same time at the bodegas in their sandals and housecoats.

If only I was old enough to drive, I thought, and then realized: "I can go to e*l Winn-Deezee* on my bike, Abuela. I'll buy the *pollos* for you. I don't mind," I said sheepishly. "Okay, I think about it. *Gracias, mi'jo*," she said and kissed me on the forehead. Abuela never agreed to anything without sleeping on it.

The next day, after we got home from school, she called me into her bedroom. "Okay, you go for me?" she asked, picking up the Winn-Dixie flyer on her dresser. *"Sí, sí,"* I replied, as if she had to ask. She pulled an envelope from her *guaquita* behind the dresser and gave me a five-dollar bill. *"Coje.* Get me *dos pollos;* make sure they charge you right—and don't lose the change," she instructed. *"Sí,* Abuela, *sí,"* I agreed, and then with angelic eyes I asked, "Should I get that *queso en lata* that we were going to buy last time?" *"Ay, sí, muy rico.* I remember," she said, recalling the taste before replying, "Okay, but only if you have enough money for *los pollos* first." Did I hear her right? Was Abuela actually craving Easy Cheese?

Still wearing my Catholic school tie and polyester trousers, I buried the five-dollar bill deep in my pocket so it wouldn't fall out and hopped on my bike. Abuela kissed me and sent me off on my mission. *"Apúrate.* Be careful!" she shouted, waving good-bye as I pedaled away. Winn-Dixie was about a ten-minute ride by car; I made it there in fifteen, pulled out a cart, and dashed straight to the snack aisle, anxious that somehow they had run out of Easy Cheese, but they hadn't. Relieved, I dropped a can in my cart and began strolling leisurely through the store, pretending I was as grown-up and American as everyone there. *This is the way the world should be—everything so quiet and neat,* I thought, watching a lady dressed in pearls and high heels gently pushing her cart like a baby carriage; *everything so clean and organized,* as I scanned the perfect rows of cans and bottles, each one pulled to the edge of the shelf, leaving no gaps; *so effortless and efficient,* as I browsed the clearly marked prices on every item and read the signs above the numbered aisles telling me where to find everything. This was the world I wanted to live in. This was America.

Chicken, chicken—the echo of Abuela's voice woke me out of my daydream and reminded me of my mission. I made my way to the whole fryers in the back aisle and checked the price—still twenty-four cents per pound. Doing the math in my head, I picked out a five-pounder and a six-pounder to be sure I'd have enough money for the Easy Cheese and still have some change left over. Abuela always liked to get change back, even if it was a few pennies for San Lázaro. Scanning the checkouts, I looked for Beatrice, wanting to be as far away as possible from her, afraid she would remember Abuela's scene. My new cashier's name was Emily. She double bagged the chickens without my asking and thanked me "for shopping at Winn-Dixie" as politely as a TV mom while handing me my change and receipt. I tucked both carefully in my pocket, knowing Abuela would insist on checking.

As I had to balance the chickens on my handlebars, it took twice as long to ride back home. Abuela was sitting on the front porch when I arrived. "*Ay, Dios,* I thought something happened," she cried, then took the bag from me and inspected the chickens. "Very good, but . . ." she began, and I handed her the change and receipt before she had a chance to finish asking me for them. She looked it over, checked the price on each item, and counted the change before we stepped inside. "*Bien,*" she approved, then thanked me, "*Gracias mi'jo.* Here, your *merienda* is ready." She had laid out a huge spread on the kitchen table for my after-school snack: Cuban crackers, *dulce de guayaba,* and chorizo, which I eagerly topped with Easy Cheese.

Not Ritz Crackers, but I had to make do. Abuela stood by, watching over me curiously. "Let me taste," she finally asked, and I handed her a sliver of guava paste topped with Easy Cheese. She took a nibble and savored it slowly, cautiously. Her eyes filled with surprised delight. *"Qué rico. Qué sabroso. Qué delicioso,"* she repeated after every bite until she finished. "Make me another one," she demanded.

And so it began: once or twice a week I'd bike to Winn-Dixie for Abuela and return with two chickens and a can of Easy Cheese. Just as I had wished, I became a regular. I knew my way around the store without having to read the signs above the aisles or ask a stock boy for directions. I began recognizing the ladies who seemed to always shop at the same time as me. I'd nod at them in passing down the aisle, saying hello with my eyes like any typical, well-behaved American housewife. I also had my regular cashier, Emily, at register 8 (sometimes 12); I'd check out with her no matter how long the line because she always smiled and asked me questions: how old I was, where I lived, why I always got chicken and Easy Cheese, and why I always came by myself. I told her my mother worked and my grandmother was sick and couldn't get out of bed—too embarrassed to tell Emily the truth about Abuela's fear of *americanos*.

I wondered if someday I would marry an exotic American girl like Emily, with her perfect English; her politeness; her blond hair in two long braids to her shoulders, clipped at the ends with barrettes, like the Swiss Miss character on the pudding cups. Would Abuela approve? Would she take a liking to her as easily as she did to Easy Cheese? "Don't forget *el queso en lata*," Abuela would remind me every time I'd hop on my bike to Winn-Dixie. For weeks we experimented with Easy Cheese. Abuela reveled in the taste of her new "recipes": Easy Cheese on fried plantains, Easy Cheese as topping for flan, Easy Cheese on tamales. But in my mind the combinations just didn't belong together—they were from two different worlds—and they tasted terrible! Still, it was better than no Easy Cheese at all, I decided, and played along. But I drew the line at Easy Cheese on my favorite dessert, *arroz con leche.*

One week I did manage to convince Abuela to let me buy a box of Ritz Crackers to have with *our* Easy Cheese, but she complained the combination was too mushy, too salty, and added a sprinkle of shredded coconut. "Don't buy any more of those," she ordered. That was it for the Ritz. But when she ran out of recipe ideas for Easy Cheese the week after the Ritz defeat, she asked me to buy something new. "Like what, Abuela?" I asked. "I don't know. What else have *los americanos* put in cans? Get whatever you want," she said, giving me carte blanche, but only two extra dollars from her *guaquita.* On the way to Winn-Dixie I ran through a mental list of all my favorites from Jimmy Dawson's house and decided I'd get instant mashed potatoes to replace the bland malanga roots that Abuela had to tediously boil and mash.

Back home, Abuela checked the receipt and counted the change as I explained my new find. "That's impossible. *¿Cómo puede ser?*" she questioned, amazed by the picture of the buttery, golden spuds on the box, "Cheese in a can and now *papas* in a box? *Cómo inventan los americanos.*" She insisted we try out the mashed potatoes that very night. I translated the instructions on the box aloud for her: two cups of *leche;* three-quarters of a cup of *agua, tres cucharadas* of butter. "*¡Increíble!*" she exclaimed as she added the flakes and watched the mixture turn into silky smooth potatoes right before her eyes. She took a taste and then added a pinch of salt, took another taste. "*Pero* it needs something—a little more *sabor*," she concluded, and then added a few dashes of Bijol, a Cuban condiment that flavored the potatoes with annatto and cumin and dyed the mash a bright yellow-orange, the color of a No. 2 pencil. Not exactly what I had in mind.

A few days later I showed up with Pop-Tarts. After hopelessly scanning the box for clues, Abuela asked me what they were. "*Tostada con* strawberries inside," I explained. "What are *estroberies*?" she asked. "*Fresas,*" I translated. "Oh, *pero* how do they get the *estroberies* inside?" she asked. "I don't know," I responded aloofly, hoping she would leave it at that, but she kept looking over my shoulder while I set two in the toaster. As soon as they popped up, she asked me for a taste. I gave her a tiny piece. "*Mm, qué rico. Cómo inventan los americanos.* You think they have these with *guayaba* instead of *estroberies, mi'jo*?" she asked. How ridiculous. I shrugged my shoulders, refusing to explain any further. But that wasn't the end of it. The next morning, instead of the usual Cuban toast, Abuela made Pop-Tarts for everyone. I never thought I'd see the day: Abuela and the entire family at breakfast dunking Pop-Tarts into their *café con leche*.

After two or three weeks, the family was getting bored of the chicken Abuela prepared almost every night for dinner: chicken and rice, chicken *milanesa, croquetas* made with chicken leftovers. "*Pollo* again! I'm going to start laying eggs!" Mamá complained at the dinner table one evening. "You're living here for free, and all you buy is chicken, chicken, chicken," she continued jabbing at her. Abuela could have returned to shopping at La Caridad, or La Sorpresita, or El Gallo de Oro, but I could tell she had taken a liking to the *americano* foods—and the bargain prices at Winn-Dixie. Regardless, she knew she had to change the dinner menu. "*Mi'jo,* get something besides *pollo* that I can make for dinner. Something different," she requested for my next Winn-Dixie run. *I'll get something really*

American, I thought as I roamed the aisles considering Hamburger Helper, Rice-A-Roni, Manwiches. I decided on a family-size box of Kraft Macaroni & Cheese.

"*¿Queso con macaroni? Qué cosa*—I never thought of that," Abuela marveled as she opened the box. "*Pero* where is the cheese?" she asked. "No, Abuela, you have to add milk and butter. This turns into cheese," I explained, showing her the foil packet with the cheese powder. "*¿Qué?* First cheese in a can and now cheese in a bag. *Cómo inventan los americanos,*" she said. "We'll make it tonight for dinner." She set a pot boiling with the macaroni as per the instructions I translated. "Now we need one cup of *leche* and four *cucharadas* of *mantequilla,*" I continued. But Abuela had something more Cuban in mind: she asked me to bring her a can of tomato sauce, an onion, two chorizo sausages, and a green bell pepper. "But, Abuela, that's not how you're supposed to make it. What are you doing?" I protested. "*Ay, deja eso, mi'jo.* Those *americanos* with all their rules. I've never followed a recipe all my life," she said proudly.

She minced and sautéed, added lard (instead of butter), then the cheese powder, a few sprinkles of garlic powder, half a teaspoon of Bijol, and violà—*Cubaroni*! That's what Abuela called it when Mamá questioned the concoction with disdain at the dinner table. "*¿Qué carajo* is this?" She took a tiny taste from the tip of her fork and savored it a few seconds before pronouncing, "It's much better than it looks. Good enough to eat." She was noticeably impressed, but as usual unwilling to praise Abuela for anything, especially her cooking. "At least it's not chicken, *gracias a Dios*. I was growing feathers already." Mamá laughed. But the mix of flavors didn't make sense to me. You had to be either Cuban or American; you couldn't be both, I thought, watching the family dig into the Cubaroni until it was all gone, along with my wish for something *really* American for dinner, just once.

I had almost given up when November came around and my teacher, Mrs. Echevarría, handed out some ditto sheets to color for Thanksgiving. The pilgrims' tall hats I colored black, the buckles on their shoes, gold; the Indians' faces I lightly colored red; the cornucopias of squash and pumpkins, all kinds of oranges and yellows; the huge turkey, an amber-brown (a turkey, not a pork roast like my family always had for Thanksgiving). As we colored, Mrs. Echevarría narrated the story of the first Thanksgiving, enthusiastically acting it out as if she had been there: " . . . Then the chief of the Indians told Pilgrim John, *We make big feast for you,* and Pilgrim John said, *Yes, let us give thanks for our new friends and for this new land where we are free.*" My teacher seemed to understand Thanksgiving like a true American, even though she was Cuban also. *Maybe,* I thought, *if I convince Abuela to have a real Thanksgiving, she and the whole family will finally understand too.*

With new resolve and colored dittos in hand, I approached Abuela that night as she sat at the kitchen table sorting through receipts and making a tally of her expenses. "Abuela, do you know what Thanksgiving is really all about—what it *really* means?" "*¿Qué?*" she said without looking up from her notebook. "Thanksgiving," I repeated. She looked up at me blankly, and I realized she couldn't understand "Thanksgiving" in my properly pronounced English. So I blurted it out the way most Cubans pronounced it, as if it were the name of a saint: "San Giving, Abuela, San Giving." "Oh, *el día de San Giving.* Yes, what?" she asked, and I began explaining: "It was because the Pilgrims and Indians became friends. The Pilgrims made a big dinner to celebrate and give thanks to God because they were in the land of the free and living in the United States." "What are *pilgreems*? And those black *sombreros*?" she asked, looking over my dittos, "We didn't wear those *en Cuba.*"

It seemed hopeless, but I insisted. "*Mira,* Abuela—*mira,*" I continued, pointing at the dittos again. "They had turkey on San Giving, not *carne puerco* and *plátanos.* We are *americanos* like them now in the United States. We have to eat like Americans, Abuela, or else they'll send you back to Cuba." "*Ay, mi'jo,*" she said with a laugh, "we're not *americanos,* but no one is sending us back. We'll go on our own, when that *hijo de puta* Castro is dead—and not one second before." "But, Abuela, I don't want to go back. I'm American. I want to have a real San Giving this year—like this," I demanded, holding up the ditto. "You, *americano?* Ha—you're *cubano,* even though you weren't born in Cuba." She chuckled. "And what is that food in those pictures? I never saw a chicken that big." "That's not a chicken, Abuela, it's a turkey. Please—I'll help you cook," I pleaded, but she kept resisting. I had no choice but to resort to coercion: "*Bueno,* Abuela, maybe I shouldn't go to *el Winn Deeẓee* anymore. If we aren't going to be *americanos,* then why should we shop there?" She took a long pause and looked over the dittos again before replying, "*Bueno,* let me think about it."

She slept on it for two days before making a decision: "Maybe you're right, *mi'jo.* Maybe we'll try San Giving how you say," she conceded, with one condition: "But I will make *carne puerco* too, just in case." It was settled. That Thanksgiving we would have turkey, as well as pork. I was ecstatic, but the pressure was on: I knew I wanted us all to have a real American Thanksgiving, but how? Abuela certainly didn't know, and the dittos weren't enough to go by. I didn't know as much about Thanksgiving as I thought I did. I needed help. That week Mrs. Echevarría had us make turkeys out of paper plates and construction paper. Surely she would know how to prepare a real Thanksgiving dinner, I thought, and so I asked her all about it. *"Ay, no,"* she told me. "My husband's mother does all the cooking for Thanksgiving. His mother is an *americana*—thank goodness. I can't even boil an egg." Great.

The next day at recess, I asked some of the American kids in class what they had for Thanksgiving. "Turkey—what else, dummy? With stuffing," Jimmy Dawson told me. "What's stuffing?" I asked. He burst out laughing, thinking I was kidding: "It's the stuff you put in the turkey," he tried to explain. "Oh, you mean like candy in a piñata?" I proposed. "No, no, dummy . . . with bread and celery and other stuff—that's why they call it stuffing," he tried to clarify. "Oh . . . okay." I pretended to understand exactly what he meant.

Nancy Myers told me her mother always made pumpkin pie. "Pumpkin? Like in Halloween?" I asked, bewildered. Patrick Pilkington said his favorite dish was candied yams. "Candied? With marshmallows? Like hot chocolate? On yams?" I asked him. They each described the dishes as best they could, but when I asked them how to make them, they couldn't explain. "I dunno," Jimmy said and shrugged, "my grandmother makes everything." Great.

Given all the fuss I had made the week before, Abuela knew something was amiss when I hadn't mentioned anything else about Thanksgiving. *"Mi'jo, qué pasó* with San Giving?" she asked. "There's only five days left. I have to start cooking, no?" "Abuela," I whined, "I don't know what to buy or how to make anything. What are we going to do?" "No worry, we can have pork and black beans like we always have—maybe some Cubaroni? That's *americano* enough, no?" she said, genuinely trying to appease me. "I guess so, Abuela, but it's not the same," I said. "*Espera* a minute," she said, and darted to her bedroom. She returned with that week's Winn-Dixie flyer: "*Mira*, look—this will help, *mi'jo.*" It was a special flyer with pictures like the ones on my dittos and full of Thanksgiving Day items on sale, including turkeys and something called Stove Top Stuffing in a box, which immediately caught my attention. Could it be true? Could Thanksgiving dinner be as easy to make as instant mashed potatoes and macaroni and cheese? With the flyer as my guide, I made a list and Abuela calculated the cost to the penny: $27.35 plus tax; she gave me $30 and off I went on my bike to Winn-Dixie, hoping Thanksgiving would be as easy and tasty as Easy Cheese.

The store was more crowded than I had ever seen it before. I roamed around for a while looking for stuffing, but it wasn't listed on any of the signs above the aisles. I noticed a lady wearing culottes and a fancy pendant necklace just like Mrs. Brady from *The Brady Bunch*—surely she was American, I thought; surely she would know all about making a Thanksgiving meal. I worked up the nerve to ask her where I could find the stuffing, pointing to the picture of it on the flyer. "Well, how sweet. You're helping your mother fix Thanksgiving dinner?" she asked as if I were three years old. "Yes," I said, seizing the opportunity, "but I don't know where to find anything." "Oh, don't worry, honey," she continued, "just go to the end of aisle eight. They have everything you'll need, pumpkin." Did she call me *pumpkin*? Why? Or did she mean they had pumpkin pie there? I was confused. "Really? Even pumpkin pie?" I asked. "Oh, I don't know, honey. I always buy the frozen ones. It's so much easier than making one from scratch," she offered. Frozen pumpkin pie? Could it be that easy?

Just as Mrs. Brady said, I found everything in the special Thanksgiving display at the end of aisle eight, including the Stove Top Stuffing. I read the instructions on the box: *Boil 1-1/2 cups water and 1/4 cup margarine in a medium saucepan. Stir in contents of Stuffing Mix pouch; cover. Remove from heat. Let stand 5 minutes. Fluff with fork.* Just as I had hoped—easy as mashed potatoes. Abuela's saying, *Cómo inventan los americanos,* rang truer than ever to me then. There were also cans of yams at the display, alongside bags of tiny marshmallows, just as Patrick Pilkington had told me. What he didn't tell me (or didn't know) was that the instructions for candied yams were right on the marshmallow bag: *Put mashed yams in casserole. Mix together margarine, cinnamon, brown sugar, and honey. Top with miniature marshmallows. Bake at 325 degrees until heated through and marshmallows are bubbly.* Even Abuela could make that once I translated for her. There were also cans of something called "Cranberry Jelly" piled up high. *Jelly in a can?* I wondered. None of the American kids had mentioned that, but I saw other customers tossing one or two cans into their carts. I followed suit, figuring it was important for something.

All I needed was the turkey. *Will Abuela know how to cook something that enormous?* I worried, staring at the case full of Butterballs. Sure, the turkeys on the dittos had looked big, but these were three, four, five times the size of a chicken. Would Abuela freak out? But I noticed the turkeys also had cooking instructions printed right on the wrapper. I read them over and discovered the turkey had a timer that would pop up when it was done—*¡cómo inventan los americanos!* The instructions also recommended three-quarters of a pound per person, so I started counting relatives and family friends who we considered relatives anyway, blood or no blood: *tío* Mauricio and my bratty cousins, Margot and Adolfo; *tías* Mirta, Ofelia, and Susana; my godparents; *tíos* Berto, Pepé, and Regino; the mechanic, Minervino, and his wife. Altogether, about twenty-something guests, I estimated, and figured I needed at least a twenty-pounder. There was no way I could carry it on my bike all the way home with the rest of the groceries. I'd have to come back just for the turkey.

Considering the number of guests, I went back to the display and got two more boxes of stuffing, six cans of yams, four bags of marshmallows, and three cans of cranberry jelly (whatever that was for), and then I picked up a frozen pumpkin pie like Mrs. Brady had suggested. Proud as a Pilgrim in 1621, I floated down the aisles with my loaded cart, ready for my first real Thanksgiving. When I got home, I set the bags down on the kitchen table and explained to Abuela that the turkey was too big and I needed to go back right away. "*Pero* how you going to carry it?" she asked, concerned. "Your Abuelo can't take you—he's at a baseball game with Caco. You'll have to wait until *mañana*." But I didn't want to wait until the next day. What if they ran out of turkeys? I told Abuela I'd tie the turkey to the handlebars on my bike. She thought it over for a moment, then handed me a piece of twine from the kitchen drawer where she kept twist ties, matches, and birthday candles.

I hopped back on my bike, darted to Winn-Dixie, got my bird, and tied all twenty-one pounds of it across the breast onto my handlebars. But getting it home wasn't as easy as I thought it would be. When I rode over the pothole in front of St. Brendan's rectory like I always did for the heck of it, one of the knots slipped and the frozen turkey slid like a shuffleboard puck down the sidewalk and into the gutter before stopping inches away from the catch drain. *No problem,* I thought; it was frozen and sealed in plastic. I picked it up and tied it even tighter with a few extra knots. But while I was cutting through the Kmart parking lot, it fell again and skidded under an Oldsmobile sedan. I crouched down and tried to grab it, but it was just out of my arm's reach. Finally I squirmed under the car on my belly and yanked it back, the turkey and me emerging grimy and blotched with oil.

By then, the sweaty condensation on the bird made it impossible to tie to the handlebars. I took off my T-shirt, wrapped it around the turkey like I was swaddling a baby, and retied it for a third time, thinking that would do the trick. Not so. Crossing Eighty-seventh Avenue it came loose again. I swerved to avoid running it over and fell off my bike. There we were: me and a twenty-one-pound turkey, lying on the pavement in the middle of a four-lane road just as the traffic light turned green and cars began honking incessantly. *Surely the Indians and Pilgrims must have had an easier time,* I thought. With one hand on the handlebar and the other barely able to carry the turkey, I managed to inch my way over to the sidewalk. "That's it!" I yelled at the bird. I tied it to the bike seat and walked my bike the rest of the way.

Once home, I washed off the scuff marks and grime with the garden hose before presenting the turkey to Abuela. There was a tear in the plastic seal, but the turkey was still frozen and intact. *"Qué grande. Qué lindo,"* Abuela praised it, none the wiser, and made room for it in the freezer. Mamá poked around and snooped inside the grocery bags. "What's all this for?" she asked Abuela, who looked at me to answer her. "We're gonna have a real *San Giving* this year, Mamá. Abuela's going to make a turkey and yams and everything," I explained. *"¿Cómo?* Turkey? Nobody knows how to make that. Especially not your Abuela. She can't even cook Cuban food too good," she jabbed. "Don't worry," Abuela said, trying to remain calm. "You sit your big *culo* down and relax—like you always do. Riqui is helping me—and he knows what he's doing." *"Bueno,"* Mamá replied, "I don't know, you better cook something else too— some *carne puerco,* just in case." *"Sí, sí, sí*—whatever," Abuela said just as the bird slipped through her hands. It slid across the terrazzo floor, bounced down the single step from the kitchen into the Florida sunroom, and knocked into the TV. It lay there, mocking us, mocking *me,* basking in the sunlight, enjoying the breeze whispering through the jalousie windows and the view of the backyard mango tree framed by the sliding glass door.

Early on Thanksgiving morning, Abuela told me to put the turkey outside. "That's the best way to defreeze it," she said with authority. I put the turkey in a baking pan and placed it in the middle of the backyard terrace where the sun could shine on it all day. And Abuela faithfully followed all my instructions as I translated them to her, without adding any additional ingredients of her own: no Bijol, no garlic, no cumin. By two o'clock the yams were ready for the marshmallow topping and we had finished a pot of Stove Top Stuffing. *"¿Cómo?* Why? Where?" Abuela asked, as bewildered by the concept of stuffing as I was, despite Jimmy Dawson's explanation, which I parroted to her: "Yes, Abuela, inside. That's why they call it stuffing." We stuffed the bird and put it in the oven alongside Abuela's *just-in-case* pork shoulder, which she had marinated overnight with bitter orange and garlic *mojito.*

28

Wafts of roasting turkey. Wafts of roasting pork. The competing scents battled through the house while I helped Papá and Abuelo set up folding domino tables on both ends of our dining table. We assembled a mishmash of desk chairs, beach chairs, and stools stretching from the kitchen into the living room to seat all twenty-two relatives. I spent the rest of the afternoon making construction paper turkeys like Mrs. Echevarría had taught us in class. I placed one at each setting, then drew pumpkins all over the paper tablecloth and cut into its edges to make a frilly trim. Abuela added a bouquet of gladiolus, which didn't fit the theme but made the table look better, despite the plastic plates and utensils.

"*¡Ay, Dios mío!* Come over here!" Abuela yelled for me. "What is that blue thing?" she asked, alarmed by the pop-up timer in the turkey, which she hadn't noticed before and I had forgotten to point out. "Relax, Abuela. It's nothing. It's supposed to pop when the turkey is cooked," I explained. "Really? *Cómo inventan los americanos.* They make everything so easy," she said, relieved, then slid the turkey back into the oven, only to call me over again twenty minutes later. "*Bueno,* the *puerco* is done. The turkey must be done too—look at it," she said. "*Pero,* Abuela, the blue thing hasn't popped up. We can't take it out!" I demanded. "*Ay, mi'jo,* look at the skin, toasty like the *puerco,*" she insisted, knocking on it with the back of a spoon. "It's done I tell you. *Además,* it's already seven o'clock. We have to put the other things in the oven before everyone gets here." "*Pero,* Abuela, we can't," I repeated. She ignored my protest. "What do you know about cooking? Give me *los yames* and *el* pie." I knew it was useless to argue any further and hoped for the best as I topped the yams with marshmallows and cinnamon and took the pumpkin pie out of the freezer.

The doorbell rang. "I told you," she said smugly. "*Ándale*—get the door." It was the Espinoza clan who arrived first—all three generations: *tía* Mirta with her showgirl hips; *tío* Mauricio wearing a tie and jacket, unwilling to accept that his days as a Cuban tycoon were over; their two children—my cousins—with fancy names: Margot and Adolfo; and their grandmother Esmeralda, who was constantly picking food out of her ill-fitting dentures. They burst through the door with kisses, hellos, and *Happy San Giving*s. *Tía* Mirta handed Mamá a giant pot she brought with her. "*Mira,* here are the *frijoles.* I think they are little salty, *pero* Mauricio was rushing me," she said. Minutes later cousin Maria Elena arrived with her hair in curlers and a Saran-wrapped glass pan full of *yuca con mojito. Happy San Giving.* Then *tío* Berto with an open beer in one hand and four loaves of Cuban bread under his armpits. *Happy San Giving.*

At first I thought it was Abuela who didn't trust that a purely American meal would satisfy. But when she was totally surprised by *tía* Ofelia's golden caramel flan, I knew it wasn't her; it was Mamá who must've asked everyone to bring a dish to sabotage Abuela's first attempt at a real San Giving. My suspicion was confirmed when *tía* Susana arrived with a platter of fried plantains in a bed of grease-soaked paper towels. "*Mira,*" she said to Mamá, handing her the platter, "*los plátanos* that you asked me to bring—I hope they are sweet. Happy San Giving." "Oh, you didn't have to bring nothing, *pero gracias* anyway," Mamá said, casually placing her palm against her cheek, a gesture that always gave her away when she was lying.

Abuela served the pork roast next to the turkey, pop-up timer still buried in the bird. A Cuban side followed every American side being passed from hand to hand. "That sure's a big chicken," *tío* Pepé chuckled as he carved into the bird and then the pork. "What's this, the innards?" he asked when he reached the stuffing. I had to explain the stuffing concept again to all the relatives as he piled generous portions of turkey and pork on everyone's plates. Papá was about to dig in when I insisted we say grace, proudly announcing I would read a special poem I had written as a prayer in Mrs. Echevarría's class.

Dear God:
Like the Pilgrims and Indians did long ago
we bow our heads and pray so you'll know
how thankful we are for this feast today,
and for all the blessings you send our way
in this home of the brave and land of the free
where happy we shall forever and ever be.
Amen.

As soon as I finished, *tía* Susana asked *tío* Berto, who then asked Minervino, who then asked Maria Elena, who then asked me what the hell I had just said. None of them understood a single word of my prayer in English. *"Bueno, ahora en español por favor,"* *tío* Mauricio requested, and I had to do an impromptu translation of my prayer in Spanish that ended with a resounding *Amen* and a roar of *"¡Feliz San Giving! ¡Qué viva Cuba!"* from the family. Nothing like the dittos.

And so the moment of truth was at hand, or rather, at mouth, as everyone began eating. Not even a minute later Mamá asked, "What's this with *canela y merengue* on top? So sweet. Are you sure this isn't dessert?" Abuela instantly responded to her spurn: "They are *yames,* just like yuca but orange and sweet—that's all. Just eat." *"Ay, Dios mío*—orange yuca! What about blue beans?" Mamá laughed, and the rest of the family joined in. "They are not like yuca. They are like boniato. It's what they ate on the first Thanksgiving," I explained. "Really . . . they had march-mellows that long ago?" Mamá quipped. She saw my face crumple. "What else do you know about San Giving, *mi'jo*?" she asked me, changing her tone and taking an interest. I went on for a few minutes, telling the tale of the Pilgrims and Indians in Spanish so that everyone could understand. But soon the conversation changed to *tía* Mirta's black beans. "You make the best *frijoles* in all Miami," Papá complimented her, and everyone agreed as they poured ladlefuls of black beans over their mashed potatoes like it was gravy. Nothing like the dittos.

"What's this *mierda roja* for?" Abuelo asked me, holding a dish with a log of cranberry jelly. I was embarrassed to admit that I hadn't figured out what it was for. "Well, it must be for *el pan*," Abuelo assumed, and he began spreading cranberry jelly on his slice of Cuban bread, already buttered. "*Oh . . . sí . . . sí.*" Everyone responded to the solved mystery and followed suit. It was the thing they all seemed to enjoy the most, besides the roasted pork, of course, which *tío* Berto couldn't stop praising as perfectly seasoned and perfectly tender. He spooned the bottom of the roasting pan and poured pork fat drippings over the lean slices of turkey on his plate. "*Ahora sí.* Much better. Not so dry," he proclaimed after a taste, and then proceeded to drench the platter of carved turkey with ladles of pork fat swimming with sautéed onions and bits of garlic. Nothing like the dittos, but at least after that everyone had seconds of the turkey.

"What's that?" Papá asked when Abuela set the pumpkin pie on the table. "I don't know . . ." Abuela shrugged and looked to me for an answer. "Pumpkin pie," I said proudly to blank faces at the table. "*Calabaza*," I translated after realizing I might as well have said *supercalifragilisticexpialidocious*. "*¿Calabaza?*" *tía* Mirta shouted incredulously. "*Pero* that's for eating when you have ulcers and diarrhea, not a dessert. *Cómo inventan los americanos*," she chuckled sarcastically. I wanted to smash the pie in her face, but instead I brought the box from the kitchen to show her it was a legitimate dessert. "Poom-quin pee-eh?" *tío* Regino read out loud, and the entire table burst out laughing. I hadn't realized that *pie* is exactly how *foot* is spelled in Spanish. A *calabaza* foot—that's what was for dessert. Not what I had in mind. "*Qué va,* there must be something else, no?" *tío* Regino petitioned, and *tía* Ofelia pranced in showing off her flan and set it on the table. Everyone began oohing and aahing. A creamy custard floating in a pool of caramelized sugar or an ulcer-curing pie? It was no competition.

No one touched the pumpkin foot, except me. I cut a huge slice and dug in. To my surprise, it tasted musty and earthy, just how I imagined the flavor of the color brown would be, though I couldn't admit it. Instead I went on faking my pleasure—"Yum! Delicious"—hoping to tempt others into giving the pie a try. But no one did, except Caco, who could never resist an opportunity to ridicule me. He reached over with his spoon and scooped a chunk off my plate and into his mouth. "Gross! Yuck!" He grimaced and began spitting out the pie. In a flash I reached over to his plate with my spoon and mushed together his chewed-up pie with his slice of flan. We were heading for an all-out food fight, but Mamá put an end to it. "*¡Basta!* Enough, it's San Giving Day, *por Dios Santo.*"

After dessert, Abuela made three rounds of Cuban coffee. *Tío* Berto and Abuelo moved the domino tables into the Florida room and played with Mauricio and Regino, slamming dominos and shots of rum on the table. "What's this, a funeral? *Por favor,* a little *música, maestro,*" *tío* Berto requested, and Papá complied. He turned on the stereo system and put in *Hoy cómo ayer,* his favorite eight-track tape with eight billion songs from *their days* in Cuba. The crescendo began and Minervino took his butter knife and tapped out a matching beat on his beer bottle. *Tío* Berto grabbed a cheese grater from the kitchen and began scraping it with a spoon, playing it like a *güiro*. With that, Cousin Danita began one-two-threeing to a conga as she served Cuba libres for the men and crème de menthe for the ladies, her enormous, heart-shaped butt jiggling left and right as if it had a mind of its own. Inspired by her moves and a little too much rum, *tío* Mauricio took Mirta by the waist and before you could say Happy San Giving, there was a conga line twenty Cubans long circling the domino players around the Florida sunroom.

When the conga finished, the line broke up into couples dancing salsa while I sat sulking on the sofa. *You can't teach old Cubans new tricks*, I thought, watching the shuffle of their feet. There seemed to be no order to their steps, no discernible pattern to the chaos of their swaying hips and jutting shoulders. And yet there was something absolutely perfect and complete, even beautiful, about them, dancing as easily as they could talk, walk, breathe. "*Ven*, I'll show you," Mamá insisted, pulling me by my hand, trying to get me to dance with her. "No, no, Mamá, *yo no sé*—I don't know how," I protested. "*¡Caramba!* You're Cuban, aren't you? It's in your blood, *mi' jo*, you'll see. *¡Ándale!* Get up!" she demanded, yanking me off of the sofa and onto the floor. She put her arm around my waist and my hand on her shoulder, leading me through the basic one-two and back. Turn. "More hip, more shoulder," she spoke into my ear while pushing my body left and right. "Yes, like that . . . *así* . . . *bien* . . . *muy bien*," she complimented me. "*Acuérdate*, even though you were born in España, you were made in Cuba—your soul is Cuban," she said, reminding me—yet again—that I was conceived in Cuba seven months before she headed for Spain with me in her womb.

As I began picking up the rhythm, Abuela dashed into the room twirling a dishcloth above her heard and demanding, "*¡Silencio! ¡Si-lencio, por favor!*" Papá turned down the music and the crowd froze waiting for her next words. "*Tío* Rigoberto just called—he said he heard from Ramoncito that my sister Ileana got out—with the whole *familia*!" she announced, her voice cracking as she wiped her eyes with the dishcloth and continued: "They're in España waiting to get *las* visas. In a month *más o menos*, they will be here! *¡Qué emoción!*" She didn't need to explain much more. It was a journey they all knew—had all taken just a few years before. A journey I didn't know, having arrived in America when I was only forty-five days old. But over the years I had heard the stories they always told in low voices and with teary eyes, reliving the plane lifting above the streets, the palm trees, the rooftops of their homes and country they might never see again, flying to some part of the world they'd never seen before. One suitcase, packed mostly with photographs and keepsakes; no more than a few dollars in their pocket; and a whole lot of *esperanza*. That's what the Pilgrims must have felt like, more or less, I imagined. They had left England in search of a new life too, full of hope and courage, a scary journey ahead of them. Maybe my family didn't know anything about turkey or yams or pumpkin pie, but they were a lot more like the Pilgrims than I had realized.

Abuela disappeared and returned with a handful of black-and-white photos of her sister Ileana with the family back in Cuba. "*Mira.*" She explained in detail as she passed each one around, "Here she is on *tío* Ernesto's old horse at his farm. Here she is in her wedding dress. Here we are by the old sugar mill . . . look, there is the old schoolhouse . . . look, there's the old clock in the park . . . Look how young we all were, remember?" Suddenly, no one, including me, was in Güecheste anymore; they weren't in Miami or Cuba; they weren't in the present, or the future, but floating somewhere in the formless, timeless space of memory. Though I had never met my *tía* Ileana, it felt as if I too remembered her and the farm, the schoolhouse, the sugar mill. There was more to my past than I had ever realized, a whole other history no book or Mrs. Echevarría ever taught me about: palm trees and mountains; men in straw hats and oxcarts loaded with sugarcane; thatch-roofed homes and red-earth roads in ditto sheets I had never colored.

"*Gracias* to your San Lázaro!" Mamá cried out and rushed to hug Abuela. "I know how much you miss her. *Qué alegría* for you. If only I could get my mother out—soon, soon," Mamá insisted. "Happy San Giving *a todos*!" she cheered. "One day we will all be together." "Happy San Giving!" everyone roared, holding their glasses of sparkling *cidra* and rum high up in the air. My frustration and disappointment faded. No matter that they called it San Giving, this *was* my first real Thanksgiving Day. Papá turned the music back on and the celebration continued louder and more exuberant than before. Sprawled on the couch, I fell asleep to the sounds of bongos and *tía* Susana's cackle; to *tío* Berto playing the cheese grater and the voice of my *tío* Minervino, who believed he could sing as well as (if not better than) Julio Iglesias; to the clang of cowbells and beer bottle taps and the soft scuffle of my mother and father dancing a slow *danzón*.

The next morning Abuela made Pop-Tarts but didn't eat, complaining she had had stomach cramps all night long. She said Abuelo was still in bed, nauseated. Mamá admitted she threw up before going to sleep, but thought it was too much crème de menthe. I had diarrhea, I confessed, as did Papá. Caco claimed he was fine. None of us knew what to make of our upset stomachs until *tía* Esmeralda called. She told Abuela she had been throwing up all night and was only then beginning to feel like herself again. She blamed it on those strange *yames*. Then *tío* Regino called and said he'd had to take a dose of his mother's *elixir paregórico*, which cured anything and everything; he blamed it on the flan, thinking he remembered it tasting a little sour. The phone rang all day long with relatives complaining about their ailments and offering explanations. Some, like *tía* Mirta, blamed the cranberry jelly; others blamed the black beans or the yuca that was too garlicky. And some, like me, dared to blame it on the pork. But surprisingly, no one—not even Abuela—blamed the turkey.

LOSING THE FARM

*A*t one time, our backyard in Güecheste was shadowed by Australian pines and dahoon hollies. Abuelo cut them down, one by one, to plant fruit trees like those that grew in Cuba—a loquat, some papayas, and an *aguacate* tree—each one yielding a little taste of his lost paradise. But he'd protest every time he bit into any of the fruit—according to him, they were never as large or as succulent or as deeply colored as the fruit in Cuba, which was blessed with soil as rich and fertile as the Garden of Eden. *"En Cuba* you could spit a seed on the ground and it would grow the next day, *como si nada,"* he'd claim, frustrated with how poorly his trees grew in *América.*

He also planted night-blooming jasmine beside the front porch where he sat every summer evening enjoying the last tokes of his six-inch-long *tabaco* for the night. Wearing his trademark Bermuda shorts and black oxfords with dress socks crinkled around his ankles, he'd cross his legs like a woman—one leg draped over the other—and dive into the pages of one of the dime-store Westerns he'd buy at the Farmacia León. Sometimes I'd join Abuelo, fascinated by the dusk settling over the neighborhood as quietly as dust and how his lips moved silently as he read or blew rings of smoke haloing above him. As soon as it grew dark enough to see the green flashes of the *cocuyos*, the jasmine flowers would release their perfume and Abuelo would take a deep breath through his nose. "*Qué rico*. You smell that?" he'd ask me, raising his eyes from the book right on cue. Like the smoke rings from his cigar, he would slowly disappear into the scent of memory: "I had a tree like that in Cuba, *pero* it was three times bigger and a hundred times sweeter. *La gente* could find my house by following the perfume to the beautiful *galán de noche* growing by my front door."

But flowers and fruit trees weren't enough for Abuelo to feel at home in Güecheste. He once suggested raising a pig in the backyard. "I'll feed it *aguacates* from my tree and *sobras* of rice. It'll taste just like the *carne puerco* we had in Cuba," he petitioned Mamá. But she forbade it, complaining that she already had enough "pigs" to clean up after and that she would never be able to wash the slaughtered pig's bloodstains from the concrete terrace. To console himself, he bought a few baby chicks from Ignacio Navarro, an old friend of his from Cuba. Ignacio worked a small farm in Homestead, at the southern end of the county. Abuelo convinced Mamá that chickens would be good for controlling palmetto bugs and roaches—and even mosquitos; one less thing for her to worry about.

The chicks arrived in a brown paper bag stapled shut at the top and pierced with tiny airholes. Their pecking twitched the bag around the back terrace as if it were being skittered around by a ghost. I followed the bag cautiously until Abuelo held it still, undid the staples, and told me to peek inside. "*No tengas miedo.* They won't hurt you," he assured me. It was true; the half dozen *pollitos* like fuzzy pom-poms were too adorable to hurt anything, even me. I picked one up, felt its tiny heart beating against my palms, then flung it into the air, thinking it would fly. It didn't, of course; it fell right onto the terrace, dazed but unhurt, and began scuttling around, pecking and pecking at nothing. My cat, Misu, looked on, crouched behind the sliding glass door, waiting for an opportunity to spring on the chicks. "You make sure Misu doesn't get outside," Abuelo cautioned, "until the chicks are *grande* and can defend themselves."

I made Abuelo promise to wait to feed the chicks until I came home from school every day so we could do it together. He kept old Bustelo coffee cans filled with leftover rice and beans and other table scraps; we tossed handfuls like confetti on the terrace for the chicks. One time, to Abuelo's absolute horror, I fed them some M&M's, thinking they'd love them as much as I did. "*¿Estás loco, niño?* They'll die eating that *mierda,*" he admonished me, though I didn't quite believe him. How could anything die from chocolate?

The chicks grew into white hens that reached my shins, and the hens' droppings splattered the terrace like a Jackson Pollock painting. Mamá hosed it down every weekend, complaining as she whisked her wet broom back and forth across the concrete like a *güiro*: "*¡Qué cagazón!* Is this what I left *mi madre* and sisters in Cuba for—to clean chicken shit? *¡Ay, Dios mío!*" But her attempts at cleaning the droppings were useless; they built up for weeks, baking in the hot Florida sun. Mamá finally broke. "*¡Basta!*" she shouted at Abuelo and me. "I have *muchísimo* to do around here without all this *mierda de gallina* everyplace! Get rid of those chickens—*no me importa* if you have to eat them *uno por uno.*"

The following few days, I fed the hens as if it were their last meal and they were our next, not knowing what would happen to them. Then the following Saturday morning I woke up to the shadow of Abuelo walking past my bedroom window. He carried several long boards on his shoulders and wore the *guajiro* straw hat he always put on to do yard work. His shadow was soon followed by the sound of a handsaw and then a hammer, the blows vibrating my windowpane. *Could he finally be building a tree house for me?* For months I had pleaded with him, but he had never heard of or seen a tree house. "*¿Qué es eso?* That must be a silly *americano* thing," he told me.

But that's why I wanted one as perfect as the tree house on *The Brady Bunch*. Mine would be made of lacquered pine with a Dutch door, cradled in the wye of our *aguacate* tree, with a rope ladder and a secret escape hatch in the floor. I'd dress the windows in red-and-white checkerboard curtains, bring up my set of Lego blocks and books. I would spend all day out of sight of the mean looks Abuela cast my way whenever she caught me coloring, drawing, writing, or playing house with Misu. My own little paradise, perched so high above the world I'd see clear to Miami Beach, I thought.

"*¡Levántate!*" Mamá startled me out of my daydream, knocking my bedroom door open. "Get up and go help your Abuelo—*está completamente loco.*" "Why?" I asked, hoping for the answer I wanted to hear, but there would be no tree house. "He's building *un gallinero*—can you believe that? *¡Un gallinero!* What did I leave Cuba for?" she said. I thought hard: *A chicken coop? A chicken coop?* Until it made sense: the coop would keep the chickens off the terrace and silence Mamá's complaints. Abuelo had figured out a way to save the chickens from slaughter, for the time being at least. I got dressed, put on year-old work sneakers, and scarfed down my *café con leche* and bowl of Froot Loops before dashing outside to see what was going on.

Abuelo had already dug four holes for the coop's posts in a back corner of the yard, which was littered with two-by-fours, rolls of chicken wire, and boxes of nails. "Riqui, *al fin*," Abuelo greeted me. "It's about time. *Ven acá*, hold this for me." As instructed, I gripped one of the posts with both hands. Abuelo drove it into the ground with a rock the size of my head. Trying not to blink or recoil each time the rock hit, I kept my eyes on the ground and my feet spaced apart. Our next-door neighbor, Pedrito, came over to help; he was in charge of mixing the concrete that would anchor the posts. "Is that one ready?" he asked. *"Listo,"* Abuelo answered, and Pedrito began plopping the concrete, like gray cake batter, into the hole around the post. *"¡Excelente! Eres un bárbaro,"* Abuelo commended him, patting him on the back and shaking his hand ceremoniously. "Pedrito is a real *hombre del campo*, like me," he explained.

They did look like brothers, almost, wearing similar straw hats that seemed too big for their short, stocky bodies. They both had thick eyebrows fuzzy as caterpillars; ears as big as bananas; and wide, muscular fingers from years of working with their hands. Pedrito was the only neighbor I ever saw Abuelo pal around with; they helped each other with yard work, traded and smoked *tabacos* together, and exchanged loquats and *aguacates* from each other's trees, bantering over who had managed to grow the biggest or the best-tasting one.

After the four posts were set in place, Abuelo asked if I wanted to keep helping; I would have preferred to go inside and watch cartoons or play with my Legos all Saturday morning, but I said yes. We had to save the poor chickens. Next, Abuelo had me sit on one end of the two-by-fours set on the work bench so I could keep them steady as he hand-sawed each one, his flexed forearm swelling up thick as a loaf of Cuban bread, rings of sweat appearing under his arms. Jiggling the box of nails like a maraca, I handed them one at a time to Abuelo, who hammered the beams to the posts, framing the coop while Pedrito unrolled the chicken wire. The three of us bent, trimmed, and stapled the wire to the frame as if we were wrapping paper around a giant gift box. When we finished, Abuelo stood back to admire the masterpiece. "It's done. *Bárbaro*. Beautiful," he announced, resting his hand on the top of my head. "Now let's bring *las gallinas*."

One by one I chased the clucking hens into their new home while Abuelo sat in the shade of his *aguacate* tree, fanning himself with his hat. He pulled out two *tabacos* to celebrate, offering one to Pedrito. "*Coje*. These aren't that bad, they're from La República Dominicana, but grown from Cuban seeds." "*Oh, gracias, compadre*," Pedrito said. "*Quizás* we'll have a real Cuban *tabaco* in Cuba next year. Remember the taste of those Cohibas we'd smoked at *el club de yates* in Cienfuegos?" "Of course, *compai*," Abuelo responded, grimacing as he rolled the cigar in his mouth. "Of course. Who could forget?" But before Pedrito could light his cigar, we heard the unmistakable voice of his wife, Caridad, calling from their living room window, which faced our backyard. "Pedrito! Pedrito!" Are you done playing *guajiro* farm boy yet?" she bellowed, and then beseeched him, "*Por favor*, you've been gone since the morning. *Dios mío*, it's time to eat *almuerzo*—get in here now!" "*¡Ya voy! ¡Ya voy! Cojones*, can't I have a day without you *jodiéndome*?" Pedrito belted back. Angry and embarrassed, he tucked his unlit cigar in his shirt pocket. "*Hasta mañana, señores*," he said to us, then jumped over the chain-link fence into his yard.

As far as I knew, no one in all of Güecheste had a chicken coop. That was something I could really brag about—it was even cooler than a tree house. The *Brady Bunch* kids never had chickens. Abuelo flung open the kitchen door and called everyone out to the backyard. My cat, Misu, was the first to dart out; finally able to roam the backyard again, he snooped his way to the chicken coop. Papá and my brother, Caco, were at their Saturday baseball game; and as usual, Abuela was on the phone gossiping with one of her sisters. No one seemed to care about our chicken coop, except Misu and Mamá. She came out right away in the rubber shoes and yellow rubber gloves she wore every Saturday while doing her housework. *"Mira,"* Abuelo told her proudly, "no more chickens on the terrace." She rolled her eyes, but had no choice but to concede: *"Bueno,* okay for now, but that's it—not one more chicken in this house—*¡ni uno!"* she warned, waving an index finger sheathed in yellow rubber before marching inside.

But Abuelo didn't heed her warning; over the following weeks, he brought home five or six more fully grown hens, one at a time, so Mamá wouldn't notice the brood increasing. Within a month, they all started laying eggs. Abuelo and I gathered them in the morning, carrying them in our shirttails and setting them on the kitchen counter for Mamá. At first, this delighted her, and the entire family as well. Abuela made fresh eggs—scrambled, fried, poached—every weekend morning and sometimes even on school days; she calculated how much money she was saving by not having to buy eggs. "These are no everyday eggs," Abuelo would point out to Mamá whenever we sat down to breakfast together. "These are *huevos criollos. Mira,* look at that beautiful yolk—orange like a sunset, not yellow like the old eggs from the store that taste like *pura mierda*. Riqui and me feed *las gallinas sobras* of real food, like in Cuba—that's why they are so *deliciosos*." Then he would dunk his toast in the yolk and chew it slowly and deliberately in his mouth, letting his palate take in all its subtleties, as if he were tasting a fine wine or a gourmet cheese; as if he were tasting Cuba itself.

Soon, however, an overabundance of eggs crowded the refrigerator. Mamá unloaded eggs onto visiting relatives, insisting they leave with at least half a dozen in their hands, unable to wave goodbye. She cooked potfuls of *natilla* custard that she bartered for free manicures and pedicures from our beautician neighbor Teresa. She even instructed Abuela to make omelets every other night for dinner. But Mamá still couldn't make a dent in the surplus of thirty-something eggs a week. I was afraid she would complain and again sentence the chickens to death. I had to do something. FREE EGGS | HUEVOS CRIOLLOS | GRATIS, I wrote with my Crayola Markers across the back of an old poster board from a science fair project, each word in a different color and outlined with glitter. Every afternoon I did my homework sitting on our front lawn next to a bucketful of eggs and my sign. It was my Cuban version of a lemonade stand, though I gave away the eggs for free. I was just glad it worked. Within days, there was a frenzy for our *criollo* eggs that most Güechestians hadn't tasted since leaving Cuba; some of them even returned twice in one day.

Everyone loved our eggs, except Caridad. "Are you sure those eggs are safe to eat? They look so dirty. I bet the whole *barrio* will get sick," she said with revulsion, not daring to touch the eggs. Abuela told me Caridad didn't know any better; she was a snobby city *princesa* from Havana who didn't like country people from *el campo* like us. Abuela said Teresa told her that Caridad had said that we were nothing but lowly *guajiros* and that we should move to Homestead or go back to Cuba where we belonged. But despite Caridad, within two weeks we were down to zero eggs. I thought about selling them for fifty cents a dozen instead of giving them away, but I didn't want to get greedy. It was enough that my chickens were saved once again.

After the egg crisis, it seemed that Abuelo, the hens, Misu, and I would live happily ever after. Then came the rabbits. At St. Brendan's annual Easter Fair, I spent all my tickets on the Musical Roulette Walk. Here's how it worked: everyone walked around a ring of numbered squares until the music stopped; then the MC would spin a numbered dial and pick the lucky winner. It took me eight tries, but I finally won the best prize of all——a white bunny in a tiny cage filled with fake Easter grass. For once, I was the envy of all my classmates, especially Jeannette Gutierrez, who was standing next to me in the game. When she lost, she sat down right on her numbered square, buried her head in her crossed legs, and sobbed into her knees.

I brought the bunny over to my brother, Caco, and gloated, "Look what I won!" "Big deal," he said and turned away from me. I turned to Mamá. "Look how cute. I can keep him right . . . right?" I asked her, kissing its quivering pink nose and whiskers through the pet carrier. "*Alabao sea Dios,* another animal!" she grumbled, and said nothing more, avoiding my stare. "Please . . . ," I continued, until I caught her eyes and she gave me the look that signaled *okay,* even though she could not bring herself to say it. As soon as I brought the bunny home, Abuelo picked it up without hesitation. He folded back its ears and peered inside, thumbed through its paws, turned it over on its back, and very matter-of-factly announced, "Female. Healthy, *pero* too skinny. They've been feeding her *pura mierda* like they do to the chickens. I can see it in her eyes. She needs real food. *Vamos.*"

I assumed we were going to the Tropical Pets store in Güecheste Mall, but instead Abuelo drove to El Milagro—*The Miracle*—where he would buy his *tabacos*. I wondered why we were going to a bodega, but I trusted him. Abuelo pried a shopping cart loose. I stepped onto the bottom rack, where Abuela often placed bags of Goya rice and sacks of kitty litter for Misu, and I held on to the front end as Abuelo pushed me for a ride through the produce aisle. Not surprisingly, he tossed a bag of carrots into the cart, but he also picked up a bunch of watercress and a bunch of cilantro. "*Aprende, mi'jo:* rabbits have to eat three different vegetables every day—and some fruit once a week," he instructed, inspecting a pint of strawberries.

Then we headed to the back of the store, through a pair of swinging doors and past the SÓLO EMPLEADOS sign into the storeroom. Abuelo approached a man in a white smock who was sifting through a box of plantains. They exchanged pleasantries in Spanish that I couldn't quite make out. The man walked away and returned with a wax-lined box of lettuce—not heads, but loose leaves. "*Gracias,*" Abuelo said, shaking the man's hand. "*Guárdame* all the leaves you can. I'll come once a week for more. *Gracias.*" On the way back home, Abuelo explained that grocers plucked the bruised leaves off the lettuce heads and just threw them away—that's what he fed his rabbits back in Cuba.

I stared at the bunny's marquise-shaped eyes and twitching whiskers for days, but still couldn't think of a name for her. I didn't want a tacky Cuban name like Carmencita, Ileana, or Ofelia—the names of some of my aunts and cousins. I wanted an American name, something uncommon, yet pretty. Then I remembered Bonnie Patterson, my first crush in kindergarten and the only girl in our class who had freckles and blue eyes. But I decided to spell it with a *y*: Bonny—my bunny Bonny—it had a ring to it, I thought. I pleaded with Mamá to let me keep Bonny in my room for the first few weeks until she got bigger. With my ruler, I drew up a chart on construction paper listing the days of the week across the top and marked down the vegetables and fruits I fed her daily after school.

After my parents went to sleep, I'd take Bonny from her pet carrier and let her hop around my bed. Or I'd prop the sheets up with wire hangers and we'd eat carrots and strawberries inside our makeshift tent in the dark. One night I forgot to put her back in the cage before I fell asleep. The next morning I woke up to the nightmare of Caco and Mamá standing in my doorway. "You see? I told you," he whined to her. "*¡No lo creo!*" Mamá exclaimed at the sight of Bonny snuggled under my chin, wiggling her nose at her. "What's that dirty animal doing in your bed? *¡Ay caramba!* Why didn't I stay in Cuba? That thing has to go outside; *mira* how *grande* it is already." It was true, Bonny had doubled in size, and I knew it was no use begging Mamá to let me keep her in my room anymore. Besides, her pet carrier was getting too small for her.

After school I told Abuelo about the incident and he came to the rescue again, promising Mamá we would build a cage for Bonny and keep her in the backyard. And we did, the very next Saturday, using the leftover two-by-fours and chicken wire. We set the cage under the *aguacate* tree so Bonny would have plenty of shade, and covered the top with an old raincoat. But the cage was just too plain and ugly for my beautiful Bonny. I dolled it up with a string of gold tinsel I took from a box of old Christmas decorations and brightened up the newspaper shreds lining her cage with strips of purple and yellow construction paper. Still, I felt sorry for her, out all day in the scorching heat and torrential thunderstorms that blasted through almost every afternoon. Before Mamá would get home from work, I'd take Bonny into my room for a couple hours and let her hop around the shag rug and all over my textbooks while I did homework. If Mamá came home early, I'd hide Bonny inside my book bag or in the laundry basket, then sneak her back out to her cage while Mamá was busy with housework.

It seemed as if Abuelo, the chickens, Bonny, Misu, and I would live happily ever after, but Abuelo couldn't leave well enough alone. A few weeks after we finished the cage, he showed up with a cardboard box and signaled me to follow him around the side of the house to the backyard. "Open it," he said, and I did. Out hopped a big brown rabbit with droopy ears that fell around his face like pigtails; he was so heavy I had to use both hands to pick him up. "Oh, a little *amiguito* for Bonny," I said, thrilled, not knowing any better. "Is it a boy or a girl?" I asked. "A boy," Abuelo answered. "*Pero* don't tell your mother anything," he cautioned. Of course I wasn't going to say a word, and since Mamá never petted Bonny, much less fed her, she'd probably never notice her new friend. But just in case, Abuelo and I moved the cage to the rear of the yard, behind the shed, beyond Mamá's line of sight from the clothesline. At first I wanted to name him Droopy, but I decided on Bernie. Droopy was too obvious, I thought, and besides, Droopy and Bonny didn't sound as nice to me as Bernie and Bonny.

A few weeks afterward, Abuelo built an addition to Bonny's cage. He clipped a hole in the chicken wire on the side of the cage and fastened to it a square box made of plywood, which he filled with torn-up rags and more shredded newspaper. At first I thought it was like a hideout or a bedroom for Bernie and Bonny, but I wasn't sure. "What's that for?" I asked him. "*Un nido*—a nest for Bonny," he said, without further explanation. "A nest? Like for birds, Abuelo? Why?" I questioned. "*Sí, sí,*" Abuelo continued, "she going to have little *conejitos;* they need a good nest so they will be safe." Even though at the time I didn't know much about the facts of life, I *did* know that neither babies nor bunnies came from storks, and I understood intuitively what had happened: Bonny and Bernie weren't friends, they were *novios,* husband and wife, in love.

Less than a month later, Abuelo came into my room just as I was falling asleep and shook my shoulder. "Riqui? Riqui? *Despiértate* and follow me," he whispered, placing his index finger over his lips. We tiptoed through the house and out to the backyard, I barefoot and in my briefs, Abuelo in his boxer shorts and oxfords, holding a flashlight. "You see the *conejitos?*" Abuelo asked, shining the beam into the nest. What I saw were four pink, squiggly worms without eyes or fur, no bigger than my finger. "Ooh, gross!" I blurted out. "*Bueno,* that's what you looked like once too, *mi'jo,* and you're not so ugly now, ¿*verdad?*" Abuelo joshed. "Don't worry, they'll look like real *conejitos* soon. But we have to keep Bernie away or he'll kill them." "Kill them! Why?" I was stunned. "Shh. Shh. *Sí,* he'll kill them— that's just the way it is, *mi'jo, así es*" was the only answer he gave me. "*Pero* don't worry, when the *conejitos* grow, we'll put Bernie back with Bonny," he added as he pulled him up by the skin behind his ears and put him in the same box he had arrived in.

Just as Abuelo had said, in a few weeks the little worms grew into bunnies with eyes and fur, and Bernie and Bonny were reunited. To Abuelo's amazement, Bonny didn't try to bite me when I reached into her nest to pet and hold the bunnies. They were so tiny they looked almost fake—like chocolate Easter bunnies. So small and perfect they didn't seem real and yet there they were—breathing and warm, twitching their ears and blinking—pure life in the palms of my hands. I'm sure Mamá must've noticed the crowded rabbit cage while watering her potted plants or taking out the garbage, but she must've looked the other way. After all, they were no trouble for her, as long as they stayed outside the house and in the cage. And besides, she was busy contending with Caco. For years he had been pleading with her for a dog, ever since she'd let me keep Misu. But now that I also had chickens and rabbits, he became even more jealous of me—and utterly relentless.

Of course, Abuelo and I wanted a dog too, but we had already pushed our luck with Mamá. We let Caco do all the begging and bargaining, knowing he'd have a better chance than we did. It took him weeks of whining and making promises around the dinner table: *I swear I'll walk him every day . . . I promise to feed him . . . Please, you won't have to do anything . . . Riqui has chickens. Riqui has rabbits . . . It's not fair!* He persisted until Mamá finally gave in: "Okay, *está bien,* now stop *jodiéndome.* But the dog goes outside. I don't want to see any dog hair or dog poop *en mi casa.*" Abuelo caught my eyes across the table. I guessed from the look in his eyes that he already had a dog in mind: a German shepherd like Papo, the dog he'd left behind with a neighbor when he fled Cuba. Even so many years later, Abuelo still liked to show off a cracked black-and-white photo of himself and Papo on the porch of his house in Cuba:

Abuelo with a full head of hair and wearing a crisp linen shirt, Papo at his side, his chin resting on Abuelo's shoe, both looking straight into the camera.

As I suspected, the very next Sunday Abuelo asked Caco and me if we wanted to go pick out a puppy at Ignacio's farm in Homestead, as if we would say no. We jammed our sneakers on in two seconds and jumped into Abuelo's baby-blue Comet, all three of us riding in the front seat. Looking out the car window, it was hard to believe that only forty minutes away from our suburban backyard there was a place like Homestead, with no sidewalks; no utility poles; hardly any houses, driveways, or hedges. Only the bumpy, lonely road we were on, trespassing through open land covered in untamed grass that met the horizon in every direction. "Was Cuba like this?" I asked Abuelo. "*Más o menos,*" he said, "*pero* with sugarcane fields everywhere, and mountains, and lots and lots more palm trees." I imagined Cuba rushing past the car windows. For a few seconds I was there with him, driving through his homeland as if there had never been a revolution, as if he had never left his *patria*.

As with Cuba, I had never been to Ignacio's farm but felt as if I had from all the stories Abuelo told me. It was just as I had imagined: a small house that looked even smaller in contrast to the expanse of land surrounding it; its wood siding weathered, its paint chipping, its windows slightly askew, as if the house were grimacing. We pulled into the gravel driveway to the sight of Ignacio waving at us from the front porch. "*¡Blanco! ¡Qué pasa!*" he shouted to Abuelo. "*Aquí,* Navarro," Abuelo responded. Ignacio and Abuelo called each other by their last names—it was a macho thing between them I noticed, like the hard pats they gave each other on their backs to offset the warm hugs they gave each other in greeting. We stood in the driveway as Abuelo introduced us: "These are my *nietos,* Caco and Riqui." I was quietly stunned by the house, the land, and the three-foot-long machete hanging from Ignacio's belt. He wore the same type of straw hat that Abuelo and Pedrito often did, and was about the same age, but Ignacio didn't have a gut like Abuelo; I could still make out the sinews of his biceps underneath the flaccid veneer of his old skin.

"You *muchachos* never been to a real *finca, ¿verdad?* Come," Ignacio said, winking at us. We followed him through a makeshift gate made of splintered wood and wire mesh into the acres of land beyond the house. It was the land he was proud of, not his house. On the other side of the gate, we stood in a large, dusty clearing with a few tufts of grassy weeds sprouting from the bare ground and several roosters roaming freely. The clearing was surrounded by chicken coops, each one ten times the size of ours, holding hundreds of hens like a single mass of white feathers clucking and scratching the ground. We trailed behind Ignacio as he led us through his rows of *plátano* trees fanning themselves with their leaves as big as windmill blades. He picked a couple tiny bananas from a tree and offered them to Caco and me; we both looked strangely at the fruit. "Taste these. They're *plátanos burros,* like bananas, *pero* more smaller and more sweet," he reassured us. Following Caco's lead, I peeled mine and took a cautious bite. *"Qué rico, delicioso,"* I said to be polite, trying not to make a face over the strange Play-Doh–like taste.

We reached a field that seemed to consist of nothing more than rows of neatly planted weeds. But then Ignacio stopped, pulled back one of the plants, and said proudly, *"Mira qué lindas,"* revealing a bunch of strawberries dangling like heart-shaped charms at the ends of the stems. I didn't wait for Ignacio to offer me any; I plucked one right away and ate the whole thing in one bite. Falling a few steps behind on purpose, I secretly filled my pockets with a dozen more strawberries for Bonny and Bernie. In my excitement, I forgot why we were there, until Caco whispered to me anxiously, "Hey, where the hell are the puppies?" I shrugged.

After the strawberry patch, we entered a field of sugarcane. I could hear wind like something alive was pushing through the stalks, setting them aflutter before moving over my face. Suddenly, in a single move, Ignacio slid his machete from its sheath, slashed a stalk of cane clean, and then began slicing off the bark as easily as if he were peeling an orange. "Taste this," he said, handing us each a piece. "It is as good as the *caña* from Cuba." Whether or not that was true I had no way of knowing. But it did feel like Cuba, at least the way I had imagined it, walking through the maze of stalks mysteriously converting the sun into sugar. Gnawing on the cane as hard, sweet, and sticky as rock candy, I lost all sense of direction, trusting that Ignacio knew the way, until we emerged back at the clearing. But still no puppies in sight.

"*Bueno,* Navarro, what about *los perritos?*" Abuelo finally asked Ignacio. "*Oh, sí–sí–sí,*" he said, breaking out of the sugarcane field and walking toward the house, "*Vengan*—come." He opened the back door, then clapped and whistled, summoning four puppies that romped unsteadily down the steps into the clearing. They must've been a few months old, no taller than my knee and still not in full command of their bodies. They wobbled around, pawing at our legs and biting our shoelaces, chasing each other and anything that moved. Just as I had guessed, they were German shepherds like Papo. "I have to keep these little *cabrones* inside still, they get into trouble out here," Ignacio explained just as one of the puppies started after a rooster, then pounced on a leaf, then wad-dled back to us with a stray feather in his mouth. "Which one you want?" he asked us.

We probably should have let Caco decide; after all, it was going to be *his* dog. But apparently Abuelo had already given it some thought. He pulled a tennis ball out of his pocket and tossed it into the clearing. The puppies pawed after the ball, rolling over it and each other in a darling match of puppy rugby. The winner emerged with the ball barely in his mouth, and much to everyone's surprise, even Ignacio's, he started making his way back to Abuelo, dropping and picking up the ball again and again. "This one," Abuelo said without reservation, then picked up the puppy and inspected it as he had done with Bonny, announcing its health and sex. "Okay, he's cute," Caco agreed, taking the puppy from Abuelo and holding it up in the air above his head. "This one!"

On the way back home, Caco and I sat in the backseat, as jumpy with excitement as the puppy that Caco couldn't hold still on his lap. "Don't touch him," Caco whined, "he's my dog. You can't touch him unless I say so." He was even more jealous than I had imagined. "Please," I begged, and he let me pet the puppy a few strokes before demanding, "Stop! That's it!" With a name already in mind, I asked him, "What are you going to call him? How 'bout Chester?" "Ches-ter? What kind of a sissy name is that?" Caco said, not surprisingly. "Okay. How about Scooby?" I proposed. "Don't be so stupid," he retorted. I sensed it was personal; any name I suggested would be met with the same derision, so I shut up. After a little silence, Caco asked, "How about Bubba?" as if he really wanted my opinion and wasn't simply looking for me to agree with him. I thought it was a silly name, but I had to be nice if I wanted petting rights. "That's nice. But I don't think he really looks like a Bubba. Do you?" I said cautiously and politely. "No, I guess not. How about Tiger?" he asked again. "Yeah, he looks like a Tiger, with all that orange and black," I agreed.

Tiger proved to be the perfect name because he turned out to be as wild as one. In less than a month, he had crisscrossed the backyard with so many ruts it looked as if it had been plowed like Ignacio's farm. He chased everything—nothing was safe, not even his own tail or shadow. Abuelo and I had to constantly fill the holes he'd burrow trying to get into the chicken coop. He'd harass Bonny, Bernie, and the bunnies, pawing at their cage and barking in their faces; they would huddle together in a corner of the cage, terrified, until I'd come and shoo Tiger away. He met his match the day Mamá came home to find he had yanked the laundry off the clothesline. Horrified by the massacre of her home-sewn dresses and the panty hose shredded to rags over the lawn, Mamá pronounced Tiger insane and ordered him tied up, "*Si no*, I'll get rid of that *perro loco* myself," she threatened. And so it was. Caco, practically in tears, tied Tiger to a five-foot chain that Abuelo staked in a corner of the yard from where the dog could do no damage.

Even though Tiger was a nuisance, I couldn't stand the sight of him chained up, whimpering and yo-yoing around the stake. I decided to try training him using a twig, leftovers I saved every night after dinner, and a free booklet I picked up at Tropical Pets, *How to Train Your Puppy*. I even watched reruns of *Lassie* to pick up pointers on how a good dog should behave. But since I wasn't allowed to pet Tiger—much less play with him—I had to train him in secret. During the afternoons, when Caco was away at baseball or soccer practice, I'd go through the exercises in the booklet with Tiger as quickly and patiently as I could. It wasn't easy. Tiger was just as kooky as Alberto Delgado, who would get up in the middle of class and run around the room sputtering out raspberries. Mrs. McShane called him "hyperactive," but we called him Alberto *Del-spazo*. Tiger was a *spazo* too: he'd become distracted by the faintest sound or slightest breeze through a tree or fixated on a leaf or a fallen *aguacate* and ignore me completely.

It seemed hopeless, and I was about to give up, until the afternoon I discovered the one thing Tiger loved as much as I did—Easy Cheese. I was squirting some right into my mouth while teaching him to sit, encouraging him with a morsel of leftover fried pork. Instead of the pork, he stole a lick from the tip of the Easy Cheese can and then sat, salivating and waiting for more like a good little doggie. I could only conclude that Tiger didn't like either Cuban food or Abuela's cooking, or both. He was German, after all, not Cuban. I broke through to him after a few weeks. He was no Lassie, but at least he learned to sit and fetch, and he stopped tearing up the yard as much. I showed Mamá, and she agreed to take him off his chain for a week to see how well he'd do. He passed her test and after a while she even looked the other way sometimes when Caco or I took him inside the house.

It seemed like me, Abuelo, Misu, the chickens, the rabbits, Tiger, Mamá, and Caco would live happily ever after. And we did for a few months—some of the best months of my life that I can remember. Every afternoon filled with a sense of purpose, taking care of *my* animals as if I were a veterinarian: tossing feed to the chickens, weighing them on our bathroom scale to make sure they were getting enough to eat, collecting and counting their eggs; hand-feeding strawberries to Bonny and Bernie, cleaning their paws with soap and water, and checking the bunnies for ear mites; teaching Tiger a new command over a shared can of Easy Cheese, then taking his pulse and listening to his heartbeat with my ear against his chest. For those few months, even Abuela commended me for the *manly* duties I had taken on instead of rebuking me for the usual pastimes I favored, like coloring and finger painting. Life was good.

Then Abuelo brought a rooster home from Ignacio's farm. He was bigger than Misu or the rabbits, with talons almost as long as my own fingers. His scarlet wattle quivered under his beak like the wrinkly flesh under Abuela's chin. I followed him around the yard at a safe distance, catching his steely, sideways glances at me with his glassy eye as if he knew what I was thinking. I was scared of him, yet fascinated by the architecture of his muted gold plumage; his waxy tail feathers like a poof of exclamation points, as bold as any peacock's. Commanding even Tiger's respect, he roamed the backyard freely, pecking and scratching and crowing every morning at dawn. He was majestic, stately, and royal, his comb like a big red crown. I decided to name him Rey, Spanish for "king." Abuelo agreed. But Abuelo didn't bring Rey home just for decoration; he had plans for him, which became obvious as soon as I saw Rey in the chicken coop perched on top of a hen, pecking at her head. Just as had happened with Bonny and Bernie, within a few weeks there were close to a dozen baby chicks darting around the coop like tiny yellow pinballs. What was Abuelo thinking? Surely Mamá would notice and become infuriated.

But it wasn't Mamá who would bring about the demise of the chickens. That would be Caridad. Her bedroom window faced my bedroom window, and at least once a week, usually just before my bedtime, Caridad and Pedrito would scream at each other, firing off cuss words in Spanish like my *tío* Emilio when he got drunk: *¡Papayua! ¡Hijo de la gran puta! ¡Singa'o!* Like gossipy old ladies, Caco and I would turn off the lights, then crouch under my window to eavesdrop on the spectacle. Shushing each other, we'd try unsuccessfully to hold back our giggles, exchanging wide-eyed *Oh my God* looks after each bad word, the last even more vulgar than the one before it. And in between the insults: shattering glass, wall pounding, door slamming, even an occasional slap. Caridad and Pedrito's epic fights were more titillating than any R-rated movie we'd ever sneaked into or any of Mamá's telenovelas on the Spanish channel.

Compelled by the ruckus from next door, so loud it echoed down the hallway, the rest of the family would eventually trickle into my room and take a seat by the window. It was a weird kind of family night for us, sitting around in slippers and pajamas as if we were watching TV, whispering comments to each other: Ay, Dios mío . . . *That's true. I saw her* . . . No lo creo . . . *How can he be so mean?* Then someone, usually Abuelo, would feel guilty for setting a bad example for Caco and me; he'd put on a half-serious tone and then coax everyone to go to bed. It was during one of those nights that we all heard Caridad scream at Pedrito, "You're as annoying as that goddamned rooster next door, waking me up every morning at dawn to get you this and that and make your damn breakfast. *¡Cómo jodes!* You'll be making your own breakfast if you keep it up, you lazy bastard! Why don't you go live next door with those filthy chickens and those dumb *guajiros* you love so much!"

When the officer from Animal Control showed up a week later, we knew it must have been Caridad who called in the complaint. At first, when Mamá peered through the peephole she thought a police officer was at the door and feared the worst. "*Ay, Dios,* Riqui

60

come—*apúrate*," she called me, pale with panic. "Open the door. Something must've happened to Papá and Caco." The officer greeted us with a "good afternoon," but as soon as Mamá returned his greeting with her formal, night-class English, "Yes, how do you do, sir," he began speaking to her in Spanish. He introduced himself as Officer Ramirez and explained, "No, *señora*, I'm not a *policía*, no one is dead, *no ha pasado nada*. I'm from Miami-Dade Animal Control. We received a complaint about chickens in your backyard." Ecstatic to learn that Papá and Caco weren't dead after all, Mamá clutched her neck, letting out a soap-opera sigh, and grabbed the officer by the hand, insisting he step inside, "*Ven, entra mi'jo*, sit, I'll make you *un cafecito*."

She was so flustered she hadn't really grasped what the officer had said or why he had come. Topping the inner basket of the espresso maker with coffee, she called out to Abuelo, "There's *un hombre* here to see you. *Algo* about the chickens, I think." Abuelo clonked down the hall in his oxfords. He looked blankly at the officer sitting at the kitchen table, sipping his *cafecito*. "*¿Qué pasó?*" he asked, and the officer explained himself a second time. "*¿Cómo? Un* animal *qué* officer? *¿Qué's eso?*" Abuelo still did not understand the predicament. "I need to look in your backyard, *¿está bien?*" Officer Ramirez asked, fastening a form to his clipboard and pulling a red pen from his shirt pocket. "*Sí.* Come." Abuelo motioned to the officer, leading him politely out the back door, asking if he wanted a beer. The officer said he couldn't drink on the job. "What job?" Abuelo asked, still clueless.

I followed them into the yard. Officer Ramirez marched right over to the chicken coop: "You know this is against the law?" he asked Abuelo without lifting his eyes from the clipboard, scribbling notes and checking boxes on the form. "*Qué's* against the law?"

Abuelo asked, perplexed. "Raising fowl in an R-zoned area," Officer Ramirez answered, as if quoting from the county ordinance. Abuelo still didn't get it. "Foul? What do you mean? *Un* foul play?" The officer began getting short with him, "No. No chickens. No *gallinas. ¿Comprende?* You have one week to get rid of the chickens, the rooster, and the coop," he told Abuelo, tearing off a carbon copy of the form and handing it to him without looking at Abuelo, who was still complaining. "*¿Qué? No gallinas* in my own backyard? That's *imposible.* Aren't you Cuban?" Abuelo asked, as if the problem were simply a cultural misunderstanding.

Perhaps realizing the gravity of the situation, Abuelo straightened up, hiked his Bermuda shorts up above his belly button, crossed his arms over his gray-haired chest, and raised his voice: "*¡Qué carajo!* What do you mean I can't have chickens? I can have all the chickens I want—*cojones*—this is a free country. That's why I came here from Cuba and now you tell me I can't have chickens. *¡Le ronca el mango!*" Trying to defuse Abuelo, Officer Ramirez kept repeating, "*Señor, cálmese.* Calm down, *señor*," as he stepped backward along the side of the house, adding, "I'll be back next week to inspect and close the case," when he was clear of Abuelo's reach. Abuelo picked up one of Mamá's potted bougainvillea, ready to hurl it at the officer, before he calmed down and mumbled to himself, "*Esto nunca hubiera pasado en Cuba*—this would have never happened in Cuba." Standing motionless in the backyard, he scanned the citation, trying to decipher the English. "FINE? That means *good*, no? If I pay him fifty dollars everything will be FINE? What does that mean?" I had to translate the bad news for him, "No, Abuelo, FINE *quiere decir* that you'll have to pay fifty dollars a day if we don't get rid of the chickens."

I thought we'd just return the chickens to Ignacio, but no. Two days later the massacre began. I couldn't stand hearing the desperate clucks of the chickens or the sound of their necks snapping in Abuela's hands as Abuelo handed them to her one by one. But I couldn't stand *not* watching the massacre. So I sat on the floor behind the Florida room's sliding glass door, watching Abuela toss the strangled chickens onto the terrace, their bodies still quivering until she finished off each one with a knife clean across the neck, decapitating them, their white feathers turning red and redder, then dunking the headless chickens into a vat of boiling water to scald the skin and loosen the feathers off.

That night Abuela made one of my favorite dishes—*fricasé de pollo*. She set down the platter with pride, the talon scratches on her hands and forearms still raw. I took only rice and fried plantains, though I could barely eat even those. I was sickened by the sight of the chicken swimming in garlic sauce studded with carrots and raisins. Perhaps because Mamá could sense her son's horror or simply because she too was repulsed, she passed the platter to Papá without taking a piece of chicken. But no one else seemed to care: Abuelo claimed it was just as tasty as the chicken he used to raise in Cuba; Papá ate two drumsticks and a breast; Abuela said the bland chicken from *el Winn Deezee* couldn't compare, and Caco agreed, as if he had ever tasted anything that hadn't been store-bought. I wasn't sure I could ever love an animal or my family again. Who were these merciless people, these murderers, especially Abuelo? Didn't he love the chickens as much as I did? Who would be next: Bonny or Bernie? Their bunnies as appetizers? My sorrow boiled into outrage until I shoved my plate aside and blurted out, "Hey, why don't we just eat Tiger next week? I hear dogs are delicious!" Then I got up from the table, stomped to my room, and slammed the door shut.

Maybe Caridad was right, I thought, maybe my family was nothing more than dumb country bumpkins. They had killed and eaten my pets. For days I avoided Abuelo's eyes across the dinner table. I didn't speak to him either, until finally, one afternoon, he offered to help me feed Bonny and Bernie. "Are you okay, *mi'jo?*" he asked me. "I guess so," I mumbled. "What's going to happen to Rey?" I asked. "Ignacio said he'll take him back—he could always use another *gallo* at his *finca*," Abuelo said, which made me feel a little more at ease.

"*Mira, mi'jo,*" Abuelo started, "*lo siento,* but don't be so upset. I never told you this, but I didn't leave Papo in Cuba. I lost him at the dog fights in Palmira when I was a *muchacho*. He was a real *campeón*, but his day finally came against a pit bull." "What! You did that to Papo?" I shouted, horrified all over again. "You killed him too? You don't love anything!" Abuelo's face changed; he became a shamed little boy. "No, no—that's not true, *mi'jo*," he said. "I still think of him all the time. I adored Papo, but I swore I'd never get close to an animal again. *¿Comprendes?*" "Not really—I don't get it. Why, Abuelo, why?" I pleaded for an explanation.

He stared straight into my eyes and then took me in his arms. It was the first time the man had ever hugged me. "I don't know, *mi'jo*, I don't know. That's just the way it is—*así es la vida*," he said without letting go. In his embrace, my pain and confusion connected with that of his past. Though I wasn't sure how to forgive him entirely, I knew that I would. He was my Abuelo, my *compadre*, my confidant, after all.

I asked if he needed any help taking apart the coop. "*Sí, claro,*" he said, placing his hand on top of my head. "Let's go." With the same tools we'd used to build the coop, we pulled apart the timbers, snipping the chicken wire loose and winding it back into rolls.

Within a couple hours the only evidence left of the chickens was a few cold eggs in a nest and the dirt patch where they had once scratched and pecked all day long. "*No te preocupes*, the grass will grow back soon. Everything will be as it was—back to normal. That's the way it is," Abuelo said.

I began fearing something terrible would happen to Bonny and Bernie and the bunnies: Would they get sick and die? Maybe there was a law against rabbits too. Maybe they would escape from their cage and never come back. A few weeks later, our principal asked students to donate items for that year's Easter Fair. I decided to donate Bonny and Bernie and the bunnies. The day of the fair, I watched as Enriquito Moreno won the Musical Roulette Walk and collected his prize. Luckily I knew him; he had sat next to me for a while in Sister Pancretila's class the previous year. And I liked him; he always let me borrow loose-leaf paper and his scented markers. I was glad he would be taking care of Bonny—but did he know how?

I walked over to him. He was already holding Bonny in his hands. "Hey, look, isn't he cool?" he said to me. "Yeah, but *he* is really a *she*. Her name is Bonny." "How do you know?" he asked. "She used to be mine, but my mom wouldn't let me keep her," I lied, and went on to explain that Bonny needed to eat three different vegetables a day, how much she loved strawberries, and that he could get boxes of lettuce leaves for free at El Milagro, just like Abuelo taught me. Number by number during the Musical Roulette, I watched as Bernie and the rest of the bunnies were given away, silently saying good-bye as they were carried off by strangers.

After losing the chickens and rabbits, I lost Tiger to Caco. He became possessive of *his* dog again, claiming Tiger was never mine, and forbade me from grooming or walking him. He took

Tiger everywhere and showed him off to his friends as if he had trained him. Tiger became *his* pal, and I returned to my usual after-school routine: homework, reruns of *I Love Lucy*, *The Brady Bunch*, and *Bewitched*, then an hour of coloring or playing with my Legos before dinner. But I couldn't forget our backyard farm. Every time I gazed through the sliding glass window, I'd see Bernie and Bonny snuggled in their cage; whenever I stepped out back to call in Misu, I'd hear the chickens clucking and pecking. The backyard felt like a place of memory and imagination, my own version of Abuelo's lost Cuba.

A few weeks after Abuelo took Rey back to Ignacio's farm, Mamá and Papá, Abuela and Abuelo, and Caco and I were in the Florida room watching TV when we heard a slight disturbance from next door. To me, it sounded like little more than the clang of a garbage can. But Abuelo knew the pop of a gun quite well from his years in *la milicia*. "*Voy a ver* what that noise was," he said nervously, but without making much of a fuss. He put on his slippers and walked out the front door. Unalarmed, we kept watching TV, but about ten minutes after Abuelo left, we heard a siren blaring down the street. Instead of fading away, the sound grew louder, then ended abruptly, seemingly in front of our house. Mamá became hysterical: "*¡Alabao sea Dios! ¿Qué habrá pasado, madre mía?*" She ran into the street in her housecoat, chased by Papá and the rest of us.

A police car and ambulance were parked in front of Caridad and Pedrito's home. Papá dashed down their walkway, but was stopped by a police officer at the front door just when Abuelo emerged. He had a distant gaze and could barely move. Papá wrapped his arm around him, helped him down the steps and toward us. "*¡Ave María!*

What happened? *¿Qué pasó?*" Mamá and Abuela both demanded. "*Pedrito se ha vuelto loco*—he's gone crazy, completely crazy," Abuelo said, his eyes glazed over, his pajama shirt and cheek smeared with bloody handprints. "*¡Qué barbaridad!* How could he—his own wife and then himself. *¿Por qué*, Pedrito, *por qué?*" The red and blue lights spun in Abuelo's eyes and washed over us, over the street and palm trees, over the mailboxes and lawns, over all of Güecheste, terrifyingly quiet and still.

THREE

EL RATONCITO MIGUEL

I "forgot" my gym clothes, again, and Miss DeVarona "understood," again, pretending she believed my excuse that my only pair of shorts got soaked on the clothesline the night before. I lied. I just had to. She had taken down the St. Patrick's Day decorations, which meant she was getting ready to decorate the classroom for Easter. If I excused myself from gym, I knew she'd ask me to help her. And she did. "Ricardo"—she called me by my formal name—"what do you think about this purple for the front bulletin board?" she asked, holding up a piece of construction paper. I seized the opportunity. "Do you need any help, Miss DeVarona?" I volunteered, looking up at her from the history textbook I was pretending to read. "I sure do, young man," she said. "Come over here. And bring your scissors and glue."

Miss DeVarona was my favorite teacher: kind, loving, and generous. She indulged me, making me feel understood and safe—confident enough that I told her, "Well, purple isn't really the right color for the background. Let's do the baskets in purple instead, then make the background a light green, like a field of grass for the Easter bunny." She agreed. We then stuffed the Easter basket cutout with sparkly plastic grass and decorated the cardboard eggs with bands of glitter. But the Easter bunny also needed something—a special touch to make it look real. "Let's make the tail out of cotton balls," I suggested. "Yes, wonderful—what a great idea!" she praised me. When the class returned from gym, she presented our *masterpiece* to everyone and then asked me to stand up. "Isn't Ricardo talented? He's so creative. Let's give him a big thanks," she said, leading them in a round of applause. I took my seat, feeling proud at first, and then ashamed of feeling proud after catching a few of the boys' sneers and Ralph Castellano's teasing remark: "Oh how cute . . . Isn't that pretty . . . Ricar*da*."

At the first parent-teacher conference that quarter, Papá told me Miss DeVarona said I was *sensitive* and *very creative* and that I should do something artistic when I grew up, like painting or architecture or writing. "*Sí*, if you want to eat your whole life nothing but *frijoles negros* and rice. You should be a doctor or an engineer," he told me dismissively. "What's wrong with her?" Papá asked me, not knowing that Miss DeVarona's face was partially paralyzed, the result of an operation she'd had years before, though she never told us exactly what kind. Her left side never smiled, never blinked, never moved when she spoke to us, or sipped her tea, or read to us from the Chronicles of Narnia after lunch.

Perhaps because she was uncomfortable having the class watch her while she read, she usually kept us busy with something artsy-crafty. Some kids filled in coloring books; others twisted and bent colored pipe cleaners into tiny animals. But most of the kids—except me—had a latch hook rug kit. They pulled pieces of yarn through the color-coded mat as Miss DeVarona pulled us into an imaginary world of magical wardrobes and talking lions. I hadn't dared to ask my parents for a rug kit; they were too expensive—ten dollars for even the cheapest one, according to Ernesto Perez, the richest kid in class. Ernesto brought in a new kit every week. Besides, I was sure Abuela wouldn't find rug-making appropriate for *un hombre*; she'd probably throw it away, just like the strawberry-scented erasers she had taken from me.

But if I kept the kit hidden in my desk at school, Abuela would never know. I decided to save up and buy one. For weeks I did without the Little Debbie cakes I ate at lunch, socking away thirty-five cents a day until I had saved twelve dollars. That very afternoon, I rode my bike about five miles to the arts-and-crafts megastore near *tía* Ofelia's house. *Diamond's—A Woman's Paradise*, the humongous sign read, painted in cursive across the entire front of the building as if a giant had written out each word by hand. Abuela always made me wait outside the store when she and Mamá went shopping for birthday and *quinceañera* decorations, but today it would be all mine to enjoy—a Garden of Eden filled with colored sand, silk roses, plastic tiaras, candy molds, glass beads, skeins of yarn in colors I had never imagined. I lingered in every aisle, dreaming of all the dazzling things I could make, if I had enough money: a rhinestone collar for Misu, hanging macramé holders for Mamá's houseplants, a Popsicle stick lamp for my room.

Over an hour into wandering Diamond's, I found the latch hook rug kits—an entire aisle to choose from: owls, sunsets, butterflies, eagles, kittens, ladybugs, sunflowers, lighthouses, unicorns. How could I decide? Most of the kits were more than twelve dollars. Even so, it took me another hour to narrow it down to two choices: Mickey and Minnie Mouse wreathed by red hearts, or a tiger crouching in jungle-green grass. I had a crush on Mickey and Minnie, as bad as the crush they had on each other. But maybe the tiger's fiery gaze and steely look would seem manly enough to earn Abuela's approval. I made my decision hoping Abuela would allow me to hang the finished rug on the wall above my bed.

Half a block from my house, I saw Abuela standing on the front porch, waiting to interrogate me. "Where you were, *cabrón?*" she demanded as I pedaled up the driveway. School had ended four hours earlier—I hadn't realized I'd been gone so long. "Umm, I was at Enriquito's house . . . We were playing . . . outside, *te lo juro,*" I swore, but she locked her eyes on my bag. It had *Diamond's—A Woman's Paradise* printed right on it. "*¿Qué carajo?* You go to Diamond's?*"* she asked, her eyes fierce. I stood silent as she snatched the bag from my hand and pulled out the rug kit. "What's this?" she barked, her eyes as big as her mouth. "It's for making a rug. It's a tiger. See?" I explained softly as she examined the kit. "A rug? *Con* yarn? What's next—ballet? I told you *diez mil veces:* it's better to be *it* and not look like *it,* than to look like *it* even if you are not *it.*" At that age, I only understood that *it* meant watching telenovelas; *it* was my paint-by-number sets; *it* was my cousin's Easy-Bake Oven I wanted for my own—all the things I enjoyed for which she constantly humiliated me. "I'm keeping this until your *padre* gets home." She took the kit into her room, closing the door behind her even as I tried to explain. "But it's for school. Everyone has one . . ."

True to her word, when Papá walked through the front door, she marched out of her room, my kit tucked under her arm. "*Mira esto,*" she began, tossing the box onto the kitchen table. "He wants to make rugs now. You want your *hijo* doing *cosas* like that? What will be next? He can't keep this." I wanted my father to shut her up for once, but he didn't, or couldn't, for reasons I was too young to understand. Why didn't either of my parents ever take my side and stand up to her?

But that day Papá must've felt sorry for me; instead of completely giving in to Abuela, he suggested we exchange the kit for something else. "Okay," my grandmother said reluctantly, insisting, however, that we go exchange it before dinner and that she would go with us. Papá, still in his necktie, drove us back to Diamond's. "Wait in the car," she instructed him as she grabbed my hand, pulling me out of the backseat and dragging me into the store. We tramped down the aisles trying to find something appropriate, Abuela tsk-tsking past the needlepoint sets and jars of glitter. Finally, she took interest in a leather wallet and key chain kit, which she held up in front of my face. "See? Leather is for *hombres*," she decreed, pointing to the photo of the boy on the box. He wore a cowboy hat as he stitched through the leather.

The leather kit was dumb and dull—I tossed it on my desk when we got home and never opened it. With nothing to do with my hands except color in my same old coloring books, I listened even more intently as Miss DeVarona read on about the White Witch of Narnia who made it always winter but never Christmas. Abuela was just as bad as her, I thought—or was she? A few weeks before the White Witch was killed by Aslan the lion, Abuela announced at the dinner table that one of her "clients" had settled a big debt with her. She then slipped a plain white envelope to my parents and said, "*Coje*, this is for you—so you can take Riqui to Disney. We'll stay here." From the warm glance she gave me, I figured it was her way of making up for the latch hook rug incident. Nevertheless, Mamá was shocked and nearly spit up her flan; Papá couldn't say anything except *gracias*. For months my parents had been telling us just how much overtime they were working to save enough money for our first weekend trip to Walt Disney World. The whole school year they had been threatening to cancel their plans whenever Caco or I misbehaved or got an unacceptable "U" grade in conduct. But all along I suspected it was probably a front in case they couldn't afford to make it happen.

The night before the trip, I thought about the bedtime story that Papá used to tell me about El Ratoncito Miguel, who tricked La Cucaracha Martina into diving into a pool of sweetened condensed milk, where she drowned. I said three Hail Marys and an Our Father, asked God to keep us safe on the trip, and fell asleep. When Mamá came into my room the next morning to wake me, I was already up and getting dressed. The sun wasn't even out yet, but I had made Mamá promise we'd get an early start so we could arrive at Disney World just when the park opened and make the most of the day. In half an hour we were all packed into Papá's immaculately clean *Malibú*, ready to go. I checked the Mickey Mouse watch that my rich *tía* Gloria had given me for Christmas: 6 A.M.—we'd be there by 10 A.M. Grateful that Abuela had given my parents the money for the trip, I was also glad she wasn't going, as I watched her waving good-bye, standing in the amber glow of the front porch light, the stars above our rooftop beginning to fade in the morning twilight.

Seven in the morning: only three more hours to go on the Florida Turnpike when Mamá smelled something funny. "*¡Ay, qué peste!* Did we go by a landfill out here?" She lowered her window to investigate whether the foul odor was coming from inside or outside the car. "Is from inside the car," she concluded, and turned to look at me. "Was it you, *mi'jo*? Did you fart?" she asked. "No, no," I said, making my best angel face: eyebrows pulled up, eyes wide open showing I had nothing to hide behind them. "Oh, who was it then, your Fairy Fart Mother?" Caco blurted out, his cracking teenage voice underscoring his sarcasm. "Shut up, butt-face," I shouted. "Did you hear what he said?" I turned to Mamá, trying to get Caco in trouble. "No, what he said?" she replied, unable to understand his smart-ass comment without translation. But how would I say "Fairy Fart Mother" in Spanish? *¿Mi Madrina de los Peos? ¿El Guardia de mis Peos?* I gave up. "Never mind."

Ordinarily I would've admitted to the act—no biggie. Caco and I had fart wars all the time, competing to see who could outdo whom with the loudest, longest, or smelliest. But this was different. *"No, te lo juro,* Mamá, it wasn't me," I repeated, not wanting anything— especially not impending diarrhea—to ruin my first trip to the promised land. But I did have to go—real bad. My stomach was in an uproar of anticipation; I was finally going to meet the most important man in my life: El Ratoncito Miguel, Mickey Mouse himself. And it was about time—I was already eleven years old, and the only kid in my class who hadn't been to Walt Disney World yet.

"You need to go to *el baño,* don't you?" Mamá asked. "No, I'm fine. I'm fine," I lied again, trying to ignore my cramps, hoping I could hold it for the rest of the three hours to Orlando. But it was no use; a loud one slipped out like a foghorn. *"¡Ay, Dios!"* Mamá yelled, waving her hand in front of her nose and lowering her window as if she were going to pass out. *"Qué va,* this boy can't wait—*va a explotar.* He's pale—*míralo.* Pull off the road someplace," she instructed Papá, who was gripping the vinyl-wrapped wheel of his Chevy Malibu as proudly as if he were driving a Rolls-Royce. The last thing he wanted to do was stop in the middle of the turnpike. "*¡No! ¿Tú estás loca?* We can't stop—what if they hit my car? You can wait, *mi'jo,* can't you?" Papá hoped, finding my face in the rearview mirror. "Yes, yes. I don't have to go, Papá," I swore, even as my stomach cramped up again. Pointing through the windshield, Mamá directed Papá, "Over there—*perfecto.* Over there—*ándale.*" "Okay, okay. *No jodas más!*" he shouted and switched on his hazard lights, inching the car onto the paved shoulder.

It still didn't dawn on me that I was about to take my first shit in the woods until Mamá pulled a jumbo roll of toilet paper from her just-in-case tote bag. "*Menos mal* I remember to bring this," she said proudly, "*por si las moscas.*" That was her favorite Cuban motto, *por si las moscas—in case of the flies*—an idiom meaning "always be prepared for the worst," and she was—always. Besides the toilet paper, she had brought a cooler full of ham and cream cheese sandwiches, grapes, and pineapple sodas in case there were no convenience stores; five cans of OFF! mosquito repellent in case one wasn't enough; a tube of Krazy Glue just in case *something* broke; and a spare set of house and car keys in case Papá lost his, again.

"*Vamos,*" she said, plucking me from the car and leading me down the embankment by the hand with the roll tucked beneath her arm. We scurried through a stretch of itchy grass that brushed at my knees, until we reached the edge of the tree line beyond which everything was wilderness. "*Allá,* behind the trees. No one will see you," she directed, pointing to a cluster of sable palms amid a clump of bushes. "Hold the tree, *y agáchate* all the way down, like a toilet but lower. Like this," she instructed, squatting down herself to demonstrate. "But what if there's something out there, Mamá? What if—" "Shh, don't worry, *mi'jo,*" she assured me. "Now *apúrate,* we don't want to miss El Ratoncito Miguel."

It was the last thing I expected: taking a dump while thinking of Mickey Mouse as cars whizzed by on the turnpike and I nervously turned over my fears. What if something bit my backside? Even worse: What if I missed and soiled my new sneakers? How mortifying. But I emerged unsoiled, zipped back up, and handed the roll of toilet paper to Mamá, avoiding her eyes and steeling myself for the wisecracks from my brother. "Did an alligator bite your weenie off?" he yelled out the window as we approached. Just when I thought I couldn't be more embarrassed, Mamá pulled her Kodak Instamatic out of her tote. "*Ponte* over there, by the tree. No, *un poquito* to the right," she said—and snap: my first shit in the woods documented on film.

No matter how ridiculous, Mamá insisted on recording every part of our lives with photos. It annoyed the hell out of us, constantly interrupting the flow of whatever we were doing, and you could tell from our grumpy faces and slouched bodies in the photos. Still, we'd try to please her most of the time, knowing it was important to her. She'd send the photos along with letters to her family in Cuba, which was the only way she could stay in touch with them and keep them up-to-date on our lives in America. I could only imagine the embarrassing narrative in the letter that would accompany the photo of me and the tree—an incident that would become infamous in our family. It became a Blanco family road trip game—*spot the tree where Riqui did number two*—that passed the time on every trip to Disney World that followed.

"*Ay, mira*, I forgot I packed this *por si las moscas*," Mamá said, pulling a bottle of Pepto-Bismol out of her tote and shaking it. Indeed, she always thought of everything. "No-no-no," Papá protested, "no drinking in the car." But Mamá insisted it was an emergency and he let me take a swig—thank goodness. "Did I ever tell you"—she started with the same old story she'd told a hundred times—"when I was a *niña* in Cuba, we were so poor we had no toilet. I had go to *el baño* every day under the guava trees behind *la casa*. I wiped myself with newspaper, if there was even newspaper. Sometimes I had to use the leaves right off the guava tree. You boys don't know how good you have it." Somehow I was a little less grossed out by her story that time. I heard and understood, for the first time, that certain tone of pride in her voice as if there were something virtuous about defecating outdoors. Perhaps I had just gone through some bizarre Cuban rite of passage with my mother. Or perhaps it was because I was relieved, and *relieved*, that it was all over and we were back on the road to Disney World.

With each passing mile north of Miami there was less and less that reminded me of where we lived. The emerald lawns of the suburbs gave way to endless stretches of saw grass shining gold in the newly risen sun. The sound of car horns turned into a quiet wind easing in through the windows. And there was nothing in view to remind me we were Cuban either: no billboards in Spanish for El Dorado Furniture or Rivero's Funeral Home's discount packages—coffin, wake, and mass for one low price; no Virgin of La Caridad bumper stickers or Cuban flags hanging from rearview mirrors; and no bodegas or *cafeterías* at which to stop for *café cubano*, though Mamá had packed a thermos full of *café*, in case of the flies. The last thing to disappear was Papá's favorite Cuban station from Miami, *Radio Mambí*, playing static-laced Cuban songs between hourly anti-Castro jabs and fist-pounding rants delivered by men whose every fourth word was *la Revolución . . . la Revolución . . . la Revolución*.

Speeding in silence along the edge of the Everglades, past stands of cypress trees rising from the plain like the buttresses of cathedral ruins, I felt we had entered another country. Papá broke the spell when he announced, "I have *una sorpresa,*" which usually meant gum or candy or money. But not this time. "Close your eyes," he instructed all of us. We heard him click off the dead radio, followed by the sound of Papá sliding back his car seat, fidgeting with something, jamming something, then clicking buttons. Suddenly, the car speakers blared with the voluptuous voice of Celia Cruz belting out her Afro-Cuban hit: *"Quimbara, Quimbara Quimba, Quimba-ba, Eh mamá, eh mamá . . ."* *"¿Cómo?* How could this be? Where is the music coming from? We're nowhere," Mamá said. Papá explained he had bought a used eight-track player at the Tropicaire Flea Market and had it installed under the seat.

Caco and I didn't agree on much, but we did agree on one thing: we both hated Cuban music. We thought it was tacky, especially when our parents really got into it. Mamá poured herself and Papá the last bit of Cuban coffee and they sang along to a cheesy bolero by Olga Guillot, glancing at each other and dueting like Sonny and Cher. Mamá had a pleasing voice and would often sing while doing the dishes or hanging the laundry on the clothesline; you couldn't make out the difference between her singing and Olga Guillot's singing. But Papá must have been tone-deaf; he sounded like someone was pulling at his sideburns, the way Sister Mary Jane did to me during hymn practice when I didn't sing loud enough. Annoying us further, he played air bongos on the steering wheel. We couldn't take it anymore.

"Papá, put in another tape—pleeez," Caco begged. With a tinge of shame in his voice, Papá said that after buying the eight-track player, he didn't have enough money to buy new tapes. So we were stuck with the same old *Hoy como ayer*—the compilation of Cuban hits from the fifties and sixties played at every family gathering for years. Unless we did something, we'd have to endure it yet again for the rest of the trip. Caco and I looked at each other, silently trying to devise some new act of defiance, but instead we resorted to the same old tactic: Caco stuck his index fingers in his ears and hummed, and I followed, both of us blathering *bla-bla-bla-bla*. It was the best we could do, but not enough to drown them out. Those songs were unstoppable.

There was something bizarre about Celia Cruz's soulful rhapsodies and Julio Iglesias's crooning as we sped past billboards advertising Motel 8s and Shoney's All-You-Can-Eat buffets. The sound track in the car didn't match the names on the highway signs—Johnston, Brooksville, Lehigh—which conjured images of general stores and bowlegged cowboys. Miles away from Miami, everything felt so exotic, so American; but inside *el Malibú* everything was still as Cuban as ever. "Come on, Papá, let's stop here," Caco and I pleaded with him as we passed the sign announcing the Fort Pierce Service Plaza ahead. We wanted a break from the barrage of bongos and congas. We swore we had to pee, but he wasn't quite persuaded. Then Caco added, "And we can wash the dead bugs off the windshield." "*Verdad*, good idea," Papá agreed.

It had taken Papá two years of twelve-hour days as a butcher at El Cocuyito to save for the down payment on *el Malibú* at Anthony Abraham Chevrolet, a landmark famous for its humongous American flag, which you could spot a mile down *Calle Ocho*. "What a country," he said, teary-eyed, when he drove *el Malibú* off the lot. It was his first car in America, and he was in love with it. Every Saturday he'd wash and wax it, then stand back to admire its metallic copper finish glittering in the Florida sun, the beguiling grin of its front grille, and its headlights as bewitching as cats' eyes. No one, not even

Mamá, was allowed to eat or drink in *el Malibú;* if we slammed the door, he'd make us open it again and close it softly; if we forgot to roll up the window and it rained, he'd hand-dry every inch of the car inside, stroking the dashboard softly, memorizing its beauty, and staring into the neon-green dials as if he were gazing at the stars. He pampered *el Malibú* more than he did Mamá, she would complain, which wasn't terribly far from the truth.

When we pulled into the service plaza, he fished a rag out of the trunk and before pumping the gas wrapped the rag around the neck of the nozzle to catch any dribbles of gasoline; then he checked the oil three or four times to make sure he wasn't running low; then he pulled out the pressure gauge from the glove box and checked the air in each tire, twice. The squeegee was useless on the bugs splattered all over the windshield and chrome bumper; he started scraping them off one by one with his fingernail. That's when Caco and I lost our patience and bolted out of the car and into the store to scope out the candy and bubble gum aisle. By the time Papá came in to pay, we had picked out a handful of Bazooka bubble gum squares. "Please . . . we're on vacation," I begged him while sliding the gum onto the counter. "Okay, *pero nada más,*" he said.

"What?" the clerk asked Papá, looking at him quizzically. The space between his eyebrows bunched up in confusion. "*Notin, notin,*" Papá replied in his best English, and then asked the clerk, "Do you have *winchil wacher?*" Caco and I knew what Papá was trying to say, but the clerk had no idea. He obviously didn't speak Spanish and wasn't Cuban, judging from the falcon tattooed on his forearm, the size of a watermelon, and the dark-red beard that came to a sharp point several inches beneath his chin. His belt buckle was the size of my hand and depicted a strange flag that, while red, white, and blue, definitely was not the American flag—the stars and bars were in the wrong places. I had never seen anybody like him, and he had probably never seen anybody like us.

"*Winchil wacher. Winchil wacher,*" Papá kept repeating, embarrassing us with every syllable of his terrible English. The clerk's blank look turned to one of disdain: "Listen, mistah, I can't understand one iota of what you be saying. You people need to get learning English. You're in America." Finally putting an end to it, Caco blurted out, "Do you have any windshield washer?" enunciating every consonant that Papá couldn't. "Yeah, over there, bottom shelf," the clerk said. "Anything else, mistah?" Papá was as humiliated as we were embarrassed; he paid for our bubble gum, the gas, and a jug of windshield washer without saying a word to the clerk, who put Papá's change on the counter, instead of handing it to him, as if he were loath to touch Papá's hand.

We got back in *el Malibú* and drove to the restaurant and gift shop at the other end of the service plaza. Mamá stepped inside slowly and cautiously scanned the crowd like a dumbfounded *señorita* Dorothy in the land of *los americanos*. No one looked Cuban, much less *felt* Cuban; none of the men smelled like cigars, none of the women had their hair up in rollers, and no one was kissing anyone on the cheek or yelling to each other across the room. There wasn't a single word of Spanish in the air and all the signs were in English only. Mamá and Papá were at our mercy; they didn't dare engage anyone without us as backup translators, and that was fine with us. It gave us a linguistic upper hand, which we had learned to take great advantage of. Back home, at our local Kmart, we'd always maneuver Mamá into the checkout line with the most American-looking, freckle-faced, strawberry-haired, English-only cashier we could find, knowing Mamá wouldn't be able to argue over the true price of items she had agreed to buy for us because we said they were on sale.

At the fast-food counter in the service plaza, Caco zeroed in on a middle-aged woman at the register. "Look at her name," he whispered, nudging me with his elbow and pointing with his eyes to the lady's name tag: Joanne. Besides her *gringa* name, she wasn't wearing any jewelry, not even earrings. Clearly she wasn't Cuban. That gave us an advantage over Mamá, when she asked us to order what we were usually *allowed* and could *afford*: a plain hamburger and a Sprite for her; a double cheeseburger and a milkshake for Papá; two cheeseburgers, small fries, and small Cokes for each of us—and nothing more. Speaking to Joanne as fast as we could, so that Mamá wouldn't understand us, we sneaked an extra cheeseburger, *large* fries, *large* Cokes, and an ice cream sandwich into our order. When the food came, Mamá questioned us, but we just gazed at her innocently, casually explaining, "Oh, she must have made a mistake." Mamá looked at us with pursed lips. Of course she knew the "mistake" was our doing, but before she could say anything, we darted away and sat in a booth. We knew she wouldn't dare make a scene and refute the order on her own in English. By the time she came over to us, we had devoured our extra cheeseburger and split the ice cream sandwich. We deserved a treat after the two hours of Cuban music we'd had to endure—and the two hours left to go.

With full bellies and wads of Bazooka gum tucked secretly under our tongues (we were not allowed to chew gum in *el Malibú*, of course), we jumped into the backseat again. As soon as we left the service plaza and merged into traffic, Papá popped the eight-track tape back into the player. Caco managed to doze off, his face smushed against the window, distorted into a drooling Creature Feature monster. He had already been to Disney World with our cousin Mirita the year before, so he wasn't nearly as excited as me. He thought he was already an expert on the park, as well as everything else for that matter. But I couldn't sleep. I didn't want to miss one second of the trip. Instead I took out the pamphlets on the Magic Kingdom that Mirita had given me.

For months, I had kept the pamphlets on my bedside table, studying their glossy pages every night. Before bedtime, I'd quiz myself on the names of the attractions I had memorized one by one, as well as their locations on the park map. Now, in the backseat of *el Malibú*, browsing through the pamphlets for the hundredth time, I still didn't quite believe such a magical place really existed: a place where buck-toothed bears yodeled while playing banjos; where openmouthed hippos rose from a river and hissing snakes hung from jungle trees; where pirates had gunfights in village streets paved with doubloons. How many hours had I spent coloring El Ratoncito Miguel's ears, wearing down my black crayon to a stub? How many nights had I imagined El Ratoncito Miguel's voice as Papá told me bedtime stories? How many times had I read my Cinderella storybook, engrossed by her lemon-yellow hair, her teal gown flowing like a waterfall, and her sparkling tiara, secretly wanting to be as beautiful as she was? How could Caco sleep?

My reverie was broken by a booming *"Al combate corred, Bayameses . . . Que morir por la patria es vivir . . ."*—my parents singing along to a rendition of the Cuban National Anthem. Caco woke up in a panic, disoriented until he realized the noise was emanating from our superstar parents. "No, not again! They should go on *The Gong Show*. We gotta do something," he said, looking at me as if it was my fault. "What if we stick toilet paper in our ears?" I proposed. Contemplating for a minute the astonishing fact that his younger brother had actually come up with a good idea, Caco finally responded, "Yeah, but how are we going to get the paper out of her bag, doofus?"

It was then that I noticed a wad of chewed bubble gum stuck to the seat. It must've fallen out of Caco's mouth as he slept. I was going to tell Papá on him, but then I thought about Ernesto Suarez from my class, who'd stuff bubble gum up his nostrils for a laugh. "I've got it! Here, stick this in your ears," I said in a flash, tweezing the gum off the seat with my thumb and index finger. "You're crazy. That's gross," Caco said, but I could tell he knew it was a good idea. He put the gum back in his mouth to soften it up again, then pulled it apart into two pieces and plugged his ears. "Well? Does it work?" I asked him. He didn't respond. I poked him and got his attention, then gestured the question silently with my face and eyes so Mamá and Papá couldn't overhear us. He gave me a thumbs-up, and so I gave my Bazooka a few chews and then plugged my ears with it. It felt icky, like getting into a wet bathing suit, but it was a brilliant idea, and it worked. At last, a respite from the painful sound of Cuba's undiscovered duet: Mamá and Papá.

My mind eased back to thoughts of Disney World as *el Malibú* zipped past the highway signs that counted down the miles to Orlando, to Disney, to paradise. Nothing but peace and quiet as the scent of orange groves drifted into the car, until a siren shattered the silence. Caco and I took the gum out of our ears and turned around in our seats to peer out the back window. A police car was tailing *el Malibú*. Papá slowed down and moved into the right lane to let the police officer pass us, but he didn't. He kept right behind us until Papá realized we were being pulled over. Mamá, who was convinced she had never done anything wrong in her life, began hysterically tidying up the front seat as if cleanliness would get us out of a ticket. Caco and I had turned around in our seats and were looking out the back window. "Cool!" Caco said, to which Mamá responded with a slap on his behind, shushing us both and making us sit back down.

Papá turned down the music, pulled over, and sat up straight in his seat. *"Cojones,"* he mumbled just before the officer stepped up to the car. "Howdy," he said, and tipped his Stetson hat. "Do you know what the speed limit is here, mistah? Where are y'all heading?" Nervous, Papá seemed to forget what little English he knew. He *ummed* and *ummed,* until Caco had no choice but to help Papá out with translation. One by one, he translated the officer's questions in Spanish and Papá's answers into English. Swept away by the Cuban oldies and high on Cuban coffee, Papá had sped up to 75 mph, twenty miles over the speed limit, the officer informed him, then he asked to see Papá's license and car registration. "Oh, y'all from *Miamuh,*" the officer drawled, the same disdain in his voice that had saturated the clerk's at the service plaza. "This here's a major violation. Y'all gonna have to follow me to town. We don't take kindly to speeding 'round these parts Mr. Blank-o," he said, pronouncing our last name in English, before tipping his hat again and walking back to his patrol car.

Keeping a safe distance behind the officer and pretending to be calm, Papá asked Mamá where she had put the gun. *"Ay, Dios mío,* that's right!" Mamá exclaimed, scrambling through her *por si las moscas* tote bag. "I thought I put it here." Papá had bought the tiny pistol a few years before, giving in to my mother's *in-case-of-the-flies* paranoia. They kept it "hidden" in the top drawer of her armoire, buried under bottles of nail polish, tiny boxes of costume jewelry, and Papá's cologned handkerchiefs. Whenever we were going somewhere Mamá perceived as potentially dangerous, she'd insist we take the pistol with us. But to Disney World? What had she been thinking? That the car could break down in a swamp and we would be attacked by alligators? That an escaped convict could be on the loose; a crazy *americano* who would hijack our car?

After a few seconds paralyzed by her panic, she found the gun in her tote. *"Ay, mira,* here it is! What I do?" she asked Papá, who told her to hide it somewhere—and fast. In a flash she scrunched the pistol into a giant bag of plantain chips, secured the bag with a rubber band, and placed it on the floor of the passenger side, all the while looking straight out the windshield so that she wouldn't look suspicious. "Okay. No one touch the chips," she said, just as we exited the turnpike.

We followed the police car through a strip of gas stations and diners, then pulled into the parking lot of a municipal building with a flat roof and metal doors; it was no bigger—and much, much uglier—than our house. The officer motioned to us, and we followed him single file into a reception area. The walls were painted with a thick layer of high-gloss enamel; a faux-marble Formica counter stretched from one end of the room to the other. And behind the counter hung an enormous bulletin board pinned with posters of "wanted" men alongside photos of lost dogs and cats. Walking into that room was like walking into *The Andy Griffith Show*; I expected some Don Knotts–like character with bulging eyes to swing around in his desk chair at any moment. Or a girl in pigtails wearing a checkered shirt. Instead we were greeted by a pudgy, jolly lady wearing a sateen blouse with a large bow tied at the collar. She was completely made up: sky-blue eye shadow, long violent strokes of rouge on her cheeks, and powder too light for her skin tone, making her face look ghostly, jumping out at you before the rest of her body. "Why, hello," the lady said, all sparkly as if she were expecting us. "Have a seat. I'll be right with y'all."

But my parents wouldn't, *couldn't,* sit down. Mamá kept tugging nervously on her blouse, which had the French word *OUI* printed in gold letters across her chest. Those shirts were all the rage that summer at the Tropicaire Flea Market, and though she knew *oui* was French for "yes," she seemed oblivious to the sexual connotation of having *YES* spread across her breasts. Papá kept clearing his throat and tucking in his shirt; he closed the two buttons to conceal the gold San Lázaro medallion nested in his hairy chest. I kept looking at my Mickey Mouse watch, trying to figure out how much time we'd lost already, nervous that we'd never get to Disney World. "Here you go. Now take your time and fill this out. Don't forget to sign the bottom," the lady said, holding out a clipboard.

Papá completed the forms with our help and returned them to the lady who immediately glanced over it. "Blanco? Where y'all from?" she asked in a genuinely curious tone, pronouncing our name in what was a close approximation of the Spanish. *"Meea-mee,"* my father answered. She kept prying: "Oh, y'all must be on your way to Disney World." *"Sí*—I mean *jess,"* my father said, loosening up a bit, though that's all he could utter to the woman as she continued, "Oh, we catch you folks speeding all the time 'round here." (. . . *Jess* . . . *Jess* . . .) "But don't you worry; you'll be out of here in a jiffy." (. . . *Jess* . . . *Jess* . . .) "I can tell your little one is in a hurry to see Mickey." (. . . *Jess* . . . *Jess* . . .) She might have pinched my cheek if I'd been within her reach.

In his state of nervousness, Papá couldn't understand a word she was saying, until she caught us all by surprise and threw out a phrase in formal but broken Spanish: *"Es muy bonita, Miami, ¿ver-*

dad?" Papá responded with sudden glee, "*Sí, sí,*" instead of "*Jess, jess,*" and asked her: "*¿Usted habla español?*" She explained that she had loved the language ever since studying it in high school; how she dreamed of meeting Julio Iglesias and going to Spain someday. Papá told her we had lived in Spain for a few months after we left Cuba, and her eyes lit up brighter than her eye shadow. She introduced herself: "Oh, where are my manners? *Hola,* my *nombray es* Sharon," and welcomed us formally as if we were guests, "*Bienvenidos. Bienvenidos.*"

Papá went on and on about Spain, the beauty of Madrid, even in winter, and Sharon kept asking questions, taking the opportunity to practice her Spanish. For a change, the linguistic shoe was on the other foot with Sharon; it was she who couldn't be understood, not Papá. He had trouble making out most of what she said, asking her to repeat words over and over again and then teaching her the correct pronunciation. He even taught her how to say Mickey Mouse in Spanish. "*El Rah-ton-ci-to Mee-gwel,*" she repeated clumsily after him with her heavy accent. *Oh brother,* I thought. Listening to gringos speak Spanish annoyed me as much as listening to my parents speaking broken English. It felt like Sharon was trying to be someone she could never be—she could never be Cuban like us, just as my parents could never really be American like her.

Fortunately, Sharon became enamored by Papá's Latino charm and slipped the speeding ticket somewhere under the counter. "*No problema. No problema,*" she said, handing Papá back his license and registration and bidding us farewell, "See you again, *hasta pronto,*" as if we were coming back anytime soon. On the way out, Mamá walked backward ahead of us. "*Pónganse ahí* and let me take a picture," she demanded, making us pose by the flagpole in front of the Town Hall, recording the incident for all time. Caption: *Four Cubans with a gun escape conviction.*

Back on the turnpike, the tension eased up and Mamá pulled the now salty pistol out of the plantain chips. She was about to break the no-eating-in-the-car rule and pass the bag around, but Papá quickly raised his bushy unibrow at her and tsk-tsked. "Oh no!" Caco blurted out, and I shook my head when Papá cranked up the music again. We were out of Bazooka, so we had no choice but to suffer through the music and singing. I focused on the billboards announcing buffet restaurants, fast-food chains, seashell shops, and bargain motels only "minutes" from the Magic Kingdom, offering discounted park tickets. We were getting closer and closer with each passing highway sign: ORLANDO 45 MI, ORLANDO 32 MI, ORLANDO 11 MI.

Suddenly, Mamá yelled, "Stop! Stop!" as if the car were on fire. Papá swerved onto the shoulder, almost going into the drainage ditch. She pulled her Instamatic out of her tote, and suddenly we knew what all the fuss was for. "No way," Caco complained, "not again." But for once I was eager to pose for one of her photos. I darted out of the car as Caco and Papá trudged reluctantly behind me, urged on by Mamá. *Uno. Dos. Tres,* and snap, standing beside the green highway sign at the gates of heaven: WALT DISNEY WORLD RESORT | NEXT EXIT. Papá with his small potbelly sucked in, Caco's silver braces shining in the light, and me so overcome I couldn't even crack a smile.

After we exited, everything began to change: the road got wider and the tarmac blacker; the signs turned from green and white to magenta and a deep Persian blue; the palm trees looked taller and fuller, their fronds like green pom-poms; and after two hundred miles of nothing but saw grass and palmettos, there were flowers everywhere. A fuzzy, cotton-candy feeling took hold of me as we drove by ficus bushes trimmed in the shapes of Donald Duck, Pluto, and Dumbo. I felt as if I were stepping into one of my coloring books. Mamá and Papá had told us we were going to stay at the *very* fancy and *very* expensive Contemporary Hotel right inside the park grounds, thanks to Abuela. Still, I thought they were kidding—we'd never stayed anyplace nice. But when I caught sight of the hotel in the distance, I could barely blink, spellbound by its sloping walls of glass and girding of balconies soaring upward like the layers of a gargantuan cake. My stomach almost erupted again in the parking lot when I saw the monorail zoom right into the hotel, like something right out of *Star Wars*.

Can I live here forever? I thought, but the spell almost wore off when Papá began unloading all the luggage from *el Malibú*. For weeks Caco and I had pleaded with our parents not to bring any of their usual Cuban cargo. But they disobeyed us and must've secretly packed the trunk before they woke us up that morning. We watched in horror as the bellhop helped Papá load the luggage cart with a hot plate and our espresso pot for making Cuban coffee in the room; grocery bags full of mangos, oranges, and half a dozen loaves of Cuban bread; the ice chest; and a whole watermelon, just in case we got hungry in the room. Topping it all off: their rubbery pillows from home, just in case the hotel pillows were too soft or too hard.

Utterly humiliated as we walked into the hotel, Caco and I picked up our pace until we were a good thirty feet ahead of them and the luggage cart, pretending they weren't *our* parents. We were way too cool for them: Caco sporting an Adidas T-shirt and matching yellow

Adidas sweatband and wristbands that coordinated with the colored stripes on his Adidas tube socks; and me spiffed out in my Minnie and Mickey Mouse iron-on T-shirt and immaculate Thom McAn sneakers. We *definitely* didn't know Mamá in her *OUI* T-shirt and faux Pierre Cardin handbag, pointing her camera straight up into the atrium and snapping photos, yelling to us in Spanish from across the lobby to come stand by Papá and the luggage cart so she could take a picture.

Inside the hotel room, safe from further embarrassment, the spell began taking over me again. I didn't want to waste a single second brushing my teeth or combing my hair, but Mamá insisted I look pretty for the photos *para Cuba*. She then took ten minutes to make a pot of Cuban coffee, sweetened with sugar packets she had pocketed from the condiments counter at the service plaza. Finally, we got out of the room and our parents were at our linguistic mercy again. Unable to fully understand the English on the directional signs to get here or there, Mamá and Papá had no choice but to follow Caco and me as we led them through the lobby and to the monorail platform.

I didn't quite understand the words *efficiency* or *engineering*, but I felt them for the first time in the spiderweb of steel trusses holding up the skylight that capped the atrium, in the smooth hush of wind as the monorail pulled alongside the platform, and in the monorail doors that opened automatically as soon as it stopped. Inside, the cab felt like a spaceship, zooming above the ponds and emerald lawns, above another world more perfect than I had imagined. Overwhelmed, I closed my eyes, wanting to make sure to take in everything with my other senses too. I didn't want to miss a sound or a scent or a feeling. Caco kept poking me in the ribs, trying to break my trance, but Mamá indulged me and led me by the hand off the monorail and down the ramp. I insisted on keeping my eyes shut, even as the attendant at the turnstile asked if we needed a wheelchair for me. Caco clarified the situation: "No, thanks, he's not blind. He's just a goon."

When I popped open my eyes inside the park, I knew exactly where we were from the brochures I had memorized. We were right in the middle of Main Street. I had heard the words *gorgeous* and *paradise* many times before, when my parents spoke of Havana and Cienfuegos, the seaside colonial town in the province where they were from. But here I saw those words come to life in the evenly spaced antique lampposts, the litter-free streets lined with dainty willows and majestic oaks, the geometric rows of impatiens and rosebushes abloom, soft music rising from speakers hidden in the flower beds, the trolleys drawn by Clydesdales clopping their pom-pom hooves, and the costumed men in top hats and women in hoop skirts twirling lace-fringed umbrellas on their shoulders. But where was El Ratoncito Miguel?

"Is this what Cuba was like?" I asked Mamá. "Oh, no," she answered, "it was even more better." *How could anything be better than this?* I thought as we meandered down the street, through scented clouds of popcorn and chocolate fudge. After photo stops at the antique clock, at the old-fashioned ice cream shop, and at a number of benches, statues, and trickling water fountains, we finally reached the circular plaza at the foot of Cinderella's castle, so perfect it hardly seemed real—a place where God might live. I couldn't wait to cross over the moat, walk through the gate, stroll the royal halls, and find my way to Cinderella's bedchamber; I'd hold her glass slippers and touch her dresses, then climb up to the tallest of the gilded spires reigning above the whole park. But I wanted to save that thrill for last. Weeks before I had plotted out a route for us that would end with a visit to the castle. "Let's go this way first," I insisted with map in hand, leading us over the footbridge and into Adventureland.

My first ride: the Jungle Cruise. Though I knew the animals weren't real, I let my imagination scare me into a little fun, exaggerating my screams as we floated past the hissing boas curled around tree limbs and the hungry lions roaring along the far shore. Despite the fact that Mamá grew up in the countryside of Cuba, defecating in the woods, she was squeamish and easily frightened. When the mechanical alligator rose out of the swamp snapping its snout on her side of the boat, she jumped up and dropped her sunglasses into the water. "*¡Ay! ¡Ave María!*" she roared above the guide's narration, making a scene—in Spanish no less—and demanding that Papá ask the guide to turn the boat around so she could fish out her faux Christian Dior glasses. "Ma'am, please keep your hands inside the boat. Ma'am, I'll have to stop the boat unless you sit down," the guide blared on his megaphone, causing twenty-something heads to turn around and witness the spectacle of Mamá in her *OUI* shirt. Caco darted into an empty seat a few rows in front of us. I wanted to dive into the water and be swallowed whole by the alligators. "*Ay*, I almost forgot," Mamá said, reaching into her handbag. "*Gracias a Dios*. I brought another pair, *por si las moscas*." She slipped on an identical pair and calmed down. But the damage was done.

Taking Caco's lead at the Pirates of the Caribbean, I convinced Mamá that it would be better if he and I rode in the dinghy ahead of them so that she could take better pictures of us. She agreed, and we thought we had put one over on her. But not really. We missed half the ride turning around to face her camera and force smiles, blinded by flash cubes that were brighter than the cannon fire erupting from the pirate ships. That's why flash photography was not allowed, but of course the sign was in English, so Mamá paid no mind to it, or the irritated faces of the others on the ride, for that matter. Papá kept shouting from their dinghy: "Look, Riqui! You saw that, Caco? Watch it, he's going to shoot you!" as if we were five years old. The man seated next to us began losing his patience too. "Shh! Shh!" he finally said. "You shh, shh, shh," Caco responded. Our parents were annoying; they were inconsiderate; they were loud. But they were our parents; no one could mess with them, except us.

I looked at my Mickey Mouse watch practically every fifteen minutes, counting down how much time we had left before the park closed. We were driving back early the next morning, so I had to make sure we got to see *everything*, including El Ratoncito Miguel. Luckily, according to my calculations, we were right on schedule, exactly halfway through the park by the time we reached the Hall of Presidents in Frontierland. It was the most elegant theater I'd ever seen, with chandeliers as big as flying saucers and carpet so plush I wanted to take my shoes off. We sank into seats so soft and pillowy, it was like sitting in a marshmallow. As the lights dimmed and the curtains parted, I feared my parents would act up again. But surprisingly they didn't. They were perfectly still and quiet, mesmerized by the assembly of mechanized presidents, as the spotlight shone on each one and their names were announced. They listened so intently that if I didn't know any better, I could have sworn that they understood exactly what Thomas Jefferson said when he rose from his chair and recited part of the Declaration of Independence; or when

Lincoln recited an excerpt from the Gettysburg Address, his hand tucked inside his coat.

The history lessons from the glossy pages of my textbook came to life. For the first time, I felt this was indeed *my* country, even if it wasn't my parents' country. After all their talk about missing their wonderful lives back in Cuba, how could they be so fascinated by *my* country's presidents? Perhaps they weren't as Cuban as I made them out to be; perhaps someday we'd be a real American family. I was confused but strangely elated, until Richard Nixon stepped forward and Papá let out two sharp whistles for his favorite president. It had been Papá's idea to name me Ricardo after Richard Nixon, who was, in Papá's opinion, the first "decent" president after that "damn *democrata*" Kennedy who had betrayed "us" at the Bay of Pigs. Mamá jabbed him with her elbow. Caco and I shook our heads in silent disbelief and sank into our seats, out of sight until the show was over.

"I'm not riding that bullshit sissy ride," Caco complained as we got in the line for It's a Small World. Ordinarily, he (and I) could cuss a lot because our parents could hardly pick up bad words in English. But that time he added, *"Esa mierda es para maricones,"* in his best Spanish to make sure his objection was understood. Mamá gave him her dreadful *just-wait-until-I-get-you-at-home* face: eyes squinted and eyebrows pulled down low. "Did you say what I think you said, *cabrón?*" she asked him, as if she didn't know. *"Esa mierda es para maricones*—for faggots," he dared to repeat, with the same scowl as I remembered on Raphael Ramirez's face whenever he called me a faggot at baseball practice. But this was my brother. Mamá wrapped the handles of her twenty-pound tote bag around her wrist and gave him a good purse-whipping across his backside, making him lose his balance. I felt sorry for him, even though I felt he got what he deserved. Startled by the commotion, a little girl wearing saddle shoes started crying behind us in the line. "What did you say?" Mamá dared him again, her tote already cocked. There was no reply. "*Menos mal*—that's what I thought," she said firmly. "Stand straight—*caramba*—and move." Defeated, he shuffled his feet all the way down the line and stomped into the riding boat.

Slouched in his seat, Caco put his fingers in his ears to block out the overjoyed dolls singing the theme song, their mechanical heads bobbing side to side like dashboard ornaments, each one dressed in the traditional garb of its country. Sissy ride or not, I sang the chorus along with the dolls, "It's a small world after all, it's a small, small world . . ." as the boat waded through the French dolls doing a can-can and jiggling their crinkled skirts, the Mexican dolls blindfolded under a piñata, the Chinese dolls counting on abacuses, and my favorite: the Arab dolls belly dancing in pink tulle and pointy slippers just like Barbara Eden from *I Dream of Jeannie*.

Mamá and Papá caught on to the lyrics, sort of, and sang along too: "Is a small world after all . . . is a small, small world . . . ," their accent thankfully drowned out by the dolls' singing. But as soon as the ride was over, Mamá ranted, "Why no dolls from Cuba? There was dolls from Puerto Rico *y México*. Why no Cuba? You know if it wasn't for *los cubanos*, Miami would still be *nada*—a swamp. *Los americanos* could show us a little thanks, no?" "Yeah, maybe they should have a doll of Fidel Castro smoking a cigar," Caco jabbed at Mamá. "Good one!" I told Caco. "*Qué estúpidos,*" Mamá said to both of us. "One day you'll know—one day." She had her tote bag cocked again, but left it at that.

Keeping a cool distance from our parents, Caco and I led the way, turning the corner at the humongous merry-go-round, where I spotted Snow White with Grumpy. Before I could even point them out, Mamá had already whipped out her Instamatic, directing me to get in line for a photo. Snow White was beautiful—just as I had imagined her from my coloring books, but already colored: hair as silky and black as my cat Misu, the bow on her head red as a lollipop, and her slender arms as delicate as the willow branches I'd seen along the Main Street entrance. But Grumpy scared me. His face resembled a dried-up mango. I imagined Grumpy smelled bad too, rotten like Caco's sweaty gym shirts. When my turn came for the photo, I blatantly told Mamá: *"Con el enano no"*—not with the midget—in Spanish so Snow White wouldn't understand what I was saying. Or maybe she did? She didn't smile at me when she took my hand and positioned me between herself and Grumpy. Regardless, I scurried to one side and pulled her away from Grumpy just long enough for Mamá to snap the photo.

Snow White sauntered back to her spot without kissing me on the cheek the way she'd kissed the other kids. I wanted to ask her if she knew where Mickey Mouse was, but I was too embarrassed after what I had just done. So I coerced Caco into asking her, threatening him I'd tell Mamá about *his* stunt with the food order at the service plaza. "Oh, he's around. You never know when he'll surprise you," she told Caco. *Around*, I thought. *Around? What? Where? When?* I didn't want to be surprised; I wanted to see El Ratoncito Miguel right then and there. I made us all wait at the Carousel for Mickey to show up: five minutes, and no Mickey; fifteen minutes, twenty minutes, no Mickey.

"This is stupid. Let's go!" Caco finally broke. I gave in after Papá reassured me that we'd see El Ratoncito Miguel later; he carried me on his shoulders through the rest of Fantasyland and into

Tomorrowland. Perched above his head, I spotted Space Mountain in the distance. As soon as I saw its silver slopes glinting in the sun and its steel needle towering above the entire park, a rush of adrenaline stiffened my legs. Not out of excitement, but out of dread. "Ooh—awesome! There it is!" Caco let out. "Are you gonna ride it like you said, chicken?" he asked me. I knew I was in for it. Weeks before the trip, he had bet me five dollars that I'd be too scared to ride Space Mountain, which he had ridden "like ten times" the year before. "It's super scary, like a roller coaster, but in the dark. You even go upside down and everything," he had explained to me; I thought he was exaggerating just to brag and scare me, so I called his bluff and took the bet.

But as we got closer and closer, I realized he had been telling the truth, and as the mountain grew bigger and bigger, my heart beat faster and faster, pulsing through my entire body. I was on the verge of pretending my diarrhea was back, but I knew Caco would still demand his five bucks right on the spot. That was all the money I had on me, which I'd saved up for weeks to buy myself something at Disney World. I was holding on to it until I found something special, something I really wanted and could afford. If I lost the bet, I'd come home with nothing to show off in class come September. At the entrance to the ride there were warnings about heart attacks and motion sickness in bold red letters full of exclamation points. One of the signs read YOU MUST BE THIS TALL FOR THIS RIDE. I figured I was tall enough, but I stepped up to the sign anyway and checked my height, bending my knees slightly, hoping for the perfect way out. But no, I had to ride Space Mountain.

My parents decided to sit this one out on a bench and started gobbling down some guava *pastelitos* Mamá had stashed inside her *por si las moscas* tote, all crumbled from the whack she had given

Caco earlier. We ignored their good-bye waves as we walked into the mouth of a dark hallway, strobed by pulsing lights, from which there seemed to be no turning back. And there wasn't. Corralled by metal stalls into a single file line that twisted and turned for thirty heart-pounding minutes, I tried calming myself down—*It'll be all right . . . It can't be that bad.* I shamed myself into courage by concentrating on the younger kids in line who didn't seem a bit scared.

But it was no use. As soon as I started feeling the tiniest bit at ease, I heard the coaster roaring overhead, followed immediately by screaming, and my hands went right to my mouth for another round of nail biting. Caco didn't help, clucking and flapping his arms like a chicken at me, still trying to get me to back out. But I didn't let him get to me. Just before we were to step into our car, Caco clasped his hand around the back of my neck and said, "Come on. You'll be all right. Don't worry. It'll be fun." Perhaps he had forgotten about the bet or maybe he knew he had been beat; or maybe he was scared too, and was comforting himself as much as he was comforting me. Regardless, I preferred to believe his gesture was one of those rare moments born out of love and compassion, from brother to brother. Guided by his hand into the car, I found a glimmer of courage.

Astronauts and brothers squeezed together in our tiny mock rocket ship, me cradled in between his legs, his hands wrapped around my shoulders (he must have felt my body trembling, my heart beating). Five-four-three-two-one-zero—we blasted off through a tunnel of fiery strobe lights and sirens. The clack-clack-clack-clack of the wheels as we climbed, and then—dip—we zoomed into the unknown, flashed past the nine planets we thought we knew. Clack-clack-clack-clack, and then—dip—we screamed together, laughed together as we hurtled past asteroid belts, through a universe as infinite and mysterious as the love between brothers at that very moment that would last a lifetime, even though only minutes later we returned to Earth. "Let's do it again," I said, walking through the exit corridor, though it was probably the endorphins talking. "Yeah right, chicken" he said, pulling five one-dollar bills out of his pocket and handing them to me. I didn't want to take the money, but he insisted and stuffed it in my pocket. "A bet is a bet." Caco was, and would always be, a man of his word.

Back at the bench, we saw Mamá and Papá cutting into a couple of mangos with plastic knives, then bingeing on the succulent slices that oozed juice all over their chins, as if they were sitting by a country road in Cuba. "*Qué*, you never seen *un* mango?" Mamá reacted with sarcasm to our looks of dismay. She would have made a small fortune on *Let's Make a Deal;* she seemed to have one of everything in her *por si las moscas* tote, including a couple of wet-naps from Kentucky Fried Chicken. "Here," she said, handing one to Papá to wipe his sticky fingers and chin. All cleaned up, we walked around the last bend in the park, ending where we started, at the circle in front of Cinderella's Castle. It was time.

Delirious, I almost started skipping all the way up the long ramp and over the moat, but then Abuela's voice haunted me: *When you going to act like* un hombre*?* I composed myself and walked as calmly as I could, counting the turrets and gold-leafed spires, trying to guess which of the dozens of windows was Cinderella's room and how long it would take to get to the top, imagining the incredible view of *my* kingdom from way up there. Just before walking through the front gate, I closed my eyes, not opening them again until we were inside the main hall, which was bathed in colors bouncing off the mosaics made of ruby, emerald, and gold glass tiles that covered the walls; each mosaic like a page from a life-size *Cinderella* storybook.

Convinced we had missed something once we reached the other end of the hall, I made us all turn around and go back inside. *Where are the stairs? How do we get in? Where is Cinderella?* My wondering quickly turned into frustration as I looked for a sign, an elevator, an entrance door in the hall. My frustration decayed into gloom when I asked a woman in a Disney World uniform how to get inside the castle. "Oh, no, you can't go up there; there's nothing inside," she said. *What? Nothing inside? No!* I was convinced she either was lying to me or was a new employee and didn't know what she was talking about. Mamá was upset too; apparently she was looking forward to touring the castle as much as I was. "What you mean, Miss? That cannot be," she began, becoming belligerent with the woman. "We stay right here until we get inside."

Finally, Papá intervened and ushered us out of the castle. All the way back down the ramp, I kept my head bowed, remaining silent except for the sound of my feet dragging. "Oh, poor baby," Caco began, but before he could keep digging into me, I kicked him in his shin and pulled off his Adidas headband, throwing it in the bushes. Caco and I broke into an all-out *fugi* fight, a martial art of our own invention in which we'd strike each other using only our index and middle fingers pressed together into what we called a *fugi*. It was our version of a karate chop, crafted by years of horseplay and watching too many episodes of *Kung Fu*. By the time Papá peeled us apart, a small crowd had gathered around our spectacle, some wearing concerned looks, others giggling.

Mamá marched over and gave each of us a whack with her tote, spilling out the roll of toilet paper I had used that morning. "That's no way to behave in Disney. After all this money we spent. *Qué pena*—how embarrassing," she reprimanded us. Frozen, completely humiliated, we stood silent for a moment, but then giggled uncontrollably at the sight of the toilet paper rolling down the sidewalk and into the castle moat. "Why you laughing? You think this funny? We're going home right now!" she said, furious, until Papá—also giggling by then—pointed out to her the ten yards of toilet paper tethered to her tote. "*Dios mío, qué pena,* look what you made me do," she said sheepishly and began walking away. It seemed she was willing to forget the whole incident, but I didn't want to take any chances. "No, Mamá, it was my fault," I apologized. "I don't want to go yet," I pleaded. I didn't mind taking the blame since I *fugi*ed Caco last, making me the winner according to our official rules of *fugi* fighting.

Caco still wasn't talking to me when we got back to Main Street, where we had started our loop around the park. He and Papá stood outside people-watching while I followed Mamá into store after store, weaving behind her through the aisles, both of us eyeing the merchandise. She kept tsk-tsking at practically everything she picked up once she turned it over and saw the price. Finally, she decided on a Mickey Mouse key ring for herself and a refrigerator magnet for cousin Mirita, who had given us her leftover ride tickets from her last visit; and she let me pick out a ninety-nine-cent "official" Disney World coloring book.

On our way to the cash register, I spotted a wall stocked floor to ceiling with every stuffed Disney character imaginable: endless rows of plastic-eyed Dumbos and Donald Ducks; Plutos and Chipmunks; Goofies and Poohs. And Mickey Mouses, of course, dressed in all kinds of outfits: Mickey in his classic red shorts and yellow shoes, in a hula skirt with leis around his neck, in a chef's hat wearing an apron, in a pirate's hat with a sword. But the one that really caught my eye was Mickey dressed as a wizard in a bright red robe and a blue hat with stars. "Wait, Mamá," I demanded, pulling her back by her tote. "Did you see that Mickey—how beautiful? Can I take a look at it?" I asked, knowing she'd disapprove of me reaching for it without permission. She took the Mickey from the shelf and looked at the price tag before handing it to me. "Fourteen ninety-nine!" she said out loud, incredulously. "*¡Qué va!* Anyway, you know Abuela will say it's a doll; she'll make you throw it out."

But I didn't care. I was determined. I was in love, just like Papá with his *Malibú*. Even with the five dollars I won from Caco, I still only had ten dollars altogether. I had to play it right. I took the money from my pocket and counted the one-dollar bills slowly and theatrically, "One . . . two . . . three . . ." giving Mamá a chance to notice her poor little son. "Oh, I don't have enough. I just won't get anything, I guess," I said looking up into her eyes with the most pitiful face I could conjure. She picked up Mickey again and pulled at the seams to make sure he was well sewn and wasn't defective in any way. I thought she was going to put it back on the shelf, but she didn't. "*Bueno,*" she said, "I'll give you five dollars more," and kissed me on the top of my head, no questions asked, no conditions demanded, like cleaning my room or taking out the trash for a month.

I still hadn't seen the real Mickey Mouse—and it didn't seem likely that I would, but at least I had a new coloring book and my own Ratoncito Miguel. Mamá and I stepped out of the store, and she stumbled on the curb, startled by the first blast of fireworks shuddering through the park. I stood mesmerized by the exploding lights like rock candy in the night sky, which dissolved slowly into embers and fell to the earth like angels behind Cinderella's castle. Despite my parents' and Caco's antics, it had been a perfect day, in a perfect place, with the perfect ending, I thought. Once the fireworks were over, we began the long, sad march down Main Street under the glimmer of the gas lamps, following the crowd over the cobblestone streets toward the exit. As we approached the turnstiles, I had a mad fantasy: What if I dashed back inside and hid out in one of the rides until everyone was gone? With the park all to myself, would I find Mickey Mouse?

On the way back to the hotel, I leaned against the window of the monorail, nearly weeping as I watched my perfect world shrink to a handful of tiny lights as far away as the stars. Was this what my parents had felt when they left Cuba, not knowing whether they'd ever see such a magical place again? In the hotel room, Mamá prepared pimiento and cream cheese sandwiches. We ate. I took Mickey out of the bag and fell asleep with him, thinking about when our next visit would be, how many months there were until Christmas break, how I would convince my parents to bring me back. The thought that I might never return to the Magic Kingdom was unbearable.

The next morning, Mamá brewed a pot of Cuban coffee in the hotel room. Papá packed up *el Malibú* and we got on the road. With nothing to look forward to, the drive back seemed half as long. Uninterested in the world around me, I didn't look at any of the highway signs, didn't care about the Cuban music playing on the eight-track or my parents singing along, or about Caco belching at the passing cars. I only cared about Mickey seated next to me and about trying to stay inside the lines as I colored page after page in my new coloring book. Now that I had been to Disney World, I knew exactly the right colors to pick for Cinderella's hair, for Minnie Mouse's dress, and for Dumbo's hat.

When we arrived home that afternoon, Papá quickly unloaded everything from the trunk and said he had to start washing *el Malibú*, claiming that if he didn't get all the bugs off, the brutal summer sun would sear them into the paint and ruin the finish. "Don't be such an *imbécil*," Mamá told him, "Nothing is going to happen. Wait until after we eat *almuerzo*." He reluctantly agreed, and Mamá walked off to the kitchen. Abuela intercepted me in the hall; she gave me a big smooch, then asked me what I had in the bag. *"Nada,"* I said, darted to my room, and closed the door.

At first, I thought I'd put *my* Mickey on the shelf right beside Caco's baseball trophies, but he'd probably make me pay him for the privilege. The only—and best—place for Mickey was right on my bed. I'd sleep with him every night. But Mamá was right—Abuela would harass me for having a "doll," and make me throw Mickey away; he'd meet the same fate as my latch hook rug kit. I couldn't leave him out in plain sight without coming up with a good explanation. After some thought, I decided I'd tell her I'd won him in a raffle, or that Papá had bought him for me, not Mamá; and if worse came to worst, I'd hide my Ratoncito Miguel under my bed.

Not long after we finished *almuerzo*, Papá bolted into my room holding a two-inch-wide belt in one hand and a silver butter knife in the other. He threw Mickey off my bed. *"Oye cabrón*, come with me," he said sternly, plucking me out of bed and dragging me barefooted to *el Malibú* in the driveway. "Look at this mess—*¡qué cagazón!"* he shouted as he opened the car door and pulled the front seat forward. It took me a moment to realize that the lava-like blob on the backseat was actually my melted crayons—all sixty-four colors from the box I had left in the car. "Now clean that up until it's like new!" he ordered, handing me the knife. Trying not to cry, I began scraping off the pool of gelatinous wax. Papá stood over me with the belt trembling in his hand: "Everything is ruined, *cojones*—everything," he said softly, his voice cracking, his face turned away from me.

FOUR

QUEEN OF THE COPA

The Seacomber was one of the last art deco hotels in old South Beach that still looked fancy. Its neon sign still worked, and its sugary pink-and-blue reliefs were still as showy and fresh as icing on a cake. The moment I saw its automatic glass doors etched with swirly *S*'s, I knew it was going to be *way* too expensive for us. Mamá and Papá didn't even want to go inside to check it out, but I pleaded, "Come on, *por favor*," until Mamá agreed, "*Está bien, pero* no touch nothing." We stepped into the lobby in a clump, afraid to look at anybody for fear they might be staring back at us. We stood stunned, as if under the spell of the gargantuan chandelier hanging above us like a spiderweb of diamonds. The palm trees reflected in the mirrored wall seemed to be growing inside the lobby. The plush sofas, like immaculate white clouds anchored to silver legs, looked as if they had never been sat on. It was all so beautiful it scared me.

"Ask how much—*dale*," Mamá ordered, her voice tinged with excitement. Papá approached the reception desk. I was conscious of each one of his footsteps as they bounced off the mirror-smooth marble that made his wrinkly pair of oxfords look even shabbier. "May I help you?" the clerk asked him in perfect English. He wore a blazer with an *S* emblem and a perfectly knotted tie fixed with an *S* pin. "Jess . . . umm . . . how much is a room?" Papá mumbled in his best *inglés*. "For which days, sir?" the clerk asked with an attitude, as if he owned the hotel. "July two to five," Papá answered. "Just a moment," the clerk said, before flipping through a binder. "Yes, we have one room available for ninety-eight dollars, sir. With a three-night minimum." Papá cleared his throat. "Ninety-eight dollars?" he repeated, making sure he had heard right. "For one night?" he added. "Yes, plus tax, sir," the clerk confirmed. "Now, if you'll excuse me." He dismissed Papá with a smile.

Mamá opened her eyes like an owl at Caco and me. "How much?" she burst out, appalled. *"Noventa y ocho,"* Caco answered her in Spanish, speaking like a ventriloquist trying not to move his lips, signaling her to remain discreet and restrain her voice. *"¡Qué va!* These people *están locos,"* she yelled as softly as she could. "We're not *los Roquefelas*. Let's keep looking. Anyway, a hotel is only to sleep." But on the way out she grabbed a bunch of complimentary postcards that pictured the hotel's two-story waterslide, the giant color TVs, and humongous rooms with mirrored closet doors. "How beautiful," she said. "I'll send these to your *tías* in Cuba. Let's go." Caco and I dragged behind, out through the fancy glass doors, with no choice but to continue scouting the strip of hotels until we could find one we could afford.

Every year, usually right after Easter, Mamá would start planning and budgeting for a weeklong vacation in the summer. But only someplace a few hours away from Miami, only as far as Papá was willing to drive us in *el Malibú*. We had been to Clearwater Beach near Tampa and Marco Island on Florida's west coast. This year,

Mamá had talked about going to Walt Disney World again. But after the tuition hike at St. Brendan's, and after having to buy a new refrigerator and repair the TV in the Florida room, a few days at a reasonable hotel in Miami Beach—*reasonable* was Mamá's way of not saying *cheap*—was all we could afford.

The St. Moritz was cheaper than the Seacomber, but they didn't have kitchenettes. Mamá planned to cook breakfast, lunch, and dinner in our room so we wouldn't have to spend money on eating out. The Sands Hotel was even cheaper, but they didn't rent out any *pin-pan-puns*—the funny name Mamá gave to roll-away beds for how one half unfolded (*pin*), then the other half (*pan*), and there it was (*pun*). Squeezing all four of us plus Abuela and Abuelo into one room was impossible at the Sands; we'd have to get two rooms, and that was out of the question.

Our next stop was the Copa, one of the many run-down art deco hotels along Ocean Drive that had been converted into pay-by-the-week apartments. The Copa, like the other languishing hotels, had been painted gunmetal gray, concealing the bright pinks and blues that wouldn't resurface until South Beach's renaissance in the early nineties. We stepped onto its front veranda, lined with vinyl patio chairs as old and broken as the hotel's residents sitting in them: rows of retirees, the men's bald heads glowing in the sun and the women's silver hair, teased into thin nests, shining like halos. Rows of feet in gummy orthopedic shoes rested as if glued to the ground; canes leaned against the balustrade; chorus lines of loose panty hose sagged at the knees and socks crinkled around swollen ankles. Their eyes were stiff, like dolls' eyes, hardly noticing us as we walked past them and into the lobby.

The lobby was the size of our living room, crammed with dark, lumpy sofas made of scratchy polyester and brown laminate tables adorned with plastic flowers stuffed into dusty glass vases. The grimy tile floor was cracked and spotted with gum blotches. "Yuck," I told Caco, but Mamá heard me. *"Cállate,"* she admonished. Worst of all, there was no air-conditioning in the lobby—only a jittery ceiling fan circulating hot air laced with a mildew smell like wet towels. "Do they have AC in the rooms?" Caco asked me. "They better," I said, as concerned as he was.

At home, to cut down on the electric bill, we were not allowed to turn on the air-conditioning until after dinner, no matter how much we'd complain or beg. Some afternoons, after walking home from school drenched in sweat, I'd strip off my polyester uniform, bathe in rubbing alcohol, dust my body with talc, then lie on my bed like a floured drumstick under the ceiling fan to cool off. Regardless, not until around 8 or 9 P.M. would Mamá give us the okay, and Caco and I would storm through the house closing all the windows before turning on the AC to super-duper high and sitting shirtless in front of the vents, enraptured by the ice-cold air against our sweaty temples, hypnotized by the hum of the compressor fan, intoxicated by the clean scent of the filtered air.

The thought of spending a week sweating at the Copa without air-conditioning—not even at bedtime—was terrifying. "What if they don't have AC in the rooms?" I said to Mamá as Papá approached the front desk. *"Bueno,* we'll see," she replied, adding, *"Air-condichon* is a luxury, not a necessity. We had no *air-condichon* in Cuba and no one died." Papá returned with good news: the room was only thirty-two dollars with a kitchenette. The bad news was that an AC unit would cost five dollars extra per night. "Is not so bad. *Está bien,* put a deposit," Mamá instructed Papá, and then paused, Caco and I anxiously waiting for her next words. "With *air-condichon,*" she added. "Yeah!" I exclaimed quietly, bouncing on my tiptoes. Caco put out his hand: "Give me five!" he said. I slapped his palm and then he slapped mine. The thought of AC blasting all day long for a whole week made up for the crummy lobby and all the old folks.

"No paradise, *pero bueno*, it's better than nothing," Mamá said aloud to no one in particular, scanning the row of travel posters that decorated the lobby, advertising places I'd never heard of: Aruba, Cancún, St. Thomas. Places with teal-blue waters, hammocks strung between coconut palms, and bays teaming with sailboats—all hung in gold plastic frames without any glass.

The day after we returned from our hotel-scouting trip, Mamá began tightening the family budget to save up for our vacation at the Copa four months away in July. She pushed back the AC hour to 10 P.M., sometimes 11 P.M. if she decreed it was a cool night. She also asked Abuela to start fixing more *reasonable* dinners and chip in the money she saved on the grocery bill. At least three times a week, we had potato omelets, boiled corn meal with *chicharrones*, or rice with a can of Libby's Vienna Sausages that were no bigger than my pinkie and as mushy as dog food. The sacrifices hardly seemed worth a week at the crummy Copa. Except for the air-conditioning, I had little to look forward to, until the phone rang one night after dinner.

Abuela answered: "*¿Oigo? ¡Bien, bien! ¿Cómo están ustedes?* Still cold *en Nueva York?*" she began, and sat down at the kitchen table in the one chair with armrests. Her "throne," Mamá had dubbed it, where Abuela spent hours on the phone shamelessly gossiping or calling in bets. As soon as I caught on that it was my *tía* Elisa from New York, I parked myself on the living room sofa with my cat,

Misu, within earshot of Abuela's voice. I loved eavesdropping on her conversations with any one of her sisters; whichever one she was talking to, they'd gossip about the other three. This time she and *tía* Elisa went on for twenty minutes about *tía* Susana's latest *problema* with Valium; *tía* Ofelia's terrible vanity; and the usual disdain for *tía* Ileana, who still corresponded with her "no-good," communist son-in-law who "chose" to stay in Cuba. The conversation was juicier than any of the telenovelas I watched with Abuela every weeknight on *Canal 23*.

Then I heard her say, "*Sí, en julio, en el* Copa, right on the beach. *Sí*, you should come and visit." Could it be true? After another round of gossip, Abuela finally hung up and announced what I had been hoping I had heard: "*Oye, tía* Elisa and Paquito said they want to come with *las niñas* to *el* Copa with us. *Qué bien*." I flung Misu off my lap and slid down the hall in my tube socks to tell Caco the good news. "Oh, brother—big deal," he responded, returning his attention to the TV.

But it *was* a big deal. *Tía* Elisa only visited us once every few years, and she was my favorite great-aunt. She always had something nice to say to me, even when it was something bad: "You chubby, *pero* you look healthy"; "You need a haircut, *pero* you look nice"; "You're too short for your age, *pero* you'll grow." And she cooked the best, most un-Cuban dishes: Sloppy Joes with shoestring potatoes; fried rice with tiny pieces of scrambled eggs; red cupcakes from a box, topped with cream cheese frosting and sprinkles—all the dishes that Mamá never made, claiming that gringo food was bad for us and would stunt our growth.

Tía Elisa and Paquito had lived in New York City since leaving Cuba in the early fifties, years before the revolution. I thought of Paquito as the *real* Ricky Ricardo: a sharp Latin-lover type who had become a big success in a big city. He didn't own a nightclub, but he had owned a grocery store on the Upper West Side, which had folded because Paquito had *"problemas,"* according to one of Abuela's gossip sessions on the phone that I once overheard.

Their daughters, my *primas,* Carla and Denise, were born and raised in New York. They were big-city girls, as American as could be, and the coolest of all my cousins by far. I only got to see them when they came down to Miami—and I could never get enough of them. Denise was the hipper, flashier of the two. She sported headbands and hot pants, and wore false eyelashes that fluttered like black butterflies. She spoke with a thick New York accent whenever she said words like *wuater* and *doowr.* Carla was the more artsy, sophisticated sister. She played the piano and wore her hair down to her waist like Cher. She dressed in paisley-print minidresses and always seemed to carry a purse. I was fascinated by them and the stories they would tell about New York: standing at the top of the Empire State Building like King Kong, seeing *A Chorus Line* eight times, walking through Times Square's ten-story billboards, and visiting the life-size dinosaurs at the Museum of Natural History.

Within a week all the arrangements were made: Papá reserved another room at the Copa and *tía* Elisa booked the flights. I marked the day they were arriving with a red *X* on the complimentary wall calendar from El Gallo de Oro market that hung on our refrigerator. Each month featured a vintage photo of some Cuban landmark, each one captioned as *the oldest, the first, the tallest,* or *the most beautiful* this or that. Throughout the year, I'd imagine Mamá and Papá walking down the cobblestone streets of Old Havana, driving down La Gran Vía in an ice-blue Oldsmobile convertible with chrome fins, or sitting on the seawall of El Malecón, behind them the waves erupting like volcanoes. Month after month, with every opening and closing of the refrigerator door, I'd catch an imaginary glimpse of their lives years before me and the revolution that I knew almost nothing about.

But for the whole month of June, instead of the past, I imagined the future, counting the days until *tía* Elisa and my *primas* would arrive from New York City. Until age four, I had lived there with my family. Though I had some memories of the city, they were faint and vague. New York felt familiar and close, yet so far away, a larger-than-life place, like Cuba, which I knew only through photos and stories.

THE DAY WITH THE BIG *X*—JULY 2—FINALLY arrived. By the time Mamá came into my room to wake me up, I was already sitting on my bed, fully dressed in my Kmart best: my favorite red-and-blue checkerboard shirt and the white leather shoes that I kept in the original Thom McAn box; they made me a half inch taller, at least. "We going to the beach, not a *Quinces* party," Mamá poked fun at me. "Get out of those clothes." But I didn't. I wanted to look extra-special nice for Carla and Denise. I took ten more minutes getting ready, parting my hair a half dozen times until I got a perfectly straight line, lacquering it in place with a generous spray of Mamá's Aqua Net, and dousing myself with Papá's orange-blossom cologne. "Look at you, Mr. Pretty Pants," Caco teased me when I sat down to breakfast with him.

I barely had enough room for my bowl of Cap'n Crunch because the kitchen table was crammed with the groceries Mamá and Abuela had laid out to take to the Copa. As mother-in-law and daughter-in-law, Mamá and Abuela never agreed on much except two things: discipline, and food—lots of it. They had stockpiled a ten-pound can of El Cochinito lard with a happy little pig bouncing across the label, a twenty-pound bag of rice as big as a pillow but as hard as a rock, and a sack of yuca. They had filled at least a half dozen brown bags with cans of black beans, jumbo-size bags of plantain chips, a couple frozen pork shoulders, assorted flavors of Jell-O packets, and two-liter bottles of Winn-Dixie brand soda, which didn't taste at all like Coca-Cola, as Abuela insisted.

What will Carla and Denise think of us lugging all this junk? I worried as Caco and I reluctantly helped Papá load everything into *el Malibú*. We thought we were done when Mamá came to the car carrying a huge plastic tote stuffed with her cooking essentials: the pressure cooker, her Hitachi rice maker, the wooden plantain masher to make *tostones*, and the extra-big twelve-cup espresso pot. She insisted she needed to take everything. Papá knew better than to argue; he shuffled things around and crammed in her wares, pushing down on the trunk until it closed, and we drove off, only five minutes behind schedule, according to Mamá's watch, Abuela and Abuelo following in the baby-blue Comet.

As the Miami Airport came within view of the highway, I began daydreaming of flying to Spain or Cuba in one of the jumbo jets on the runway, as big and dumb as a dinosaur, lifting magically into the sky as easily and gracefully as a seagull. I imagined the runway lights from above like strings of giant rubies and emeralds, or like colored stars against the ground instead of the sky. In the terminal, I took in the sweet, mingled scents of perfume and bubble gum drifting from the gift shops. Overhead, dreamy voices made announcements in languages I didn't know, though I listened carefully, trying to guess: French? Portuguese? German? The fluorescent lights bouncing off the polished floors felt as anonymous as the droves of people bustling past us and each other, arriving and departing from places that were only black dots on a map to me. How many cities were there in the world besides Miami: Caracas, Chicago, Buenos Aires, Denver, Montreal? I began counting while gazing at the monitor until *tía* Elisa's flight flashed ARRIVED | ARRIVED | ARRIVED.

Abuela made the sign of the cross twice and thanked San Cristóbal, the patron saint of safe passage. I spotted them walking down the concourse: *tía* Elisa wrapped in a fur-trimmed stole; *tío* Paquito decked out in a jacket and a tie as black and narrow as his pencil-thin mustache and darker than his hair; Denise clicking her gum, wearing an iron-on T-shirt with a yellow smiley face distorted by her large breasts, and carrying a radio-cassette boom box; Carla in her two-inch platform shoes, wearing a shin-length skirt and carrying a leather handbag. They were so cool, but I was too nervous to say anything. After the swarm of hello kisses and hugs, Denise bent down to greet me. "Come here, cuz, gimme some sugar," she said. I didn't know what she meant by *sugar*, but I walked into her wide-open arms and kissed her cheek. Then Carla noticed me. "Richard— you look so handsome," she said, holding me by the shoulders. Carla was the only one in the family who called me Richard—and I loved it.

At the baggage claim, I wondered just how much trouble I would get into if I dared to hop onto the luggage carousel. I debated, wanting to unravel the mystery behind the plastic partitions spitting out and swallowing up suitcases like magic. But then my eyes locked on *tía* Elisa's *neceser,* her vanity case. "Sí, sí, let me take it. It's not heavy," I insisted, practically ripping it out of her hand, not because I was that well-mannered, but because it was like carrying a giant purse. Mamá had one just like it in olive green with double stitching in white and the same dainty clasp. I knew what treasures lay inside:

a tiny mirror trimmed with ruffles, silk lining, pockets with bottles of French perfume, eye shadow sets, and tweezers I played with secretly for hours in her closet.

I reached for *tía* Elisa's *neceser.* "Leave that alone, *niño*. Carry a suitcase *como un hombre*, will you?" Abuela said calmly. She wouldn't dare make a fuss or call me names in front of *tía* Elisa. I knew I could get away with it, this time at least. I flaunted the *neceser*, swinging it from my wrist all the way back to *el Malibú*, where I bodychecked Caco so I could sit between Denise and Carla. "I'm smaller," I declared, looking innocently at Mamá for backup. "I fit better than him in the backseat." It worked: Mamá banished Caco to Abuelo's baby-blue Comet and let me sit nestled between my *primas*. Their arms touched my arms, their skin white and matte as eggshells, as if it wasn't skin at all but a thin silk under which I could trace their faint veins.

Unaccustomed to the heat and humidity of Miami, they asked Papá to turn on the air-conditioning, though it wasn't even ninety degrees, yet. I flinched, thinking Mamá was going to embarrass me with one of her ramblings about the gas-guzzling luxury of driving with the *air-condichon* on. But she didn't; she rolled up the window, cuing Papá to slide the lever on the dash all the way left. The cold air on MAX rushed past my ears as I sat between my favorite *primas*. It was going to be the best vacation ever, I thought.

"There it is—*ahí*—on the right," Mamá said, managing to spot the nearly washed-out letters of the Copa printed in cursive over the tattered green awning above the entrance. Feeling a bit hammy, Papá honked the car horn as he drove up: *pum-dee-dee-pum-pum—pum-pum*, startling the old folks on the veranda out of their daze.

"Feh! What's all that hoopla for? For God's sake!" one of the old women yelled, fanning herself. Papá must have thought she was insulting him and responded indignantly, *"¡Vete pa'l carajo, vieja!"* betting the woman knew as little Spanish as he knew English, but he was dead wrong. *"¡Tú para el carajo!"* she mouthed off in broken but clearly pronounced Spanish.

How mortifying. That was Denise and Carla's welcome to the Copa. "Let's go inside," I urged them, not wanting them to witness the unloading of our Cuban Noah's Ark. "Well, this is certainly charming," Carla said. "Groovy-nice." Denise followed. They didn't seem as disappointed as I thought they'd be, after having heard so many of their spectacular stories about their amazing New York. Perhaps because of my excitement, the lobby didn't seem quite as horrendous as I remembered it. Maybe *reasonable* wasn't exactly the same as cheap after all.

We walked out to the deserted pool deck. "Look how blue the pool is—how inviting," Carla said, always needing her older sister to confirm her opinion. "What do you think, Denise? Isn't it gorgeous?" *Gorgeous* was one of those cool words, like *scrumptious* and *groovy, spectacular* and *outrageous,* that my *primas* used all the time, like another language to me. The pool was indeed *gorgeous*: the water perfectly still, reflecting the sky and the palms like a watercolor with a beautified version of the hotel façade, its age rendered unperceivable in the reflection. "Outta sight," Denise said upon seeing the two-story diving platform, which wasn't getting much use, I figured, thinking of the old men and women from the veranda.

Caco and Papá met us outside, but Papá gave Denise the room key since she was the oldest, he said, and then announced: "We have three rooms, and they connect, so we all stay together." It was too good to be true, but it was. *Tío* Paquito had splurged and gotten an extra hotel room, Papá explained, so that all the cousins—Caco, Denise, Carla, and I—could stay together in one room, and the adults would be more comfortable. This could turn out even better than staying at the Seacomber, I thought, a whole week with AC and my *primas* in the same room. Without Abuela patrolling me, I could blow-dry Carla's hair, put lipstick and eye shadow on Denise, maybe even paint my fingernails with clear polish, I dared to day-dream.

We met up with the rest of the family by the elevator, the men struggling to push the luggage cart loaded with all our Cuban must-haves. As soon as the doors closed, Denise reached over my shoulder and tore off a piece of bread from one of the dozen loaves Mamá had brought. "Cuban bread—far out," she mumbled while chewing, the crumbs falling inside her smiley-face shirt. "We haven't enjoyed *pan cubano* in months," Carla followed, tearing a piece off for herself. "How divine. You're lucky, we can't get Cuban food unless we go all the way to Union City in Jersey, right, Denise?" How weird. Why should my *primas* crave anything Cuban? They were practically 100 percent American. "I'm glad you like." Mamá smiled. "Wait till you taste *el flan* I made."

By the time we reached our floor, there was a feeding frenzy; everyone—except me—munching and talking with their mouths full, leaving a trail of bread crumbs from the elevator all the way down the hall. The room looked more or less how I had imagined it: a rickety dresser missing a couple drawer pulls; a mirror tarnished in spots so that I had to bob around to see myself in it; and a beige ro-tary phone on a night table stained with water rings. The shabby paint job had left visible brushstrokes on the walls, and the light switches were crusted over with paint. The polyester bedspreads matched the pattern on the curtains: a collage of faded birds-of-paradise that had bled out most of their colors. But surprisingly, right in the middle of the room was a new twenty-six-inch color TV with an extra tuning antenna.

Carla placed her suitcase down on the bed and stood by the window, looking out at the ocean. "This is stunning," she said, taking in a deep breath of ocean air. "Can you see Cuba from here?" she asked, turning to me. "I dunno. I guess so," I answered. It was a silly question—Cuba was way too far away—but I didn't want to make her feel dumb. Caco immediately darted for the air conditioner and started turning the knobs until it sputtered on and a cool stream of air began pushing through the room. Denise plopped her boom box up on the dresser and tuned in to "Shake Your Booty" by KC and the Sunshine Band. "Come on, Carla, let's show our *primos* how to do the Bump," she said, turning up the volume.

They both bumped each other and me all around the room with their hips, snapping their fingers perfectly in time with the beat. "Come on. Get your butt over here and dance," Denise said to Caco, trying to rouse him. "Naw—that's for girls," he protested, but I knew the truth: he was a terrible dancer. Instead of dancing, Caco pulled out a pillow and yelled, "Pillow fight!" leaping back and forth between the two beds, showing off in front of my *primas*. "Come on—fight!" he egged me on, throwing the other pillow at me. "Come, let's get him!" Carla yelled, then armed herself and jumped onto the bed, followed by Denise.

Thinking I could edge out a victory over Caco with the help of my *primas*, I jumped into the ring of pillow thwacks and giggles. Then one of them—I didn't know who—smacked me in the face; the zipper on the pillow cover struck me right under my eye. It hurt, but I didn't say anything; I didn't want to get either of my *primas* in trouble, just in case it was one of them who hit me. Instead, I moved to the floor, safely out of reach of their cross fire, to quietly get over the pain. As if she knew, within seconds Mamá rapped on the connecting door between the rooms, "*Qué pasa* in there?"

After a few suspicious seconds too many, Caco opened the door. "Nothing," he lied, but his heavy breathing and the sweat above his lip gave him away. Mamá scanned the room, trying to figure out what we had been up to, and then she saw the welt on my cheek. "*¿Qué te pasó?*" she asked me, turning my face to the light so she could get a good look at my war wound. I remained silent as she scolded us: "*Caramba,* we only here an hour and already trouble. Look at this—you almost broke his eye! What happened? *¡Dime!*" In a panic I squealed, blaming it all on Caco.

I knew I was Mamá's "little baby," and would play up to her notion that Caco "should know better" because he was older. But she didn't quite go for it that time. She spread the blame evenly, separating us into different corners of the room. We were hoping that was the worst of it, but then she made us turn off the radio. "Now sit *tranquilos* till I say. Not a single word out of any of you," she ordered. "And keep open the door so I can keep *un ojo* on you, *cabrones*. If there is any more trouble, no pool, no beach, no *air-condichon*— *nada*." Boredom was the cruelest punishment of all, but not knowing how long we'd have to stay quiet and still—for two minutes or two hours—made it torturous.

"Thanks, doofus," Caco muttered when Mamá turned her back, returning to her room. "But I didn't do nothing," I said, thinking my *primas* would defend me again, but instead they sided with Caco. "Yeah, what a tattletale," Denise said. "That wasn't nice, Richard," Carla added. The scorn beaming on me from all six of their eyes was insufferable in our mandatory silence; I broke involuntarily into sobs, turning my face away from them. But they heard my sniffles anyway, and kept shushing and shushing me.

Mamá's punishments could last hours, but she must have felt somewhat sorry for us since we were on vacation. Only ten minutes later she came back into our room flapping her new sandals covered in plastic daisies and sporting her faux Pierre Cardin sunglasses that made her look like a giant fly. "*Bueno*, are you going all to behave?" she asked as if we were going to answer anything else but yes, yes, yes. "*Bien*, put your bathing suits on," she said, tossing Caco and me our new swim trunks that she had let us pick out at Kmart. Caco had chosen a pair with the NFL team logos—typical—and I had picked out a bright yellow pair with dozens of floating shamrocks. I just had to have it.

My *primas* rummaged through their suitcases, darted into the bathroom, and then emerged: Denise in a hot pink bikini, and Carla in a more modest blue two-piece. Their breasts were not quite as big or pointy as Mamá's or Abuela's torpedo-teats, as Caco called them, and their thighs were even more pale and translucent than their arms. Like *decent* Cuban girls, they were only allowed to shave their legs up to their knees, leaving their thighs full of fine dark hairs matted against their skin. "Shall we go to the pool or the beach?" Carla asked. "The pool—that's where it's happening, girl. I'll bring the boom box," Denise said. "Why don't we go to the beach first?" I proposed, but they ignored me.

I went in the bathroom to change, eager to show off my shamrock trunks, but when I popped out, they had all left without me. I expected such shenanigans from Caco, but not from my *primas*. He probably talked them into leaving me behind. I stomped barefoot out of the room, down the hall, through the lobby, and out onto the front veranda, wanting to get as far away from them as possible. I wanted to be alone, but there was only one empty chair, next to an old woman in a baby-blue dress. I felt as lifeless as she and the rest of the old folks seemed; all of us like seagulls peering out into the ocean at nothing and everything. Why didn't my *primas* like me anymore? And why was Caco such a jerk?

My self-pitying thoughts were interrupted by the sounds of the old woman next to me, who kept sniffling and dabbing her nose with a linen handkerchief. My eyes were drawn to her fingernails, thick with age but perfectly manicured and painted an icy blue that matched the aquamarine cocktail ring as big as a lollipop that covered half of her middle finger. I turned my head slightly for a moment, catching a glimpse of a diamond pendant on a gold necklace pinched in the folds of skin around her neck, her wrinkled earlobes weighed down by pearl-drop earrings. *She must be rich*, I thought; so what was she doing at the crummy Copa?

"Oy, I must be allergic to you," she blurted out, pulling off her rhinestone-trimmed glasses and letting them hang from a chain around her neck. I wasn't sure how to respond to such a weird comment, and wanted to keep to myself. But she continued anyway, "So where you from, dahling?" "Here," I told her. "What, you live here at the Copa? And so young too. Who knew?" she said in jest, beginning to erase the pout on my face. "No, not in Miami—in Westchester," I explained, and told her I was here with my parents on vacation. "Oh, you're the family that schlepped in today in that fancy Chevrolet. What a loud bunch you are," she said, and began fanning herself. That's when I recognized her; she was the lady who'd had words with Papá. Embarrassed, I felt obliged to be nice, though I was also curious about her strange accent, which I couldn't place, and the way she made statements using questions. I'd never heard anyone talk like that before.

"How about you? Where are you from?" I asked, and she was good for fifteen minutes: "Oh, dahling, I'm a little from everywhere, but I've been living here for five years come September, ever since Harry passed—may he rest in peace. He was a hell of a good husband, but no good at business. He lost everything. I miss my old meshuggener, even if he left me nothing except memories and bills, and a few of these tchotchkes. Look at this one. Didn't he have good taste?" she said, holding out her hand in front of her to show me the ring, joggling it in the sunlight as if to make the stone glimmer. "Who could part with this sparkler? Not me, even if I have to eat cabbage the rest of my days."

She cleaned her glasses with the handkerchief, slid them back on, and turned her body toward me. "Let me take a good look at you. You're a cute one. A little meaty, but not so bad. So, dahling, you got a name?" "Um . . . Ricky," I said awkwardly, taken by her bluntness and wondering if I should ask her the same, but I didn't have to. "What, you don't want to know *my* name? Yetta, Yetta Epstein. Nice to meet you, Ricky," she said with a chuckle. Her candid humor drew me in. I wanted to hear more from her and less of my own whining about Caco and my *primas*.

"So, where did you live before, with Harry?" I asked. "Oh, we had a gorgeous house off Alton Road, not too far from here, but on the bay side. What a palace—original marble floors, two-car garage, swimming pool, a big kitchen—the works, I tell you, the works. Harry and I knew all the stars back then: Sinatra, Lena Horne, Jackie Gleason, Dean Martin. It was like Hollywood here. And this crappy Copa? It was one of the most la-di-da hotels on the beach, nothing schlocky about it back then. The lobby was to die for. On Saturday nights they had a band by the pool. Harry and I were regulars—danced everything from the fox-trot to the mambo under the moonlight until all hours. Who would've known that when he passed, I'd have to move back here. Like my *mamele* used to say, *we make plans and God laughs.* But I have good memories inside these walls. So what if it's falling apart like the rest of us."

"Mambo?" I interrupted, a bit puzzled. "*Ay, sí, caramba,*" she broke out in Spanish, "We knew how to do *el* mambo, rumba, montuno—you name it. Harry and I popped over to Havana all the time; he knew everyone at all the best nightclubs. Picture me, dahling, twenty-five, in heels with my bazongas out to there in a halter top—bah! Those Cuban men couldn't keep their eyes off of me. And Havana! It was even more beautiful than Miami Beach back then. Those late-night walks through the empty streets of *La Habana Vieja,* all the shutters closed and the balconies empty. It was like Harry and I had the whole city to ourselves. But I've heard it's all falling apart now, just like Miami Beach. Who would've thought?" Her story made me think of the photos in the wall calendar from El Gallo de Oro. I pictured her and Harry the same way I had pictured my parents in Cuba.

"Cuba? That's where I'm from," I interjected again. "Oh, I thought you were from Westchester, dahling? Which is it? You sure move around." "Well, my parents are from Cuba. I was born in Spain, then we moved here," I explained. "So what does that make you?" "I'm American," I said, sure of my answer at first, but then added, "I guess." "Oh, you guess, do you?" she said, taking off her glasses again and lifting her penciled-in eyebrows. "Well, I'm going up to fix lunch. *Hasta luego,* dahling," she said, folding her handkerchief into her patent leather pocketbook. She stood up, patted out the wrinkles on her linen dress, and slowly shuffled away. Throughout the rest of the afternoon I kept playing Yetta's weird words in my mind—*mamele, meshuggener, schlep, schlocky*—and her not-so-weird question: *So what does that make you?* No one had ever asked me that before.

For dinner, *tía* Elisa offered to make grilled cheese sandwiches for me and Caco and my *primas*. Mamá reluctantly agreed, but made her stuff the sandwiches with slices of roasted pork so they would have *some* nutritional value. After our Cuban grilled cheese dinner, the conversation between Caco and the *primas* in our room began to sound like gibberish to me. They went on and on about the latest R-rated movies and high school pep rallies; they argued over who sang better than whom: Barbra Streisand or Karen Carpenter; Michael Jackson or Andy Gibb. Who cared?

Bored with their chatter, I blurted out "Where are you from?" at Caco, who was standing in front of the mirror with his hands in his mouth, strapping new rubber bands onto his braces. "What do you mean? I'm from Miami—where else, dummy?" he answered. "What about you, *prima*—where are you from?" I asked Denise, who was putting on a fresh coat of lip gloss. "From New York City," she responded proudly. "Me too—the Big Apple," Carla chimed in, combing the tangles out of her hair. She bounced the question back at me, "Why? Where are you from, Ricky?" "I'm not sure," I answered. Caco promptly wisecracked, "Sure you are. You're from Ur*anus*!" Embarrassed, I clammed up; they had no idea what I was trying to ask anyway.

They rushed out the door, telling me they'd be right back, but I knew better. I could tell they just didn't want me to tag along. Still, I didn't protest. I spent the night alone in the room, watching TV and browsing through the phone book to pass the time, looking up the names of relatives and classmates, counting how many Blancos lived in Miami, and I found Yetta—Yetta Epstein. There was only one.

WHEN I WOKE UP THE NEXT MORNING, CACO AND my *primas* were already gone. Hurt, I realized they must have snuck out of the room early while I was still asleep. I hurried down to the pool and spotted my *primas* on lounge chairs, their long, svelte bodies smeared with a thick coating of sunscreen. I dragged a chair beside them as if nothing had happened. "Oh, hello," Carla said kindly, lifting her sunglasses to look at me. "Hey, cuz," Denise said, acknowledging me with a smile. They were friendly again, but not Caco—of course not. "Nice shorts. You belong at the kiddy pool," he wisemouthed, and then turned his face away. "Dig it! Put that up!" Denise said, and turned up the volume on the boom box. She and Carla began singing along to "Disco Inferno," their eyes closed to the sun, tapping their painted fingernails on the aluminum armrests and wiggling their bodies to the music. Even Caco joined in, flapping his hairy toes to the beat.

"This song is outrageous," I offered, trying to ease my way back into their favor. "Oh shut up, blubbo," Caco said. "You don't even know who sings this." My *primas* giggled. I had to save face. "Yes I do, butt-brains. It's The Trammps—and it's from *Saturday Night Fever*—I saw the movie too! What do you know anyways? You can't even dance!" It was true. Caco was a terrible dancer. He knew it, I knew it, and he knew that I knew it from the nights I spent dancing with him after he practically begged me to help him practice his disco steps. For days afterward, I'd have to wear Band-Aids on my mutilated toes. But I didn't mind. For an hour, sometimes more, we were not bratty brothers—we were tribesmen dancing barefoot in our Fruit of the Loom boxers, entranced by the percussion beating through our bodies. Though sometimes we'd dress up for the part in silky shirts and polyester slacks. Regardless, as soon as he'd lift the needle off the LP, the threats would follow: "I'll kill you if you tell anyone, I swear. I'll tell Abuela about you dressing up like a girl in your sheets."

"You really don't know how to dance?" my *primas* asked Caco, giggling even louder. "He's a total nerd," I answered for my brother, who was unable to come back at me with anything more than "Shut up, or else." "Or else what, John Duh-volta?" I said, tripping my *primas* into a full-blown cackle, holding their tummies. In a flash he scooped me out of my chair—my feet wiggling as he carried me to the pool and flung me into the deep end. I could sense my *primas* laughing even as I swam underwater to the other side of the pool.

When I came up for air, I saw them tugging at Caco's arms, teasing him out of his chair to dance with them. I sat on the pool ledge alone with my best poor-me face, hoping I'd get my *primas'* sympathy, or at least their attention; hoping they'd wave for me to come back and join them. But they didn't. They were too busy showing Caco their fancy New York dance moves, trying to get him to follow their steps, his clumpy feet splashing up puddles of pool water everywhere like a bear on his hind legs trying to do the Hustle.

I could dance ten times better than Caco. I wanted to march back over to them and embarrass him with some of my fancy Latin Hustle moves. But before I got the nerve, they stopped dancing and followed Caco to the diving platform. Taking baby steps, my *primas* pinched their noses all the way to the edge of the platform, only to turn around and run back petrified. Then it was Caco's turn to show off. He took a running start and leaped off, headfirst into the water like a pelican diving for fish. He was a natural athlete, and I was a klutz. I knew I couldn't compete with him on the diving platform, so I played it cool. I lay down on my stomach along the ledge of the pool and rested my head on my arms, pretending to be oblivious, but I watched his every move through my squinted eyes. He pulled himself out of the pool, jogged confidently back to the ladder, and climbed up to the platform again as my *primas* clapped and whistled. In an instant, Caco became their hero, coaching them down the platform until the three of them finally held hands and jumped together, feetfirst, into the pool. My *primas* became his *primas*.

━━━━━HAVING HAD ENOUGH OF CACO'S WISECRACKS AND my heartbreaker *primas*, the next morning I went to the beach with the grown-ups. It took an hour of hauling the umbrellas, beach chairs, towels, sunscreen, and the ice chest filled with sodas and snacks. As well as Mamá's *por si las moscas* beach tote: a colander to catch pesky jellyfish, kerosene to remove tar stains from the bottoms of our feet, fishing reels in case anyone was in the mood, mosquito netting to keep the flies from the food, a vial of Mercurochrome, a bottle of rubbing alcohol, and a box of Band-Aids. All that, and yet the hotel was only steps away from the beach.

Abuelo had invited *tío* Pipo and *tía* Gloria to spend the day with us. They showed up with greasy brown bags of *chicharrones* from El Cocuyito and a bottle of whiskey, trudging through the sand with a card table and folding chairs for playing dominos. After a round of hello kisses, everyone migrated into two camps. On my right, *las mujeres:* Mamá, Abuela, and *tía*s Elisa and Gloria taking snapshots of one another with Mamá's Kodak Instamatic. They posed by the shore like beauty pageant contestants in one-piece swimsuits, pushing their busts out proudly and showing off their painted toenails, the coconut tanning oil on their arms and thighs glimmering like gold leaf in the sun. On my left, *los hombres:* Papá, Abuelo, and tíos Paquito and Pipo, stirring their highballs with their fingers, shuffling the dominos over the table, the sea breeze tickling the tufts of hair on their chests and under their arms.

And between the women and the men, I sat playing chef, preparing my specialties: sand cupcakes decorated with seashells, and seaweed spaghetti with sand meatballs, all the while listening to snippets of stories and banter in Spanish. In my left ear: "*Cojones,* remember the ass on Irene *la mulata* who lived by the railroad tracks in Hormiguero? If Nixon were still president, Castro would have been finished by now—finished. I heard that Ramón from Palmira came over as a political prisoner. *¡Coño!* Where did you learn to play dominos—in Canada?" And in my right ear: "Can you believe how much it costs to send shoes to Cuba? I don't know why, but the yuca here just won't soften up. Eugenia wrote that Tania just had another girl; she says she sent photos but they never arrived. Would you go back to Cuba if things changed?"

And in both ears, the same rant they'd get into every time we went to Miami Beach: "Look at all that seaweed and that muddy water. *De verdad,* nothing more beautiful than our beach at Varadero. Remember, the sand like sugar, the water so clear you could see a dull *centavo* down at your toes. This isn't a beach, it's *un pantano*—a swamp!" I took their insults personally. After all, it was *my* beach they hated. How could anyplace be more beautiful?

I stood up and walked over to my mother. "Mamá, why do you

all hate Miami?" I asked. Amused by my question, the women chuckled, before Mamá answered: *"Ay, mi'jo,* I don't hate Miami, but I'm from Cuba. This could never compare to home. You know that. We're all *cubanos."* "Me too?" I asked, which is what I really wanted to know, hoping for a simple yes or no, but instead she replied, *"Bueno,* yes, you're *cubano,* but you are also a little *americano; and un galleguito* from Spain, where you were born." I looked out across the sea, the same water that connected this shore with Cuba's shore and so many other shores that seemed so far away. It seemed like everyone knew for certain where they belonged except me and Yetta, I thought, remembering what she had told me, *I'm a little from everywhere.*

I toweled off and told Mamá I was going up to the room to watch TV, but instead I went to check if Yetta was on the veranda again. And there she was in the same seat, as if she hadn't moved since yesterday, only she had changed her outfit and her jewelry to match: a cluster of rubies on her finger, which were the same bloodred as the quarter-size buttons on her blouse and a silk headband pushing her bouffant up another inch. "Hi," I said, standing at a polite distance. "Oy, it's a hot one today," she complained, patting her forehead with a red handkerchief. "Come, sit down, sit down— sit, will you? So what's the trouble today—nothing again?" she asked boldly.

"Well . . ." I hesitated, feeling too transparent. "I guess I'm just confused." *"Ai,* you're too young to be so verklempt. What about?" she asked, trying to tease the words out of me. I wanted to ask her where she was *really* from and confess to her that I didn't know where I belonged, but instead I replied, "I don't know." "Well, if you don't know, Yetta can't help you," she said, and then changed the subject. "I have an appointment at the beauty parlor. Look at this, what a mess this hair. Come on, come with Yetta." I almost said no, but then I thought, *Why not?*, no one would notice me gone for an hour or so. I helped her up on her feet, though it didn't feel as if she really needed my arm at all. If it hadn't been for her bouffant, I would've been almost as tall as her, which meant she was under five feet. She put her glasses in her pocketbook and took out a pair of movie-star sunglasses that covered half her face.

It seemed as if Yetta knew at least one person sitting on the veranda of each hotel we passed. "Yetta! Are you going to the discount?" a woman in a housecoat and rollers called out from the Tiffany. "No, I'm going to Sylvia's for my hair. You should try it sometime," Yetta joked. At the Cardozo, a woman in a one-piece raspberry swimsuit hailed us: "And just who is that handsome boy with you?" There was that word again, *handsome*. "Who else? My new boyfriend," Yetta said, and left it at that. And from the Sea Winds, a shirtless man with hair covering his shoulders flirted: "There goes the Queen of the Copa. What, no hat today, gorgeous?"

"Oh, *bubbeleh*, don't pay that fool no mind," Yetta said coyly. "*Bubbeleh?* What does *bubbeleh* mean, Yetta? Is that French?" I asked her. "French?" she roared. "You have no idea, do you? I'm Jewish. It's a Yiddish word for someone you like—the way your parents call you *mi'jo* or *mi cielo*, in Spanish. Yetta's not French, dahling, I'm from Poland." All I knew of Poland was that it was somewhere in Europe; and all the dumb Polack jokes that the boorish Ernesto Suarez said in class all the time. Of course, Yetta was nothing like those jokes. Still, all Sister Maritza ever taught us about Jews was that they wrote the Old Testament and they didn't believe in Jesus, and that's why they killed him, but not to hold it against them because Jesus came here to die for our sins anyway. What would Sister Maritza think of my palling around with Yetta? Why wasn't Yetta from Israel if she was Jewish; how could she be a Jew and be from Poland? What was Yiddish? Was there a country named Yidd? And how did she end up here in Miami Beach? Is this what she had meant by *I'm a little from everywhere*?

Before I knew it, we were outside a storefront, standing before a window decorated with a hand-painted rainbow and stenciled gold letters that simply read SYLVIA'S across the glass. In the window there was a display of mannequin busts with dead eyes and frozen expressions like guillotined heads, a wig pinned to each one, the sale price written out by hand on a three-by-five index card. Was Yetta's bouffant really a wig? I wondered. As we stepped inside, the wind chime hanging from the door handle announced our arrival.

A woman wearing gold lamé pants and a zebra-print blouse greeted us. "Yetta! I thought you weren't going to make it today. Come give your Sylvia a kiss," she said referring to herself. So that was Sylvia, I figured; she looked about half as young as Yetta, with a bouffant twice as big, and her hair was reddish instead of silver. "When have I ever missed an appointment? Never," Yetta answered her own question. She turned to the rest of the ladies in the salon who had the same hair as she did, a gathering of tiny gray clouds floating in the room. All the ladies' eyes were on us. They looked like turtles peeking out from underneath the shells of their dryers.

One of the ladies finally asked what they were all itching to ask: "So, is Yetta going to introduce us to this nice young man?" "He's my grandson, David," Yetta lied. I tried not to flinch, somehow trusting there was a reason why she'd said what she'd said. "What! I thought you didn't have any grandchildren, Yetta. How's this?" another lady asked, inching her hair dryer above her ears to get a good listen to Yetta's answer. "Well," Yetta began, and fabricated a whole story about me, saying that her husband had had a long-lost illegitimate daughter in Cuba, Reyna, who was my mother. After a collective gasp by the ladies, Yetta concluded, "Anyway, this is Reyna's son, David. Except it's Dah-veed in Spanish—he's three-quarters Cuban, you know. But Reyna is Jewish too. Cuban Jews, can you imagine? Jewbans they call themselves. Who knew?" Turning her face away from the ladies, she winked at me and whispered in my ear, "If it's gossip they want, gossip they'll get." I understood she was just having a little fun, like my own Abuela.

Sylvia called Yetta over to her chair, next to which stood a cart heaped with rollers in all shapes and colors like toy blocks. She parted Yetta's hair, wrapping small locks one by one with a square piece of white paper into an itty-bitty roller while holding a comb in her mouth. The process seemed so delicate and artful, and yet equally painful: all the pinning and yanking and binding of her hair. When all the rollers were set, Sylvia doused Yetta's head with a stinky liquid. The fumes permeated the room and irritated my nostrils. None of the ladies seemed bothered by it, but the noxious smell and the heat from the hair dryers made me dizzy and I dozed off in my seat.

I woke up to Yetta standing over me, her hair exactly the same height, shape, and color as when we had entered the salon. She gave a few dollars' tip to Sylvia, who promptly tucked the money inside her brassiere. "Muah—muah—muah," Yetta sounded out her kisses good-bye to Sylvia and all the ladies as we exited through the chiming door out onto Lincoln Road again. "What was that all about? Why did you make up that story?" I questioned Yetta. "Oh, dahling," she said, "I love telling a good story. That's all I got—stories, even if they are lies. So today you are my Jewban grandson." I wondered if that was made-up too. "Is there really such a thing as Jewbans?" I asked. "Yes of course, there are Jews spread out all over the world—just like you Cubans. We get around."

As we continued walking, she explained that Lincoln Road was a "people mall," a street for shopping, eating, and "whatnot." The place to see and be seen when Harry and her were a young couple. "But now look at it—oy—it's a real dump, isn't it?" she said. And she was right, everything looked as run-down as the Copa: the storefront awnings faded and tattered from years of sun and rain, the concrete walks crumbling like chalk, and weeds growing taller than the unkempt shrubs in the landscape islands. All the store windows looked grimy, filled with old mannequins with broken fingers and dressed in fuddy-duddy clothes. They seemed as out-of-date as the Woolworth's we passed by with its chrome-edged lunch counter and row of apple-red stools stretching all the way to the back of the store.

There was an eerie sensation of emptiness all through Lincoln Road, a loneliness I couldn't explain, only felt in the conspicuous silence. But as Yetta filled in the blanks with her memories, I caught glimpses of just how glamorous it must have been back in her time: the coral stone fountain still trickling in front of the glass doors of the former Saks Fifth Avenue where Yetta used to shop *when things were good;* the empty corner storefront of the former Cadillac dealership where she and Harry had bought their first fancy car; and everywhere the timeless royal palms like indestructible columns standing as straight as ever.

"Let's get lunch at Wolfie's. We're hungry," she said, speaking for both of us, and we turned off Lincoln Road at the next corner. From a couple of blocks away I could see the giant marquee: *Wolfie's* spelled out in cursive letters made of strands of neon, lit up even during the day. We took a seat at the counter, which looked as ancient as the one at Woolworth's. But unlike Woolworth's, Wolfie's was teeming with people mostly Yetta's age—or older. She handed me one of the menus pinched between the napkin holder and the ketchup bottle on the counter. "The liverwurst is to die for," she said. Liver was gross enough, but what was liverwurst? The worst part of the liver? I scanned the menu: pastrami, gefilte fish, lox, blintzes, and a slew of other foods I'd never heard of, finally finding something I could pronounce and loved: grilled cheese sandwich.

The waitress in white nurse-like shoes was slim with graying hair cut short and close so that you could make out the shape of her head. Of course, she and Yetta knew each other. "The usual, Yetta?" she asked, moistening her index finger with her tongue to turn the page in her order pad. A Reuben and a bowl of borscht, Yetta confirmed and then turned to me. "What are you going to have? Try the borscht—you'll love it," Yetta insisted. After she explained (to my horror) that borsht was beet soup—served cold—I declined and asked for a grilled cheese sandwich, no tomatoes. "Okay, then," Yetta said to the waitress, "a Reuben, a grilled cheese, two Cokes, and two bowls of borscht." Before I could protest, she assured me, "Trust me—it's to die for."

As we waited for our food, Yetta explained that all the celebrities used to eat at Wolfie's. It was hard to believe Yetta's claim, but there was proof on the walls, which were covered with framed photos of ladies in strapless cocktail dresses with diamond hair combs and men in double-breasted jackets, smoking and having fancy cocktails in the very same booths that surrounded us. "So why don't the stars come here anymore?" I asked. Yetta sighed and then explained, "Oh, that was in the fifties. Miami Beach is kaput now, what with all the drugs and the mafia. It's a shame, I tell you. People go to the fancy new resorts nowadays. Everything changes—and not for the better so much. Look at me. One day I'm twenty-four with a twenty-four-inch waist, hobnobbing with celebrities, and the next day I'm an old meshuggener sitting here telling you dumb stories. Like you care. Remember this much, *bubbeleh:* change can't be changed. One day, when you're old like me and look at the world not like it is, but like it was, you'll know what this means."

I couldn't grasp what she meant, but I felt it: it was the same emptiness I felt on Lincoln Road; the same loneliness I saw in the eyes of the old folks sitting at the Copa, lost in time; the same undertow of sadness pulling at my parents whenever they spoke about their lives back in Cuba. Like Cuba, like New York City, Miami Beach—Yetta's Miami Beach—suddenly became a place I had never been to either. "I like your stories, Yetta," I assured her. "You can tell me all the stories you want."

The waitress set down the two bowls of borscht. Yetta filled her spoon and savored it with her eyes closed, and then urged me to try it. I stared at my bowl awhile, swirling my spoon around, trying to get over the thought of it being blood instead of soup, and finally tasted it. Blood might have tasted better, but I didn't have the heart to tell Yetta. "Mmm, delicious," I lied, and she nodded her head. "You see, I told you you'd like it. You gotta try everything once—that's Yetta's rule."

At last my grilled cheese came and I was able to cleanse my mouth of the muddy taste of beets. I ate slowly, hoping Yetta would finish before I did so then I could just say I was full and we could leave. Yetta did finish before me, but she excused herself to the restroom, telling me to finish up before she got back. In a panic, I dropped a couple of spoonfuls of borscht into her bowl, a few under the counter, and mixed the rest into my half-empty glass of Coke, just before Yetta returned wearing a fresh coat of lipstick. "Now, finish up your soda," she insisted. I had no choice. Taking a deep breath and holding it in, I stuck the straw way back in my mouth and drank my Coke and borscht. "Good. Now let's shimmy back to the Taj Mahal; it's getting late."

Riding up the elevator at the Copa, Yetta insisted I visit her for lunch the next day for pierogi, which sounded just as weird as borscht and liverwurst, but I wanted to hang out with her again, so I agreed. "It's number six-oh-three. *¡Hasta mañana!*" she said as the elevator doors closed. When they opened seconds later on my floor, it was to the terrifying sight of Abuela sitting on a bench by the elevator, arms and legs crossed, waiting for me with her Godzilla face on. I knew I was in trouble for being gone all day without telling anyone, but the question was: How *much* trouble?

Abuela scolded me all the way down the hall to Mamá's room. "*Caramba*, where have you been?! *Ay, Dios mío,* we almost called *la policía*." Mamá, relieved at first, kissed me and pulled me to her, but then she reprimanded me too: "What you thinking? *¡Te voy a entrar a palo!*" I began pleading my case. "I wasn't doing nothing bad—I swear. I was with this cool lady who lives here; her name is Yetta." "Yetta?" Abuela questioned. "That's a strange name. Is she Cuban?" "She's not strange, Abuela," I explained, "she's just Jewish. What's the big deal anyway? All we did was eat at some place named Wolfie's. That's all—*te lo juro!*" "*Bueno,* it no matter,"

Mamá continued. "I don't want you with crazy strangers. Who knows what could happen to you with a Jew! Anyway, you lied to me, *cabrón*."

Mamá grabbed the back of my shirt collar and plopped me down in a seat at the dinette table. Somehow she had managed to get her hands on a pencil and a stack of loose-leaf paper. On the topmost sheet, Mamá had written out one line: *Nunca me desapareceré otra vez como hice hoy,* meaning, "I shall never disappear again as I did today." Pointing to the paper and pen, she commanded, "Five hundred times." Mamá had been a grade school teacher in Cuba and she still punished Caco and me by making us write lines—but in Spanish, so we wouldn't forget our mother tongue. I hoped that was all the punishment I was going to get, but before closing the door behind her she added, "Tonight you sleep in our room. Tomorrow no beach, no pool, no *nada*."

I shall never disappear again as I did today . . . I shall never disappear again as I did today . . . I began mindlessly scribbling, taking a break every fifty or so lines to ease the cramps in my hand and gaze out the window overlooking the pool. Squinting my eyes to blur out the cracks in the deck, the battered lounge chairs, and the burned-out pool lights, I pictured the Copa in the fifties: Yetta in a white tulle dress, pretty as Marilyn Monroe, dancing a slow song with Harry, the palms swaying like their bodies to the music, the pool sparkling as bright as the aquamarine ring on her hand resting on Harry's shoulder, and the stars like a thousand tiny eyes fixed on them. I could even imagine a young Yetta in a polka-dot bikini, leaping off the diving board, bouffant-first into the pool.

As I continued daydreaming, the Copa came to life—a real place with a history years before me, not just some dumpy hotel with air-conditioning. As I kept writing . . . *I shall never disappear again as I did today . . . I shall never disappear again as I did today* . . . I kept disappearing into the past, into Yetta's stories, into another Miami Beach, the way I had seen my parents and grandparents disappear into the Cuba of their past.

━━━━━━➤I CASUALLY SLIPPED ON MY SHORTS AND SANDALS the next morning, testing whether or not Mamá had reconsidered my punishment, but she hadn't: "*¡Eh!* Where you going? No-no-no. You stay in the room till it's time for *almuerzo*." I could live with that, I thought; at least it was only half the day and I could still sneak up to Yetta's in the afternoon. There was no way Mamá was going to give me permission to go see Yetta—*esa judía vieja*—after the fuss she made the night before. Mamá would never understand. Like most of my family, she seemed scared of anyone who was different, meaning anyone who wasn't Cuban.

I spent the morning flipping through TV channels, again, and looking out over the pool, again, watching Caco and the *primas*. I opened the window and called out to them, but they couldn't (or pretended not to) hear me above their jibber-jabber and the music blaring from Denise's boom box. Mamá returned at noon and prepared lunch for everyone: a mountain of fried plantains and a pallet of *pan con lechón* sandwiches on Cuban bread, wrapped in wax paper and packed into boxes. I stole two sandwiches and hid them in the refrigerator to take with me to Yetta's as backup in case I didn't like what she had made for lunch. After helping Mamá carry the boxes down to the beach, I stalled for a few minutes and then excused myself, telling her I had to go to the bathroom and that I'd be at the pool afterward.

"*Está bien,* but don't disappear *otra vez,*" she warned, giving me the key to the room, where I picked up the stolen sandwiches and then went up to Yetta's efficiency.

The door was a dark brown, but it must have been painted over a dozen times. It was chipping, and each chip exposed a color from another time: lime green, sky blue, peach. "You're late," she said, only a slice of her face showing in the gap between the door and the jamb, before unhooking the chain and opening the door. She was all done up: lips painted vivid red, cheeks rouged, hair perfectly teased, and dressed in a light-brown dress and a yellow scarf coordinated with the gem-du-jour: a cat's eye brooch staring at me. "What? You brought lunch? What's that in your hands?" she asked. I explained they were pork sandwiches. "*Bubbeleh,* you really don't know *nada;* Jews can't eat pork—it's not kosher—it's against our faith," she said. That made no sense to me. How on earth could eating pork be wrong—a sin? "What about if you are Cuban? Can Jewbans eat pork?" I wanted to ask.

She pulled out a chair for me at a square table between the open kitchen and the living room, set with souvenir placemats from Niagara Falls, a paper napkin folded into a triangle beside each plastic plate, small glasses that looked like old jelly jars, and a half-frozen bottle of Coca-Cola as a centerpiece. While she finished cooking the pierogi, I panned my eyes around her apartment, which felt familiar. Just like at our house, the dining chairs and the sofa in the living room were upholstered in protective clear vinyl, the lampshades were still wrapped in clear cellophane, and centered on the coffee table was a glass bowl full of plastic grapes. The walls were decorated with faux oil paintings, one of them from a faraway village with blankets of snow and high-pitched roofs with chimneys; a place that seemed as far away and unreachable as the vintage photos of Havana in the complimentary calendar from El Gallo de Oro that hung in my house.

Setting down a platter, Yetta seemed just as proud and coy about her cooking as Mamá and Abuela were about their own. "Eat. Eat. I made these myself from scratch, though they're not my best," she said, piling a few on my plate. They looked like Mamá's empanadas: toasty brown half-moons of fried dough. But would they taste the same? I looked at them cautiously, hoping they weren't filled with something even grosser than borscht. Luckily, they tasted as good as they smelled, I discovered, as the warm gooey filling oozed through my mouth. "They're delicious—really," I said, "even better than grilled cheese." "Good, good. Eat, eat. Even if you don't I'll say you did," she said. Yetta smiled and then unsmiled: "Pierogi. I remember my *mamele* every time. The two of us back at our house in Kraków, in the kitchen gossiping as we cooked. Who knew so much would happen so soon. *Gott in himmel!* How wonderful and terrible it is to remember."

Her voice thinned and her gaze drifted toward something only she could see in the empty space of the room. She looked just like my parents and relatives when they disappeared into talk of Cuba and how much they missed what they missed of that world that was invisible to me: *their* beach at Varadero, *their* peanut vendors' calls in *La Habana*, *their* rain falling over *their* burning sugarcane fields. I felt compelled to ask Yetta more about her life, but before I could figure out how to phrase a question, she changed the subject. "This is no time for schmaltz," she said. "Eat this last pierogi—don't let it go to waste."

"Can I be a Jewban—for real?" I asked—the only thing I could think of saying to console her, though I indeed had begun feeling so comfortable around Yetta that I wondered if I truly belonged where she belonged—wherever that was. "Oh—such a dahling—you're adorable. I wish I *did* have a grandson like you." she said, glowing. "When you grow up, sure, you can become Jewish if you want to. But being Jewish is a feeling too, dahling. Like the way your parents probably feel Cuban no matter where they are. Do you feel Cuban?" she asked. I rambled in answering her. "Sometimes I do, but sometimes I hate being Cuban—like when my parents do tacky things or can't understand what I'm saying in English. Sometimes I feel very American—like when I eat grilled cheese or hear 'The Star-Spangled Banner'; but sometimes I don't feel American. Then I feel like nothing." "Don't worry about it, *bubbeleh*," she advised. "Some days I feel Polish, some days American, and some days even a little *cubana* too. So what? So we're a little from everywhere—not so bad I think. Not so bad."

"*Ay, caramba*, look at that—it's almost time for bingo. *Vámonos*, I don't want to be late. Yetta is never late." From the counter she took an old mayonnaise jar filled with change and handed it to me, then slung her pocketbook on her wrist. Before I could say anything we were scurrying down the hall. In the elevator mirror she brushed on some rouge and put on a fresh coat of lipstick before the doors opened on *M* for mezzanine, a word as strange to me as any I had heard in Yetta's Yiddish.

We entered through double doors into a musty banquet hall with dingy carpets and a dusty chandelier pocked with burned-out bulbs. Walking to the front of the room, Yetta fished seventy-five cents from the jar and bought three bingo cards: two for her and one for me. "You're not old enough to gamble. Let's just say you're playing that card for me," she said, and winked. Amid the elderly people fussing over the best seats, we spotted two empty chairs and sat down. "I feel lucky, I tell you, lucky," she declared. As the caller began announcing numbers, I gazed at the sunlight streaking into the room through the windows that faced the pool, slipping into my imagination again, until Yetta broke me out of my trance, shouting, "*Bubbeleh! Bubbeleh*—the numbers! Watch that card, will you? This is rent money you're playing with, dahling."

On the next game, I only needed N-35 and I-18 to win when I heard a familiar voice feigning a whisper behind me, calling me by my full first and middle names, "Ricardo de Jesús!" which always meant I was in serious trouble. Jarred, I turned around and came face-to-face with Mamá in her giant fly glasses, Abuela at her side, both of them wearing Godzilla faces again. "So you were at the pool, eh? That's not what Caco told to me, *cabrón*," Mamá said, clenching her jaw, her eyes getting bigger and bigger. She pulled off one of her plastic daisy sandals and raised it in her hand; Abuela followed suit, threatening to thwack me with one of the thick man-sandals she wore because they were cheaper than women's sandals. "What I tell you last night, *cabrón*? So this is the crazy *judía* you're sneaking with?" Mamá continued berating me.

Panicked, I shouted, "BINGO!" hoping to cause a distraction and somehow defuse the situation. The announcer stopped calling out numbers and the bevy of bouffants turned around to look at the winner, but instead their eyes met Mamá and Abuela. The room filled with gasps and whispers at the sight of the two of them standing like sergeants with their sandals cocked and aimed, ready to fire on my backside. Yetta, who had said nothing, surprised us all when she shouted, "*Pégale bien duro*—spank him real hard right in the *tuches*. I don't blame you. *Qué cabrón*, schlepping around with an old Jewish bag like me—and gambling too! He deserves a good *shmits*—go on, let him have it—*suénalo para que aprenda*."

Disarmed by Yetta's brute remarks, in Spanish no less, Mamá

and Abuela froze and lowered their weapons. But they were reluctant to admit defeat: "*¡Vámonos entonces!*" Mamá said, demanding we leave at once. "*Adiós,*" Yetta said, and winked at me before Abuela snatched me away by my wrist. Hobbling on one sandal each, Mamá and Abuela retreated from the room with me in tow. I glanced back at Yetta, not knowing if I would see her again. She was looking back at me with a smile, and kept smiling even as the bingo game picked up again: . . . *B-13* . . . *0-71.*

Through the lobby and up the elevator, Mamá and Abuela didn't say a word. I thought they were so upset with me that they couldn't even yell at me, but when we got back to the room they acted as if nothing had happened. Abuela asked if I had won any money at bingo, and if there would be another game that night. Before I could answer Abuela, Mamá interrupted. "We're not going to play bingo— *¿estás loca? Esta noche* we're all going to watch the Fourth of July fireworks on the beach," she told Abuela, then turned to me. "*Bueno,* you should look nice. Go take a shower *y péinate el pelo,*" Mamá said, with her Glinda the Good Witch face on. I did as I was told without questioning her, or why she no longer seemed angry at me. I guessed she felt a little guilty, after having seen that I wasn't doing anything wrong; she had nothing on me. But more so, I sensed she had caught a glimpse of herself in Yetta's feistiness. Yetta became a real person to her, not just *una judía.*

After sundown, my family gathered on the beach. I sprawled out on my towel next to Caco and the *primas* around a bonfire *tío* Pipo had started, burning driftwood, paper wrappers, and anything else we could find on the beach. The fireworks began and we tilted our heads up to the lights flashing over the dark sea and in our eyes, fixed in silent reverence. "How long we been here?" I heard Papá ask Mamá, who replied immediately and without hesitation, "Eleven years next March, the sixteenth. Eleven years, *mi amor.*" "It's true, *parece mentira,*" Abuela said, seated next to *tías* Elisa and Gloria, the three of them waving tiny American flags that *tía* Elisa had brought from New York. "I've been here twenty-three years," *tío* Paquito offered, speaking without taking his eyes off the sky, "almost longer than I lived in Cuba. Sometimes I forget where I am from anymore. Can you believe that?"

The fireworks became stars exploding, giant roses blooming right before my eyes. I pictured Harry dancing the cha-cha with Carla and Denise at the top of the Empire State Building; Mamá as a little Polish girl in pigtails, playing hopscotch in the snow; me with Fidel Castro and Ricky Ricardo munching on *pan con lechón* sandwiches at Wolfie's; and Yetta in her movie-star glasses, cruising along Ocean Drive with Papá in his *Malibú* convertible, wearing a green head scarf to match her emerald bracelet flickering in the sunlight. For a moment I was everywhere at once—Miami Beach, Cuba, Güecheste, the Copa, Poland, New York.

"WHAT, YOU NOT GOING TO SAY *ADIÓS* TO YOUR friend?" Mamá questioned me as we walked down the veranda and past Yetta. I couldn't tell if she was being facetious or genuine, but nevertheless, I turned around and walked back up the steps. "Come here, you little *sheygetz,*" Yetta said as I approached her. She pressed my face between her palms and kissed me on the forehead, leaving a big smudge of lipstick that she wiped off with her handkerchief. "*Zei gezunt, bubbeleh!* See you *mañana,*" she said. "*Hasta mañana,* Yetta," I returned, then darted to the car. "Who the hell was that?" Caco asked me. "Nobody," I said with a smirk. "Don't worry about it."

"She looks far-out," Denise said, followed by Carla's "Indeed, where's she from?" "Oh, she's a little from everywhere," I said, and smiled. I propped myself up in the backseat, looking through the rear windshield and waving good-bye to Yetta, the Queen of the Copa, sitting on her throne on the veranda, waving back at me, becoming smaller and smaller and smaller as we drove off into memory.

FIVE

IT TAKES *UN PUEBLO*

*M*y *primo* Rafi was twice as tall as me and had three long whiskers he loved to show off, tiny tentacles growing from his chin. I was petrified of him. One afternoon while my family was visiting his, he bullied me into a game of tag football with the rest of my cousins. "Hey Lardo! Catch!" he yelled as I trotted down the street, my belly bouncing up and down. He knew I'd miss the ball, and I did, fueling an unstoppable fit of laughter from my cousins. They laughed until they could barely breathe and had to call for a "do-over." But there was no do-over for me. After that fateful game, I was known as Lardo instead of Ricardo. *What's up, Lardo? Get a life, Lardo. Shut up, Lardo.* Soon even my *tíos* and *tías* began calling me *Lardito*.

When I was younger, I was a finicky eater. "You look like *un gargajo,* a piece of phlegm—skinny and frail like a girl. *Los hombres* need to eat a lot," Abuela insisted, and began fattening me up with a concoction of sweetened condensed milk mixed with Coca-Cola, all the Easy Cheese I wanted, double portions of rice with *frijoles negros* at dinner, and mandatory desserts: *arroz con leche,* guava marmalade, bread *pudín*. But now that I was twenty pounds overweight, she was mortified: "Bad enough being a sissy—but a fat sissy—*¡qué va!* You have to lose all that *gordura*." And so began her campaign to slim me down. She made me ride my bike ten times around the block every day after school, and roller-skate twice a week for an hour up and down the front walkway, wrapped in garbage bags so I would "sweat out the fat." She even agreed to my request for a pogo stick just like the one my cousin Marlene had, after I convinced her that pogo-ing would be good exercise; although she immediately cut the plastic tassels off the handlebars. She banned all my favorite foods—the same foods she had used to fatten me up into *un macho*.

After weeks of watching Abuela torment me, Mamá spoke up, albeit with caution. "*Bueno,* he's not that fat," she told Abuela. "He's more like *hoosky,*" she said, mispronouncing the English word she had learned from the husky section of the boys department at Kmart, where she bought all my clothes. Riffling through the racks, she'd load her arm with a dozen gabardine blazers and pleated trousers. I'd step out of the fitting room, branded with the giant H on the tag hanging from my sleeve, modeling each piece with my head bowed until we found something that fit. Or almost fit. *Hoosky* was still embarrassing, but it was better than *Lardo,* I supposed.

──────I WAS LOOKING FORWARD TO THE SUMMER: RUN-ning errands all day with my grandparents in their baby-blue Comet that smelled like oranges; playing Aquaman at *tía* Ofelia's swimming pool; watching *The Price Is Right* and reruns of *I Love Lucy* all afternoon, sitting on the couch in my underwear, munching on cheese puffs. But that all changed a week before school let out. "What Riqui needs is hard work, a good *trabajo*. That will make him *un hombre*. He's old enough; it's time," Abuela announced at dinner, speaking to my parents about me in the third person as if I weren't sitting right across from her. "*Además,*" she continued, "working he will lose weight so that his *pipi* will grow. You know, if he doesn't lose all that fat before he turns thirteen, his *pipi* will shrivel up—become *nada*."

I gulped. My *pipi* shriveled right then and there. Except for Caco choking on his food as he tried to stifle his laughter, complete silence followed Abuela's announcement. She shoved another mound of black beans and rice onto her fork with her pudgy thumb, stuffed it into her mouth, and continued talking with her mouth full, pausing only to chew. "Remember what happen to Juan *el bobo* back in Cuba? I warned his mother, *pero* she didn't listen to me. Then it was too late, he had to have an operation to pull it out." There was *always* some character Abuela knew, in some town in Cuba, who served as a perfect example of good or bad fortune.

She continued with her plan: "*Ya hablé* with Don Gustavo. He'll let him help out at El Cocuyito all summer for fifty-five dollars a week." Don Gustavo was my *tío* Pipo's father-in-law and the chief of that side of the family, while Abuela ruled our side. She continued, instructing my father: "You drop him at the store *por la mañana* before going to work, and then pick him up." Exiled Cubans who ran family-owned grocery stores, like Don Gustavo, were exempt from child labor laws, apparently. Then Abuela delivered her ultimatum: "He goes to work or *si no* he goes back to baseball at Flagami." No! Anything but baseball, I thought, flashing back to those dreadful ninety-eight-degree afternoons in left field, shooing away gnats, terrified of fire ants, the fly balls I could never catch, and the boos every time I struck out at bat. I hated baseball and Abuela knew it; she knew I wouldn't object to working at El Cocuyito given the alternative. Once again, my parents didn't protest. *"Bueno,* we'll see . . ." was all Mamá could say to her. "Maybe . . . *vamos a ver,"* Papá said, but I knew the deal was done.

When I was a young child, before Abuela and Abuelo had moved to Miami and could babysit me on weekends, my parents had to take me with them every Saturday and Sunday to El Cocuyito, where they worked at the time—he as a butcher, and she as a cashier. I'd spend the day playing hide-and-seek by myself, crouching between dusty boxes stacked like giant toy blocks in the storeroom; or chasing the old guard dog, Napoleón, as he limped through the stockroom. When there were no customers at the checkout, Mamá would plop me on the conveyor belt—my magic rubber carpet. When Don Gustavo went home for lunch, Papá would let me wear one of his white smocks that reached my ankles like a dress; he would take me into the meat locker, a room full of death and bitter cold that somehow also felt magical: the hanging sides of beef towering over me like dinosaurs in a museum, the bags of frozen cow tongues as big as my arm, my breaths floating away like tiny clouds, which I followed in awe until they disappeared. El Cocuyito was a magical part of my childhood, and despite the reason for my employment, I looked forward to working there.

When I arrived at 7:30 A.M. that first day of work, I was reminded of that childhood, and just how little El Cocuyito had changed over all the years I had continued visiting the store with Abuelo and Abuela. I noticed the same translucent emerald letters hand-painted on the plate-glass doors, announcing: EL COCUYITO SUPERMERCADO | CARNICERÍA—MEATS | CAFETERÍA—CAFÉ CUBANO, set aglow by the rays of the sun; the same narrow aisles, tiny canyons four feet wide; the metal shelves painted a pale green, the color of mint ice cream; the same chipped linoleum tiles, worn and bleached almost white from years of mopping; the fish bowl filled with gumballs still atop the cafeteria counter; and the same smell of *papas rellenas* frying and *café cubano* brewing.

There were no customers yet, only the cashier, Sonia, wearing a knit sweater and rubbing her hands to warm herself up in the cold air of the store, chilled overnight by the open-faced refrigerator cases. But she greeted me warmly: "*¡Hola! Ave María,* look how big you are! *Bueno,* let's get started; I could sure use *una manito* around here." She showed me how to stack the brown grocery bags in the cubbyholes and how to wipe down the conveyor belt with Fantastik. The next day I graduated to more challenging tasks like bagging groceries and price checks. By the third day, we already had a routine. I'd spend the mornings bagging groceries for housewives who would twaddle on about what a good job I was doing, how mature and responsible I seemed for such a young age, and how I reminded them of one of their sons or nephews. After lunch, I'd walk down the spotless aisles with a broom and dustpan looking for a bit of dirt to sweep up, or I'd clean the already clean shelves with a feather duster like a French maid. When things slowed down and there were no customers in line, Sonia would let me ring up a few "practice" items as she looked over my shoulder, shaking her head whenever I was about to hit a wrong key.

The first week felt like I was playing grown-up rather than working, but this didn't last for long. Don Gustavo began keeping an eye on me as he patrolled the aisles day after day wearing the same bland uniform: gray polyester trousers with a cracked leather belt; a short-sleeve shirt, white and starched and tucked in; and black lace-up shoes with rubber soles. Like his clothes, he was no-nonsense, a call-them-as-he-saw-them man who seemed to leave no room for arguments or excuses. He gave me a sideways glance every time he caught me chatting with Migdalia, who staffed the cafeteria counter, and tsk-tsked whenever he saw me munching on a *pastelito* and sipping a soda.

He was waiting for the right moment to pounce on me—and it came. During one of my afternoon breaks, I grabbed a magazine from the tabletop rack at the cafeteria and sat at the counter, pretending I could read Spanish as easily as English, paging through new words and new faces of Latino heartthrobs with bushy eyebrows and hairy legs. Suddenly, I felt a bony tap on my shoulder and turned around to face Don Gustavo, who was in cahoots with my *abuela*. "You want *un cafecito* while you read, *señorita*?" he asked. "You think this is a country club? I'm not paying you to sit on your *culo*. *Vamos,* come with me," he commanded.

I followed the squeak of his shoes down the cereal aisle and into the storeroom. "Put these on the cart," he ordered, pointing to a tower of boxes marked Mazola Corn Oil. "Drop one, *caramba*, and you be cleaning oil off the floor all day." I was barely able to get a grip on the first one; it slipped out of my hands and landed with a thump on the cart. "*Vamos a ver*, let's see if you are as soft as your *abuela* says," he egged me on, a smoldering cigar dangling from the right side of his mouth, puffs of smoke spewing from it like dragon's breath. I was too scared of him to protest; instead, my fear was channeled into brute force. I loaded the next box, and the next, and the next—all eight of them. "Now what?" I asked cockily, feeling a little more courageous but still unable to look him in the eyes, magnified behind the thick lenses of his glasses.

Don Gustavo took me, or rather, *crushed* me, under his wing. I began reporting to him every morning. Hard of hearing (though he never admitted it), he was a human bullhorn, yelling instructions and commands over my shoulder all day long. The whole store could hear him and the corresponding silence of my embarrassment. Lesson number one: No! Nunca *sit on the floor. Kneel like* un hombre *when you're working on the shelves at the bottom.* Lesson number two: Coño—*move the older eggs to the front; if they go bad, I'll make you eat rotten eggs for a week.* But my apprenticeship went beyond learning the stock boy's trade. In Don Gustavo's view, hard work made a man, and being a man came with its own subset of lessons. Lesson number three: *Only women use straws* (he never let me drink anything, not even mamey shakes, from a straw). Lesson number four: *Real men don't work in shorts; shorts are for little mamacita's boys.* Lesson number five: *Real men are not afraid of getting dirty,* he'd say every time he made me climb into the Dumpster to stomp down the heap of putrid trash.

By midsummer I was worn out physically and emotionally. I thought about quitting, even though it would mean spending the rest of the summer in Little League. But then Don Gustavo asked me to help him stock and fix up the fruit and vegetable aisle, his pride and joy. I noticed a tenderness in the way his callused hands cradled the guavas as he took them one by one from the box, praising the choicest—*¡Qué linda!*—and tossing the ones that were too small, scarred, or bruised. With the patience of a sculptor, he shaved the fuzzy nap off each yuca and malanga root. He showed me how to pick out the ripest mangos. Lesson number six: *Press the flesh with your thumb. Smell the sap at the root of the stem.* ¡Qué rico! *Hold it to the light. Can you see all the colors?*

After several weeks, he let me stock all the produce, even allowing me to pile the oranges into pyramids, watching my every move, nodding his head in silent approval. And he broke out of character, sharing snippets about himself as we rotated the ripest avocados to the top of the pile or separated the *plátanos verdes* from the *plátanos maduros*. *You know I owned three* mercados *in Cuba till that* hijo de puta *took them for his* Revolución. He lost everything. According to family lore, his wife smuggled a one-thousand-dollar bill rolled up her butt when they left Cuba. He used the money to set up his own business buying fresh produce in rural Homestead and then selling it for a profit to grocery stores and restaurants all over Miami. *You know, when I got here in 1965, there was* nada, *not even a place to get* un cafecito *or a loaf of* pan cubano. By 1968, he had saved enough to open El Cocuyito. Since I'd been a child, he had told stories about the hundreds of *cocuyos* that had lit the night sky of his village, Palmira. He'd chase the fireflies with his father and trap them in jars—just as I had done with Papá in Güecheste. He also told me about the *señoritas* who'd wear *cocuyos* clipped to their earlobes and their dresses to vie for the attention of *caballeros* at the village square.

Soon after he opened El Cocuyito, it became a renowned and treasured place where Cuban exiles could satisfy their nostalgic hunger for foods that were almost impossible to find elsewhere. *You know,* a veces *it's the simple things people miss*. He stocked the store with sweet boiled ham imported from Spain; tropical fruits like mamey, papaya, and loquats from the Dominican Republic; and canned *dulce de coco* and guava marmalade from Puerto Rico. Puedes creer *I got that oven in the back for a hundred dollars from* una pizzería vieja. *My abuelo taught me to bake* pan cubano *and those* pastelitos *you keep eating all day*.

Despite the store's success, Don Gustavo still put in fourteen-hour days. El Cocuyito was more than his livelihood, it was a substitute for the life he had left behind in Cuba. *You know,* mi familia *had a big farm in Palmira*. Through his words, I saw him as a child sitting with his father in their groves, slicing into dozens of oranges with their fingernails. I watched the sugarcane fields set ablaze after each harvest, the ashes dusting the entire town like a tropical snow. One day, he took me into the office and opened the safe. From the safe he took a small pouch—it held a handful of dirt he had taken from his farm thirteen years earlier. "Smell it. *Anda*, smell it," he said. "That's what Cuba smells like. It's all I have left—this little bit of my *tierra*." Lesson number seven: Exilio *will kill a man. May you never have to leave this country of yours.*

SUMMER ENDED AND I BEGAN EIGHTH GRADE. SIS-ter Margaret decided to seat the class in alphabetical order, which landed me next to Julio Benitez. He was a bit nerdy like me, and alongside me, he was one of the heaviest boys in class—very *hoosky*. But unlike me, he had guts and gusto. For the talent show that year, he dressed up as Jimi Hendrix in a psychedelic shirt and headband. He went onstage with talcum powder that looked like cocaine smeared under his nostrils, lit a cigarette, and began playing a rendition of "Purple Haze." Sister Margaret's face flushed beet red; she stomped onstage ten seconds into his performance, slapped him across the face, then pulled him by the ear straight to the principal's office. He was suspended for a week, but became one of the most popular kids in class—not necessarily a "cool" kid, but a crazy-fun one, a misfit that everyone loved, including me. It was a case of opposites attracting. I was well behaved, shy, and book smart; I'd help him with his homework or let him cheat off me, sometimes. He, on the other hand, was street-smart, fun-loving, and gutsy; he'd dare me to make faces behind Sister Margaret's back or draft me into all-out spitball wars.

One day he invited me to his house after school and we spent the whole afternoon together goofing around. He played "Hotel California" over and over, trying to teach me a few chords on his electric guitar; then we played "Stairway to Heaven" backward, trying to hear the satanic verses that were allegedly masked into the recording. After that we shaved our faces in his parents' bathroom; Julio swore that the more we shaved the sooner our beards would come in. We then changed into shorts and cannonballed into his pool until our butts were sore. Just before dinnertime, we rode our bikes over to Jennifer Izquierdo's house—whom he had a crush on—and threw pebbles at her window. Nothing. Though Julio and I were an odd couple, I felt I could be myself around him in a way I couldn't be around other boys. He liked me for me—and vice versa. Thankfully, Abuela approved of him; in her own words, he was *un hombrecito*. She'd let him come over anytime, or let me ride my bike to his house whenever I wanted—no questions asked. We spent the rest of the school year hanging out together: me trying to keep him out of trouble; he trying to get me into trouble.

HAVING A BEST FRIEND FOR THE FIRST TIME IN MY life, I gained a new sense of confidence. I hoped our friendship would survive the summer apart, when I returned to El Cocuyito to work full-time. Julio's shaving technique had proven to work: I had sprouted about a dozen whiskers on my chin—and was quite proud of them. I wasn't quite yet a man, as Don Gustavo reminded me every day, but I wasn't quite a boy either. My body had begun to change and so had I. I understood Don Gustavo and his lessons, and

I began chitchatting with the regular customers like Felipe, who was obsessed with boxes. All week I'd set aside flattened boxes for him— the sturdier ones that had held cooking oils and sixty-four-ounce cans of Hawaiian Punch. Religiously, every Friday afternoon he'd arrive freshly showered, his gray hair slicked back, his neck and chest generously dusted with talc, wearing Bermuda shorts and loafers without socks.

Looking for me, he'd call out through the aisles, *"¡Oye, muchacho!"* a term of endearment, though I suspected he had trouble remembering my name. "You keep some boxes for me?" he'd ask every time, as if I wouldn't remember what he was there for. Sometimes, just to tease him, I'd say I had given them away to someone else, or that my *tío* Pipo had used them all up to line the floor of the meat locker. Felipe's wrinkly eyes would stretch open, instantly transforming him from a seventy-something man into a boy, until he figured out I was joking, again. He'd follow me behind the soft drinks into the stockroom and I'd pull out the boxes. He'd inspect each one for tears, stains, bends, choosing only the best ones from the batch: *"Esta sí . . . . Esta no . . . Sí . . . No . . . No . . . Sí . . ."* Then he'd thank me repeatedly as he walked away, the boxes tucked under his arms like giant folded wings. *"Gracias, muchacho,"* he would repeat, as if he could never repay me for a few dumb boxes that would have ended up filling our Dumpster. *"Gracias, muchacho,"* as if I had just given him a hundred bucks. *"Gracias. Gracias."*

After weeks of the same routine, I finally asked Felipe, *"Carajo,* what do you use all these boxes for?" "For beauty," he answered vaguely, and then added, *"Ven,* help me carry these home and I'll show you." We walked down the block to his 1940s-era house with its stucco walls like icing and jalousie windows he kept open, letting in the breeze that moved through the tamarind trees bathing the house in shade. Following him inside, I stepped into another world. "*Mira*, this is what I do with the boxes," he said casually, gesturing at the dozens of cardboard models spread out on the sofa, sitting on top of the TV set, stored in the china cabinet, and covering the dining table. Building by building, Felipe had reconstructed *La Habana Vieja*—the old colonial section of Havana—out of cardboard.

"*Coño*—this is amazing! How long did it take you to make all these?" I asked. "Oh, *más o menos* six years, so far. I pass the time all by myself here *todos los días*. But I still need more buildings to finish," he explained, and then showed me the model he was working on: "This is La Bodeguita del Medio, the famous restaurant in Havana on Calle Empedrado, where the mojito drink was invented. All the Cuban writers used to go there—even Hemingway. My wife and I saved up our *kilitos* for dinner there *de vez en cuando*. It's still there, I think. I need to finish painting in the windows and cutting out the roof, *pero* I'm starting to forget what it looked like. I have to find an old photograph somewhere in a book or a magazine. *Ay, muchacho*, it's getting harder and harder to remember *La Habana*. I think I've forgotten more than I remember."

The following Friday, I volunteered to help him carry a load of boxes home; he returned the favor by making *un cafecito* for me and spreading out snacks for *merienda*. Munching chorizo and Manchego cheese, I asked him about one of his models. "Oh, that one?" he said. "You don't recognize it, *muchacho*—the famous Catedral de La Habana? My *papá* and I used to sell flowers there *en la plaza* where all the *enamorados* would meet at night, holding hands and sneaking *besitos* behind the lampposts. *Imagínate*, all horny right in front of *la Virgen* and *Jesús*!" His favorite was the model of El Floridita, a corner building with long windows crowned with lunettes of stained glass that he made out of colored tissue paper, and balconies he propped up with toothpicks, hanging above the make-believe street. "That's the nightclub where they invented *el* daiquiri," he said. "They never let me in. I was too poor." Felipe explained that he had been born into a family of street vendors in Havana. "But me and *mi amigo* Sergio peeked in the windows all the time. *A veces* across the street drunk and flirting with *las mujeres* walking out. The women as beautiful as the place—full of chandeliers, marble, and velvet. You should see it, *muchacho*."

In truth, the models were somewhat crude. Felipe was never able to go to college, much less study architecture. But his knowledge of the city he had roamed every day of his childhood had kindled in him a lasting fascination with the city and its architecture. The places he named and stories he told echoed with the same enthusiasm I'd hear in my parents' and grandparents' voices whenever they'd speak of Cuba. Even though I wouldn't actually *see* Havana for years, Felipe brought the city to three-dimensional life. Every Friday, spread out before me, right there on his dinner table, was a Havana I could touch, a Cuba I could hold in my hands.

ERNESTO NUÑEZ, KNOWN BY EVERYONE SIMPLY AS Nuñez, was living proof of Cubans' well-deserved reputation for *hablando mierda,* talking a lot of bullshit. Every afternoon that same summer, I noticed him lingering at the cafeteria counter, pestering Migdalia, as if she would ever be interested in an old man like him; and I could hear him too, blurting out Cuban *piropos* at her while she waited on customers. *"Oye, si cocinas como caminas me como hasta la raspa,"* he would say: *If you cook the way you walk, I'll even eat your table scraps.* Indeed, she was a knockout: her hazelnut-brown skin perfectly offset her blue-green eyes, which caught the light like gemstones. Young enough to be his granddaughter, she usually brushed him off with a pursing of her lips, but one day she gave him an ironic wink and told him to go soak his dentures, then take his afternoon nap before he fell asleep standing up.

Even that dismissal didn't deter him from coming around again and again to flirt with Migdalia or, if that failed, strike up a conversation with anyone who would pretend to listen. Unfortunately, I was one of those people. Though I usually managed to dodge him, one day he came over to me with a whole *colada* of *café* as a bribe for a few minutes of conversation. But I didn't have to say much—I couldn't; he talked enough for both of us, carrying on about almost anything. I mostly nodded and pretended to be amused by his wisecracks. This became a ritual; he'd come find me every afternoon for a few minutes of chitchat, offering a shot of Cuban coffee from his *colada*. I soon learned he was a master of *dichos*, Cuban sayings. Practically everything that came out of his mouth was idiomatic; he didn't speak Spanish, he spoke *Cubichi*.

"Mono de seda, mono se queda"—*a monkey dressed in silk is still a monkey*—he'd say under his breath every time Erundina—one of the regulars—would come waddling into the store in high-heel shoes, all dressed up for nothing, her face streaked with rouge, wearing panty hose that didn't match her skin tone and which rustled as she walked down the aisle. *"Llegó el bobo con fiebre"*—*here comes the retard with a fever*—he'd scoff when Esperanza's nerdy son, Alberto, would come in flapping his size thirteen shoes, his pants hiked six inches

above his belly button. Nuñez had also mastered the fine art of *nombrete*, Cuban nicknaming, dubbing the gossipy Michelle *El Cura*—the Priest—because she could make anyone confess their secrets. One day, Tamara, the part-time cashier, who was about a hundred pounds overweight and never used a girdle, made the unfortunate choice to wear a bright red muumuu to work; from that day on, thanks to Nuñez, she was known to all at El Cocuyito as *Chambelona*—Lollipop—or *Chambi* for short.

After so many afternoons *hablando mierda* with Nuñez, and buzzed on thimble-size swigs of *café*, his talents rubbed off on me. Watching my *tía* Carmencita at a family gathering pile three pounds of pork on her paper plate, I dubbed her *La Nevera*—the Ice Box. With no curves and shoulders as wide as her hips, she damn well looked as square and heavy as a refrigerator too. I wasn't exactly proud of my new talent, but at last I was able to take revenge on my *primo* Rafi for naming me Lardo. At six feet two and 130 pounds, he looked like *una tripa,* and that's exactly what I called him—the Intestine—right in front of my cousins, who roared with laughter as we waited in line to ride the Tidal Wave at the St. Brendan's Carnival. He stomped away without a comeback, never to bother me again. Not even Nuñez was safe. One afternoon, watching him walk down the aisle toward me, I noticed he had dyed his eyebrows and hair jet-black and was wearing the latter slicked back like Béla Lugosi in *Count Dracula.* "¡*Oye! ¡Qué pasa, Vampiro!*" I shouted, and it stuck. He was the Vampire of the bodega from then on.

Thanks to Nuñez, I became fluent in *Cubichi*, one Cubanism at a time: *Juega con la cadena y no con el mono*—play with the chain, but not with the monkey; *No te ahogues en un vaso de agua*—don't drown in a glass of water; *No te cojas el culo con la puerta*—don't close the door on your ass. I greeted Nuñez every afternoon with the same saying: *Dímelo cantando*—tell it to me singing, and he would reply: *Dime algo aunque sea mentira*—tell me something even if it's a lie. In *Cubichi* I could understand what it meant to sing what I needed to say, to tell lies when the truth just wasn't enough. In *Cubichi* I could think like a Cuban, be a *cubano* without translating words or myself into English.

——————▶RAQUEL WAS A TRUE BODEGA GROUPIE, A MIDDLE-aged woman who popped into the store three or four times a day for a can of this or a bag of that, or to pick up her daily just-out-of-the-oven loaf of Cuban bread for dinner. At first we shared nothing more than the usual pleasantries—*Buenos días, ¿cómo andas?*—as she passed me in the aisles, clutching her sequined coin purse stuffed with crumpled bills and food stamps, zeroing in on her staples for the day. She knew where everything was, never needing my help. In fact, sometimes it seemed she knew more about the store than I did.

"*Mira*, these black beans have the wrong price. *Yo no soy* cheap, but these should be one sixty-nine, not one ninety-nine," she brought to my attention one day, and she was right. "Okay, *está bien*. I'll fix it," I said, a bit peeved, taking out my pricing gun as she continued: "If you ask me, they should give these away, they're terrible, nothing like my *frijoles, pero* I don't have time to cook today. Work, work, work—that's all we do in this country. *Ay, Cuba*, how I miss you! What is your name, *mi'jo?*" she asked. I answered, "Ricky," before she began again: "Riqui? *Ay*, that was my son's name too. Let me see," she said taking hold of my chin and moving my face from side to side, catching the light at different angles. "You know . . . you look like him *un poquito*. He would be about your age now. *Bueno*, enough talk—*hasta mañana*."

Day after day, she divulged more details of her life in bursts of three-minute conversations in the cereal aisle, the canned goods aisle, the soda aisle—wherever she happened to find me. She claimed her father had been a high-ranking official during the Batista dictatorship; that they lived in a ten-bedroom house in the Vedado district of Havana; that they had three housekeepers, a chauffeur, and a cook who served breakfast every morning on the terrace; that she could remember the sound of palm trees brushing against her bedroom window every night. I listened politely, but I didn't believe a word she said. I thought she was just one more of those exiles Mamá criticized for embellishing everything about Cuba, including their own wealth and position. "If you add up all the farms and land that Cubans say they owned, Cuba would have to be *más grande* than the United States," Mamá would joke.

But Raquel brought me proof of her life. *"Mira,"* she surprised me one afternoon, pulling out a square photo from her coin purse, "This was *mi casa*," she said, grabbing the reading glasses she wore on a chain around her neck and parking them on her nose. "See that window on the second floor? That was my bedroom." Indeed, there was her mansion, just as she had claimed, with a twelve-foot double door made of oak and wrought iron, the bougainvillea weaving themselves through the marble balustrades of her balcony, the palm trees at her window, no longer lies. And there she was in the photos too, a young lady in black-and-white, standing on the keystone walkway to her house. "I was pretty, *¿verdad?* You would've fallen in love with me in a second," she joked, pointing at the image of her younger self in a chiffon dress down to her shins, her licorice-black hair straight to her shoulders, a smile as sensual as the arc of pearls between her collarbones. "*Mira*, I still have those *aretes*," she said, pointing to the *azabache* earrings she wore in the photo, which she had on that very day. They dangled from her ears like black teardrops, still protecting her against evil eyes.

Now her earlobes were wrinkly, her hair gray at the roots and so thin I could see through to her scalp. She lived across the street from El Cocuyito, in a cramped two-bedroom, one-bath duplex, with her two sisters who were widows like her. No more mansion, no more palms, no more Cuba. Even though it was all true, it was all gone, including her son Riqui, as I learned during one of our tête-à-têtes in the aisle. "*Te lo dije*, he looked exactly like you. He would be fourteen this month," she said, gazing at a photo of Riqui in her hand. There was some resemblance: his nose was long and narrow like mine; his eyebrows were thick and close, like mine; and he had dimples on his cheeks, like me. But we didn't look *exactly* alike, not as much as Raquel wanted to believe, wanting to see her son again in me. I felt I should ask what happened to her son, but hesitated. What did I know about death? What could I possibly say to this woman, this mother? Sensing my awkwardness, she changed the subject: "Why, you should come to my house for *almuerzo*. *Ven, ven*, I make the best black beans you've ever tasted. We'll have time to talk—and more pictures."

I accepted the invitation, and come lunchtime crossed the street to her house. "*Pasa, mi'jo. Pasa*," she welcomed me, flinging the screen door wide open and kissing me on the cheek as if she hadn't seen me just moments before at El Cocuyito. I followed her into the house, squeezing through the crammed living room. She kept two velvet sofas so plush they seemed bloated, tufted with silver-dollar-size buttons that looked as if they were about to pop. The coffee table was as big as a coffin, resting on legs carved into lion claws. Each of the four end tables was topped with a wrought-iron lamp holding up an umbrella-size shade. Nuñez had taught me a Cuban *dicho* most appropriate for this: *Quiere meter La Habana en Guana-bacoa*, the equivalent of saying that she was trying to fit New York City in Key West. Everything was oversize, doubled, out of scale; every empty space filled, as if she had brought over all the furniture from her mansion in Cuba.

I felt like a king at the immense dining table, large enough for a medieval feast, facing the china cabinet crowded with dime-store fig-urines of eighteenth-century gentry in romantic poses alongside stat-uettes of Santa Bárbara and San Judas. Even the plates were big—as big as birdbaths. I had barely finished my first serving of black beans when Raquel asked, *"¿Más?,"* filling the bowl again before I could say no. The beans were indeed delicious, with pieces of ham hock and minced onions, but not as good as my mother's, of course—too much bay leaf. But why tell her? *"¿Te gustan?"* she asked, as if I would say anything but *"Sí, sí. Exquisitos."* *"Puedes creer* that I never had to cook or work until I came to *América,"* she explained proudly.

After I pushed the empty plate away, she led me toward the back of the house into the Florida room: *"Mira,* come over here. This is what I do all day now—make beautiful dresses for other women—just like the ones I used to wear. *Caramba,* now I can't even buy the dresses I make!" The room was stocked with an assembly line of sewing machines, cutting tables heaped with fabric swatches, spools of thread arranged by color like a rainbow, rolls of fabric like giant Popsicles, and half-made dresses tossed around like unfinished paint-ings. In contrast to all that color and beauty, the walls were covered with black-and-white photos of people and places that had already come to pass. There were hundred-year-old baby pictures, yellow photos from old newspaper clippings, framed collages of small snapshots, and large hand-colored photos that looked realer than real. More proof that her life was her life.

"Who was this?" I asked her. "*Ay,* that was my father. He was handsome, *¿verdad?*" she said, her eyes fixed on the man in the photo. And indeed he was, standing a foot taller than her at a garden party, holding a flute of champagne, wearing wingtip shoes and a linen guayabera through which I could make out his strong shoulders and full chest of hair as dark as his pencil-thin mustache and his eyes, hypnotic as smoke. "He looked just like that the last time I saw him—when that *hijo de puta* killed him." No one in my family had been killed by Castro's regime. Feeling Raquel's sorrow and anger as she took the photo off the wall and held it in her hands, I fully grasped for the first time the deep hatred so many exiles had for Castro, why his name was almost always followed by *that bastard,* or *that son of a bitch.*

Raquel continued from photo to photo like a docent, pausing at each one with a sigh or sad smile and captioning it with a story. "This was me and my husband, Ramiro, at Rancho Luna, our favorite beach in Cuba. We went every year; this was the last time. Little we knew *lo que nos esperaba.*" There she was, floating in his arms, both of them up to their waists in a black-and-white ocean they'd never see again. "You never been to Cuba, so you don't know, but this is what the park at El Prado looked like. Your parents must've told you about it. It was my favorite place *en toda La Habana.* I took Riqui there every Sunday for hours, feeding bread crumbs to *las palomas.*" There they were, mother and son framed by a colonnade of palms, surrounded by pigeons, fallen petals from a royal poinciana tree scattered like confetti at their feet.

"What happened to him?" I felt comfortable enough to ask. "*Ay, mi'jo,* you don't want to know; you're too young for such a sad story. *En fin,* Riqui is still here, and here, and here" she said, pointing to the photo, then to her heart, and then to her temple. What did I know about loss or despair? What did I know about anguish or loneliness? Nothing except for what I saw in Raquel's photos, what I heard in her strained voice, what I felt in her long pauses. "This what I live on now—memories and pretty dresses—and my delicious *frijoles,* of course. Is like my own little museum," she said half in jest, before changing the subject. "*Ándale,* you need to get back to your boxes and me to my dresses. *Trabajar, trabajar, y trabajar*—that's all we do in this country—work. It's a miracle I'm not dead yet."

───── EVEN THOUGH I DIDN'T NOTICE IT THE FIRST SUM-mer, by that second summer I couldn't help but see that Don Gustavo was able to do less and less around the store. Despite his airs as head honcho of El Cocuyito, he was past his prime. The heiress apparent was his daughter, my *tía* Gloria. She had learned the family business inside out and gradually transformed the bodega from a patriarchy into a matriarchy. She even checked up on Don Gustavo's work, un-covering his mess-ups almost daily. "*¡Papá—caramba!*" she'd let out, outraged with the soup cans he'd mixed up once again: *Chicken Noodle* with *Chicken and Stars* with *Cream of Chicken*—to him they were all *sopa de pollo;* or the merchandise that he'd constantly mis-price because he could barely read the numbers on the dial of the pricing gun: boxes of Pampers at $1.99 instead of $11.99; jumbo rolls of Bounty at $8.90 instead of $0.89. Then she'd bellow for me,

"Riqui! *¿Dónde está* Riqui?" And I'd come to the rescue, sort out and rearrange the cans, scrape off the price stickers with my box cutter, and reprice everything, following her directions.

I had become quite the sharpshooter with the pricing gun, able to nail a dozen cans in less than five seconds. I could open boxes with my bare hands and tear them up like tissue paper. I could double-bag groceries faster than any cashier could ring them up. And *tía* Gloria noticed; she began calling on me to help her all the time. One Monday morning she handed me the order book from Associated Grocers and I followed the jingle of the keys she safety-pinned to her waistband as she marched down the aisles, poking through every item on the shelves, calling out orders for me to mark down: *Two boxes of Strawberry Pop-Tarts . . . One box eight-ounce Libby's Peach Nectars . . . Five boxes of this . . . Three boxes of that . . .* and on and on for eight aisles. I could barely keep up with her as I strained to find the millimeter-size line in the book to scribble in a number in the quantity box. But of course, she checked the order book herself, twice. She was as direct, methodical, and commanding as her father, Don Gustavo—and my *abuela*.

But according to family stories, back in the fifties, *tía* Gloria was a pampered debutante in Cuba. She dressed in freshly pressed linen every day and took piano lessons well into her twenties; she was chauffeured to and from high school, and later, to the university where she studied political science. It was difficult to reconcile the once demure and sophisticated *señorita Gloria* with the *tía* Gloria I worked with every day at El Cocuyito. She wore athletic socks showing under polyester pants hemmed an inch above her ankles; a faded polo shirt pinched under the elastic waistband, segmenting her body; her hair in a loosening bun jabbed through with a pencil; and a half dozen rubber bands tied around her wrist. A woman who never wore necklaces or earrings, never smelled like soap or perfume, never painted her fingernails or her face, except on special occasions. And yet there *was* something very feminine and enviable about her satin-black hair and her flawless skin that appeared poreless even under the unforgiving fluorescent lights of the store. She didn't seem to fit any stereotype; maybe that's why the two of us made a great team.

One Wednesday she called for me. "Riqui, *ven pa'ca*, I'm going to show you how to fix *los vinos*." El Cocuyito was known for its wide selection of wines, catering to exiles of the Cuban elite and their nostalgia for the *buena vida* they could barely afford anymore. *Tía* Gloria, having once been a member of that elite, had dedicated an entire side of an aisle to spirits. El Cocuyito was the only Cuban bodega in Miami where you could pick up an eighty-dollar bottle of Dom Pérignon champagne along with a fifty-cent bag of home-fried pork rinds. As *tía* Gloria explained: "*Los miércoles* are always wine day. *La gente* come Friday to buy wine for the weekend. We must have what they want on the shelves."

With a fresh rag in her hand, *tía* Gloria took inventory, inspecting every bottle row by row and cleaning the shelf with Fantastik as she went along, calling out the vintages to be restocked. I followed behind her, jotting down the names as best I could on scrap pieces of cardboard, which seemed too ordinary to hold such soft, beautiful words like *Pouilly-Fuissé, Sauvignon, Beaujolais Nouveau, Châteauneuf-du-Pape*. We also stocked vintages from Chile and Spain like *Casillero del Diablo* and *Sangre de Toro*, which sounded so poetic in Spanish, I thought, and yet so ghoulish in English: *The Devil's Cellar; Bull's Blood*.

Keeping the list in my back pocket, I pulled a dozen boxes from the special shelves *tía* Gloria had built above the freezers to keep the wine cool and returned with my cart stacked, a fresh blade in my box cutter, and my pricing gun loaded. One by one, I priced each bottle. "*El precio* goes on the back, below the label. Never on the front!" she instructed. I held each bottle, silently reading the label, pretending I could speak French—*Appellation Pauillac Contrôlée, mis en bouteille au domaine*—pretending I was more than a stock boy, that I was as sophisticated as the châteaus, the cursive lettering, and the fancy emblems on the bottles I handed to her.

She held each one like a baby in both her unmanicured hands, dusted off the face of the bottle with her palm, then held it up to the light to check the color and the cork before tenderly placing it on the shelf. "Every label has to face perfectly forward, *¿entiendes?* Every bottle must be perfectly behind the other," she explained. Like pork rinds and champagne, *tía* Gloria was a contradiction I loved: chewing a wad of Juicy Fruit gum while teaching me the difference between Chardonnay and sauvignon blanc; a toothpick dangling from her mouth as she explained how a rosé is made by leaving the grape juice in contact with the skins. She rotated and moved every bottle around as if arranging a bouquet of flowers. By the time we finished, it looked beautiful, every sparkling bottle bathing the aisle with light, the colors reflecting in the linoleum tiles. "*Coje,*" she said, stuffing a ten-dollar bill in my pocket while I was tossing the empty wine boxes in the Dumpster. "You did good today."

You'd think she'd had vineyards in Cuba, or that she went to France every summer, but she didn't. In fact, once she settled in Miami, she never left, never took a vacation or traveled. Every morning at dawn, she'd mop the entire store spotless before opening the front doors at 7 A.M. Like for her father, El Cocuyito wasn't just her livelihood, it had become her life, a way to replace her losses, or at least not think about them. *Tía* Gloria wasn't a fifties

Cuban princess anymore—but she was a *queen* in polyester pants and sneakers, proudly and benevolently dedicated to her people in exile. She knew all the regulars by name and let them buy on credit by simply signing the back of the register receipt. No one ever went hungry. She always had enough time to ask about the children and grandchildren she had watched grow up inch by inch; she had me deliver groceries to anyone who was too sick to shop or recovering from an operation.

On her birthday that summer, *tía* Gloria pulled off the shelf a bottle of Merlot that had a torn label and uncorked it in the back stockroom. On the same pockmarked table where Don Gustavo and I gutted papayas and melons, she served *dos deditos*—two fingers' worth of wine in Styrofoam cups to all the employees and any customer who happened to be around. Among boxes of toilet paper, canned peaches, and laundry detergent, her people raised their cups in a toast: *¡Salud! ¡Qué viva Gloria!*

SUMMER ENDED AND I STARTED FRESHMAN YEAR at Christopher Columbus, an all-boys Catholic high school in Güecheste, along with many of my eighth-grade classmates. Alberto, the suavest and handsomest boy of the class, who seemed to never go through an ugly phase. Little Ralph, who earned a black belt in karate to compensate for his puniness—no one ever messed with him. And there was Eric, the class daredevil, who always had a scrape, a sprain, or a broken bone. All together we were about a dozen boys who stuck together as we navigated our new lives in high school. We sat together in the cafeteria every day. They were a familiar bunch and I felt comfortable around them, but I couldn't quite relate to them the way I did to Julio. Not surprisingly, Julio hadn't been accepted to Christopher Columbus because of his poor grades and horrible conduct. We managed to get together almost every weekend and maintained our friendship. Still, I missed seeing him every day like I had in grade school.

I also missed working at El Cocuyito and being with *mi gente*. One day, on a visit to the store after school with Abuelo and Abuela, I caught up with *tía* Gloria in the storeroom and asked if she needed any extra help. "*Pues claro,* Riqui, it's always busy here," she said, "You would be a big help. Maybe you can come in on Saturdays? But you need to ask your *padres* for permission first." "Yes, of course," I said. On the way back home, I told Abuela, knowing she would be all for it and be my ally. Together, we approached Mamá that evening and I asked for her permission. She was concerned that working would affect my studies, but I promised her it wouldn't, and that I would make up study time on Sundays. Abuela also chimed in: "*Mira* how much weight he's lost. Do you want him to turn back into *Lardito?*" Mamá agreed to a trial period until my first quarter report card, and Papá agreed he'd drive me.

On that first Saturday back to El Cocuyito, *tía* Gloria explained that I'd be in charge of setting up displays for the weekly specials. Some weeks she chose canned goods: cling peaches or garbanzo beans or soups. I'd start with a square base, then add layer upon layer of can atop can, slowly building a pyramid with a single can crowning the top, as easy as playing with Legos. Some weeks she chose bags of rice and toilet paper, which were a bigger challenge. I'd have to stack boxes in the middle and then build around the pile like a fortress to keep them from collapsing. The displays were usually nice enough, but always seemed to be missing that extra something, just like Miss DeVarona's bulletin boards.

One Saturday, I took a few sheets of onion-skin paper that my mother kept in her night table for writing letters to Cuba. On one of the thin sheets I traced the word *Campbell's* from a can of soup and perfectly reproduced the fancy script onto a placard. I used my Crayola markers to color in the background bright red, and then drew thick, stylized numbers all slanted to the left: *2 x $1.00.*

"*Qué curioso.* That looks beautiful." Sonia commented. Even Don Gustavo complimented my work, sort of. "Well, what about the other displays?" he said, meaning he approved of what I had done. And *tía* Gloria was impressed too: "That's perfect. Who taught you that?" She had me make signs for all the weekly specials. I traced the big heart-shaped *O* of the Del Monte peaches, the Cuban flag for the cans of Ancel guava marmalade, the toucan from the Froot Loops cereal, and the owl from the Wise potato chips.

At the end of November, *tía* Gloria cleared a space in front of the store to display the holiday items. I spent part of my pay on an arsenal of decorations from Diamond's: tinsel and garlands I used to trim the tables stacked with pyramids of Spanish almond *turrones* and fancy *panetelas;* velvet bows and twinkle lights I used to create a centerpiece with a FELIZ NAVIDAD sign in gold glitter. Customers oohed and ahhed, complimenting *tía* Gloria, who gave me all the credit. But my arts and crafts proved to be too girly for Don Gustavo. The day after I finished my Christmas masterpiece he told me, "Enough playing around—there's real work to do around here. Go help your *tío* Pipo with *los lechones.*" El Cocuyito was *the* place in Miami to get the best *lechón asado*—a whole roasted pig that was a must for a *real* Cuban *Nochebuena.* Starting in early November, customers began placing their orders with *tío* Pipo, *tía* Gloria's husband, who ran *la carnicería*, the meat and deli counter. As instructed by Don Gustavo, I reported to *tío* Pipo, who was in over his head. I helped him devise a foolproof tracking system using a spiral notebook in which we recorded the customer's name, telephone number, approximate number of pounds, and a "pig number" copied onto a piece of white butcher paper for each customer to keep as a receipt.

Slicing bloody steaks and gutting chickens all day long didn't fit *tío* Pipo's disposition. He was like a Cuban laughing Buddha, with a paunch that stretched out his smock and a sparkle in his eyes that gave him away as a flirt. His weakness: middle-aged women with dyed blond hair, like Elsa Gomez. Though I'm sure he never cheated on my *tía* Gloria, there were rumors for days after Elsa would come in clicking her open-toe heels, sashaying her Rubenesque figure up and down the aisles in plain view of *tío* Pipo, and shamelessly addressing him by his given name: "*Hola*, Gilberto." *Tío* Pipo's currency was meat: he gave Elsa deep discounts on filet mignon, an occasional free string of sausages, or an extra pound of ham; he scribbled black hearts and smiley faces with his wax pencil on the packages he'd hand to her with a wink of his sleepy eye and a soft tug on her earlobe. It was *tío* Pipo's most distinct, if not bizarre, trademark, one I couldn't quite explain and never questioned. Since I'd been a child, he'd greet me with a pull on my earlobe, his thumb and index finger always cold from the meat locker and tinted pink from the blood that never quite washed off his hands.

Impressed with the pig-tracking system I created, *tío* Pipo asked me to join his crew of friends and help out with roasting the pigs the day before Christmas Eve. Right after the store closed, we set up an assembly line starting with Regino (aka *Enano*, the Midget), who was in charge of marinating the carcasses with *tío* Pipo's special blend of cumin and bitter orange, which he prepared secretly in empty two-liter Coke bottles. Then came Rafael (aka *Narisón*, Big Nose), who cracked the carcasses open and laid them flat, snout up, on an aluminum roasting pan. Alberto and I followed, tagging each pig in the ear with its own PIN (Pig Identification Number) following the list from my notebook. It was a bit repulsive, though I pretended it wasn't; a real *hombre* wasn't supposed to feel sorry for the poor animals, their faces frozen in the expression they'd worn at the very moment of their death. One by one, *tío* Pipo slid each clammy-white pig into the oven.

While the pigs roasted, the crew got toasted on all the free beer they could drink, right out of the refrigerator case in the store. It was their only compensation for "volunteering" to help *tío* Pipo with the all-night roast-a-thon, which soon turned into a drink-a-thon. "*Coje*, take one. It's okay tonight," *tío* Pipo said, twisting off the cap from a frosty Heineken and handing it to me. I took the bottle and a swig: "*Ay*, I needed that," I said, like it wasn't a big deal, like I drank beer all the time. Just then, Enano walked up to us with a *Playboy* magazine opened to the centerfold. The mood changed instantly. "Look at that—what a *mujerona*," he said and passed the magazine around. Cautiously but greedily, each one of the men made comments about breasts and asses under their breaths as if their wives were listening, watching. When the magazine was passed to me, I pretended to be swept away, though I couldn't bring myself to say anything more lascivious than "Wow! *¡Coño!*" and quickly passed it on. The magazine was then retired to the bathroom, visited by each of the men, one by one. "Don't you need to go to *el baño?*" *tío* Pipo asked me with a wink of his eye. "The magazine is under the sink." "No, no, *tío*," I said nervously.

To pass the time while the pigs roasted, Narisón set up a domino game table in the store's backyard, under the floodlights and stars.

"*¡Oye Riqui, ven pa'ca!*" Narisón called me over. "We need a fourth player." I spent a good part of the night as one of *los hombres*, playing dominos and drinking, exchanging wisecracks and listening to their memories about the last *Nochebuena* they celebrated in their own country, the homes they missed, the friends they had lost. "May we be in Cuba next year for *las Navidades*!" Narisón shouted a toast, his raised beer spilling onto the table and dominos. "*¡Come mierda!* Now we have to start the game all over!" Alberto yelled, soaking up the spilled beer with a rag. The two exchanged insults, which somehow turned into a fight over who was to blame for the Revolution—Batista or Machado—and what *really* went wrong, the *real* reason for the Revolution that "ruined their lives."

"We need to take the last of the *lechones* out—they're ready, I think," I interrupted to ease the tension. "Okay, *vamos a ver*," *tío* Pipo said, walked over to the oven, and slid out one of the toasty-brown pigs, the color of burned sugar. He snapped off a tiny piece of the crackly skin and savored it for a few seconds before declaring, "Ready," and repeated the taste test for the next pig, and the next, and the next, until the last one came out of the oven and the sun broke through the sky.

Tío Pipo gave me the keys to open up the store. Once again—as I had always remembered—the sunlight shined on the plate-glass doors and set the emerald letters aglow as if they were themselves made of fireflies that had swarmed together to spell out: EL COCUYITO SUPERMERCADO | CARNICERÍA—MEATS | CAFETERÍA—CAFÉ CUBANO. I remembered Don Gustavo's story of the fireflies that lit up his village in Cuba. El Cocuyito wasn't just a grocery store anymore, it felt like that village to me, a pueblo where everyone knew each other and where, for a few minutes every day, they could pretend they were still in Cuba, surrounded by their own fruits and vegetables, their own sweets and cuts of meat, their own language and fireflies, as if nothing had ever disrupted their lives. I thought about Raquel's photos and her sad stories, Felipe's cardboard Havana, Nuñez's *Cubichi* lessons, and all that Don Gustavo had lost. I thought about all I may have lost without knowing. Perhaps El Cocuyito was my village, my pueblo too.

——A FEW WEEKS AFTER CHRISTMAS BREAK ENDED, loudmouth Nuñez warned me that the cashier Sonia and her daughter Deycita were shopping around for a partner for Deycita's *Quinces* debut. But according to Cuban protocol, he explained, it wouldn't be proper for either of them to simply ask me to be her *Quinces* partner—that would be too forward and unladylike. They had to manipulate me into asking. To many, Deycita was as pretty as her name; they'd compliment her silky mane of hair, her seductive eyes, and her Amazonian stature. But not me. While I could admit she was attractive, I wasn't attracted to her. The truth was, I didn't find any girl *that* attractive. I figured I just hadn't found the one who could really turn me on.

Sonia was determined and barraged me with snapshots of Deycita in not-so-subtle and suggestive poses: Deycita in a bikini sipping a piña colada on a chaise lounge, Deycita in a little spaghetti-strap dress and stilettos, Deycita with her hair teased out and tossed wild, Deycita with her hair blow-dried straight to her shoulders, Deycita putting on lipstick in front of her dresser mirror or dabbing on perfume behind her ears. Deycita. Deycita. Deycita. I'd smile and play along as Sonia flipped through the photos and drop obvious hints: "*Mira* how pretty she looks in this one? Doesn't that dress look delicious on her? *Ay, qué pena*—she hasn't found the right boy yet for her *Quinces*. She's so picky." Every Saturday Deycita would casually stop by El Cocuyito in the middle of the afternoon, done up in eyeliner, rouge, perfume, sitting for an hour or two on the stool at the cash register with her agent, Sonia, who would suddenly need me for a price check or to help her bag groceries, as if I was not only dumb but also blind.

I held out until Abuela got involved at Sonia's request, as I suspected she would. One day during dinnertime at our house, she started on me: "Don't you like Deycita? She wants you to be her *compañero. Qué te pasa*, you don't like girls?" Mamá came to my defense: "*Déjalo tranquilo*, he's only a boy." "A boy?" Abuela said, "He'll be ready for marriage in just a few years. He needs to start looking *ahora*." Abuela dropped the conversation until later that evening. She came into my room in her robe and curlers and gave me her same old advice: "*Mira, es mejor serlo y no parecerlo, que no serlo y parecerlo,*" she said, which meant: *it's better to be it but not act like it, than to not be it and yet act like it.* By *being it* she meant being gay—*un maricón.* I understood implicitly. "Whatever, Abuela," I muttered.

The next morning, I found in my book bag an envelope with the same phrase written on it—and a twenty-dollar bill inside. A bribe, no doubt. I kept it just to spite her, though she had already shamed me into asking Deycita. On Saturday that week, I approached Deycita, who was sitting at the cafeteria counter. "Hi," I said, thinking she'd be thrilled. "Oh, hi," she said, looking up casually from the magazine she was paging through, pretending she was surprised to see me. "Listen, I heard you haven't picked anyone for your *Quinces.* I'll be your partner," I said with confidence, thinking she would say yes without hesitation. "Oh, well . . . I hadn't really thought about it, but that might be nice. Let me check with my mother, okay? I'll let you know," she said coyly, as if I didn't know the whole ploy.

Deycita's parents had only been in the United States a few years, and they were still struggling to get on their feet, but that didn't matter. Sonia had saved up for months for the celebration—it would be a grandiose testament to achieving their American Dream, cloaked in the Cuban tradition of *Los Quinces*. For weeks, it was all Sonia and Deycita talked about to each other, to the customers, and to me. At first I pretended to be interested, but their enthusiasm was contagious, and the details began to engross me too. Deycita was having the girls' satin shoes dyed champagne pink to match the color of their dresses. Her custom-ordered cape was made of peacock and pheasant feathers. Sonia rented the most expensive silver-plated tiara that Diamond's had. And I helped design and assemble the party favors: miniature ceramic baskets filled with white Jordan almonds and baby's breath, wrapped in the same tulle as Deycita's dress. It wasn't just a party; it would be an extravaganza, with a sit-down dinner from Manny's Buffet, real champagne, and an open bar.

The only compromise they made was with the production company. They couldn't afford the clamshell-themed option in which Deycita would emerge like a beautiful pearl out of a giant mechanical shell. Instead, they went with the Cinderella theme. Nevertheless, it was to be a two-hour choreographed dance with a court of fourteen girls in hoop skirts and their escorts in coats and tails. Sonia organized weekly practice sessions on Tuesday nights in the parking lot of El Cocuyito, after the store had closed. She claimed that Osvaldo, the choreographer from the production company, had produced *Quinces* for many notables, including one of Gloria Estefan's cousins. Stepping out of his 1970-something Jaguar, Osvaldo would arrive for every practice clutching a clipboard and wearing leg warmers despite the unbearable humidity. He'd plop a three-foot-long boom box on the roof of his car and then blow a whistle strung around his neck. "Okay—places, people—places, *por favor*," he'd say, clapping his hands before cuing the cassette tape. Circling us like a house cat, he watched everyone's moves. One night he grabbed Elio, one of the hopelessly left-footed boys, who couldn't get the steps right. Osvaldo danced with him, leading him around with a hand on his waist before poor Elio knew what had happened. The girls burst into giggles and the boys whistled at him. "What? It's not funny!" Elio shouted. I felt his embarrassment as I thought about Abuela and what she would say or do if she ever saw *me* dancing with Osvaldo like *that*.

Under the brassy light of the streetlamps and over the cracked pavement and scattered litter, we practiced all the traditional dances— danzón, salsa, mambo—for hours. One short blow of Osvaldo's whistle cued the boys to twirl the girls once; two blows meant two twirls, and so on. One long blow, and the girls would stop, curtsy, and open their silk fans, slowly. When we got tired and restless, Osvaldo reminded us that without practice and dedication we'd ruin the most important night in Deycita's life—the moment she would be transformed from a girl into a woman before everyone's eyes. One night we were especially rambunctious. He stopped the rehearsal and asked us to close our eyes and imagine Deycita as a princess, wearing a pearl-encrusted gown, arriving in a carriage gilded with plumes and rhinestones, drawn by six white horses. Then he asked me to picture myself as her dashing prince, carrying a sword and wearing patent leather boots, taking Deycita's hand, kissing it, leading her into womanhood. *Me, a prince?* I amused myself with the thought: *His Royal Highness, Don Richard Jesus White, Sovereign of los Lechones,*

Keeper of the Vintages, Protector of the Village of El Cocuyito, Prince of los Cocuyos—of the Fireflies.

There would be no sword or boots, but it was the first time I wore a tuxedo. I stood in front of the bathroom mirror, fussing with my hair and the pink bow tie that matched Deycita's dress. Gazing at my reflection, I remembered a photo of Papá at about my age in a suit and tie, and for an instant I was my father. *Is this it? Am I a man?* I wondered, looking into my eyes for an answer and thinking of how much my life had changed. Mamá rapped on the bathroom door, snapping me out of my reverie: "*¡Apúrate!* We're going to be late! Sonia will kill you!"

"Why don't boys have *Quinces?*" I asked Mamá in the car on the way to the affair. "*Bueno,* girls like all the fuss. It used to mean that a girl was ready to get married. But now it's just *una tradición,*" Mamá answered as best she could. "*Qué,* you want to wear a dress now?" Abuela blurted out. "No—and so what if I did? *Cállate vieja.* Leave me alone," I barked at her as we pulled into the parking lot of the Casablanca Banquet Hall. I dashed around the building to the backstage entrance as Osvaldo had instructed me. He was fanning himself with one of the programs Sonia had printed, and walking from couple to couple, adjusting the girls' hoop skirts and the boys' boutonnieres. He was as nervous as a whore in church, I thought, remembering one of Nuñez's more apropos sayings. But so was I. "Okay everyone—this is it! Just like we practiced. Don't let me down," Osvaldo said, and he signaled the DJ to start the opening music. The first couple stepped out arm in arm, pacing themselves slowly toward their place on the dance floor.

It would take another twenty minutes for the last of the fourteen couples to do the same. But Osvaldo didn't take any chances. He called Deycita out of her dressing room. She looked as lovely as Osvaldo had said she would: her painted eyes were suddenly a woman's eyes, deep and mysterious; her ringlets danced around her face soft as light; her skin sparkled with glitter as if there were tiny stars nested on her shoulders and arms. I was proud to be her partner. "You look beautiful—really," I told her. "Do you remember all the steps?" she asked me, too nervous to reply to my compliment. "Yeah, don't worry. If you forget, just hold on to me," I reassured her, before Osvaldo whisked her away and helped her into the carriage set up backstage. I took my place out onstage; Osvaldo started the fog machines and cued the DJ, who announced: "And now, *damas y caballeros*, presenting for the first time ever, the beautiful, the exquisite, the charming, *señorita* Deycita Gomez-Moreno."

The curtain parted to roaring applause as the smoke cleared and Deycita appeared as if out of thin air. As Osvaldo had promised, she was Princess Deycita, wearing a tiara and waving to her court from inside the dreamy carriage decorated with plumes and gold leaf, drawn by four make-believe horses cut out of plywood but decorated with real horsehair tails and rhinestone reins. Her father helped her down from the carriage, kissed her on the cheek, and presented her to me. I bowed to her and she took my arm, just as we had rehearsed. We stepped off the stage and onto the middle of the dance floor, encircled by the fourteen couples in her court. The DJ changed the music and everyone started dancing a traditional *danzón*, the slowest and easiest of all the dances in the choreography. As we twirled and sashayed from side to side through the salsa, waltz, and merengue, I caught spinning glimpses of *mi gente* from El Cocuyito: Emilio out of uniform, wearing a three-piece suit and wingtip shoes; *tío* Pipo with his arm around *tía* Gloria, whom I almost didn't recognize in her halter-top dress as red and sexy as her lipstick; Raquel waving her hand to catch our attention and look into her camera, snapping photo after photo of us as if we were her own children.

After the choreography ended, Deycita and I made rounds among the guests, who grabbed us to take photos with them and paid us compliments about how beautiful she looked and how handsome I'd become. Many of them had seen both of us grow from children into teenagers. The women whispered in my ear, not too subtly hinting that I get together with Deycita: "She's ready . . . I heard she cooks as good as her mother . . . *Apúrate*, before someone else steals her away." The men were more obvious and vulgar: "You'll be the first one at bat . . . Don't wait until that mango falls to the ground and rots." Nuñez spoke in my ear: "Eat. Eat and don't leave anything on her plate," and patted me hard on the back. Mamá had run out of film by the time we got to her table—thank goodness. Abuela was beside herself: "If you get married, I'll pay for the wedding—*¡te lo juro!*" she said. I hugged Deycita to mess around with Abuela. "*De verdad*, how much?" I asked Abuela. "Whatever it costs," she said, "*lo que sea*." Her face lit up, as if I was serious.

Prompted by the DJ, the crowd quieted down for the happy birthday sing-along. Deycita blew out her fifteen candles, giving one to me and one to each of the girls in her court. Then the DJ announced a surprise, which wasn't really a surprise, but a tradition. The fourteen couples had chipped in five dollars each to buy Deycita a memento for her *Quinces*; I had tossed in Abuela's twenty-dollar bribe so that we could get Deycita something extra nice. Sonia presented the gift—a genuine pearl-and-gold-filled brooch—and helped her pin it to her dress. Then the DJ announced another surprise, which was a real a surprise to me: "*La señorita* Deycita and Sonia want to present a gift to our handsome *caballero*, our *príncipe*,

Riqui." Sonia and Deycita kissed me simultaneously on either cheek and handed me a small box and a card.

All eyes were on me, my hands trembling as I tore the box open: a gold pen and pencil set engraved with my initials, and a card signed by Deycita: *Ricky, thank you very much for making my* Quinces *so special. You are a great dancer! Good luck and I hope we can keep in touch.* And also signed by everyone from El Cocuyito—they had banded together and chipped in for the gift: Para *my make-believe son, may all your dreams come true,* mi'jo. | *Riqui,* acuérdate *everything I taught you. You are not* un hombre, *yet!* | Muchacho, *may you see the real Havana for yourself someday—not out of cardboard.* | ¡Camina por la sombra que la mierda se derrite! *Shit melts—walk in the shade, wherever you go and you be fine!* | Para *my nephew,* gracias *for all your help—you're the best* bodeguero *in all Miami!* | *Study hard, Riqui, and put this pen to good use—you don't want to roast* lechones *for the rest of your life!* I finished reading the card, looked around the ballroom at the faces of *mi gente* smiling back at me; *mi pueblo* clapping and cheering. Indeed they were my village, and for this night, I was their prince.

SIX

LISTENING TO MERMAIDS

A few weeks after sophomore year began, Julio called me at home after school: "Blanco, be ready in ten minutes. I'm gonna pick you up." I was confused. "What do you mean? Is your mom picking us up? Where are we going?" I asked. "I can't explain—I got a cool-ass surprise. Just tell your Abuela that you're coming over to my house, but hide your bike somewhere," he said, and hung up the phone. What was Julio up to now? Without Abuela or Abuelo noticing, I took my ten-speed from the back terrace and hid it behind the storage shed in the backyard. When I answered the door, Julio held his index finger over his lips, signaling me to keep quiet. "I'm riding over to Julio's," I yelled to Abuela. "*Está bien*—come back in time for dinner," she said—no questions asked.

I followed Julio halfway down the block to a convertible Corvette painted a glittery apple green. "What the hell is this, man?" I asked. "I told you my parents were getting me a car for my birthday. This is it—I got it! Fuckin' beautiful, isn't it? Get in, Blanco," he said.

I wasn't much into cars, but I had to admit the Corvette was gorgeous: red leather seats, wooden stick shift knob, chrome-trimmed dashboard. It didn't feel like a car; it felt like a painting, like we were riding inside a work of art doing sixty-five down the suburban streets of Güecheste: me still in my Catholic school uniform; Julio wearing a Hawaiian-print shirt and Ray-Ban aviator sunglasses. I was thrilled. I was petrified. I knew that Julio—like me—only had his learner's permit. When I questioned him, he said his parents were out of town and he was just taking the car out for a spin to test it out. "Be careful, man. If a cop stops us, you're screwed. We should get back," I cautioned. "Come on, Blanco—don't be such a chicken!" he said. "Let's go to the Hardee's drive-thru and show off."

While placing his order, he flirted with the girl at the other end of the intercom: *What's your name? What school do you go to? You got a boyfriend? I bet your eyes are blue?* She seemed somewhat amused, but when we pulled up to the pickup window and she saw the Corvette, she beamed. Julio kept sweet-talking her and managed to get her to write down her phone number on the receipt. "You see—that's the way it's done, Blanco," he said smugly as we drove off. We parked in the lot and started chowing down on our cheeseburgers. "So you kissed a girl yet?" he asked. "No . . . no, not yet," I said. "Damn it, Blanco—what are you waiting for? You gay or something? I'm gonna hook you up this weekend, bro. César Gutierrez is having an open-house party on Saturday—and we're going in this baby. My parents won't be back until Sunday night."

I thought about protesting, but knew he wouldn't listen. Besides, the Corvette *was* cool, and Julio had a way of bringing out the rebel-without-a-cause in me. Together, we concocted a plan. On Saturday, I asked my father to drop me off at Julio's house to hang out with him; his parents would bring me back home later. We left the phone off the hook, in case my parents happened to call. We jumped into the Corvette, and Julio eased out of the garage. Once we cleared his block, he popped in a Jimi Hendrix tape, floored it, and peeled out, leaving a trail of burnt-rubber smoke.

When we arrived at the party, the crowd had already spilled into the front yard. Julio drove slowly up and down the street at least three times, revving the engine so that everyone would notice us and get a good look at the Corvette. Heads turned, people stared, and I caught myself enjoying the attention. Being with Julio always made me feel cool. After we parked, we walked through the side yard of the house and straight into the backyard, where the rest of the action was. César had gone all out: a DJ, strobe lights, fog machine, and about twenty boxes of Frankie's Pizza. At every turn, Julio was greeted with high fives and hello kisses. I followed him through the crowd as we made our way to the keg of beer César had set up behind the storage shed, out of his parents' view. But Julio—who always had one up on everything and everyone—pulled out a flask of whiskey from the pocket of his denim jacket. "Here," he said to the boys gathered around the keg, "this is the real thing—Jack Daniel's," and passed the flask around. Like most of the boys did, I held back from gagging when I took a swig, pretending I liked the taste, though my grimace gave me away.

A little buzzed and feeling loose, we wove our way through the crowd. Julio pointed out a girl named Anita who was a friend of an ex-girlfriend of his, and therefore off limits to him, he explained. "But man, is she a fox or what? Come on, Blanco, don't chicken out," he said as he grabbed me by the neck and prodded me toward her. "Julio? Hi! How've you been?" she said, and kissed him on the cheek. Julio cut right to the chase. "Great, great. Hey, I want you to meet my friend Blanco—I mean Ricky. He was just telling me he thinks you're beautiful." I faked a smile to fill the awkward silence, until Julio gave me a pointed look. "Yeah, you look beautiful," I said, feeling a little courageous after the whiskey. "What school do you go to?"

Julio leaned into me and spoke in my ear. "Get her number," he said, before he drifted away into the crowd, leaving me alone with Anita. We spent a few minutes on small talk about friends we had in common, and the grade schools we'd each gone to. I didn't know what to say next. Unlike Julio or the other boys I knew, I didn't know how to "rap" with girls, and I wasn't sure I could learn. I almost walked away, but I held back, knowing I'd have to face Julio's digs if I did. Then one of my favorite songs came on—"Rio." Maybe I could impress her with my dance moves instead of my words. "You like this song?" I asked. "Oh, god yes—I love Duran Duran. You know, you kind of look like Simon Le Bon," she said. "You have his eyes." Her compliment gave me just enough confidence to ask her to dance. She said yes and tied back her jet-black hair, revealing more of her heart-shaped face and porcelain skin. I thought: *What would I do next if I were Julio?* Still feeling a little buzzed from the whiskey, I took her hand. "Let's go," I said and led her to the dance floor.

Turned out she was a great dancer too. The DJ played two more Duran Duran songs in a row, driving both of us to really let go. We giggled as we spun, we clapped as we read each other's eyes, we touched as we showed each other new dance steps. I had never danced so intimately with a girl before; it seemed all the dancing I *had* done with my *tías* at family gatherings was paying off with Anita. Then the DJ put on a ballad, and most of the dance floor

cleared out, leaving Anita and me in plain sight. Without saying anything, I took a chance. I stepped toward her; she leaned into me. I
placed my hands lightly around her waist, she draped her arms
loosely around my shoulders, and we began to sway softly to the
music, keeping a respectable distance between us.

I had never slow danced with a girl, though Julio had given me
plenty of tips: *Blow in her ear . . . pull her tight against you . . . trace
little circles on her back with your fingers.* But I couldn't. Avoiding eye
contact, all I dared to do was whisper, "Hey, you dance great." She
let out a coy giggle and said, "You too," then came in closer and
leaned her head on my shoulder. I tried to feel how Julio said he felt
whenever he danced slow with a girl: *excited . . . horny . . . dizzy . . .
out of control.* I *wanted* to feel those things. But nothing. I had only felt
that way those times I'd snuck a peek of Francisco Hernandez's body
glistening in the shower room. But I couldn't admit that to myself
then. Instead I convinced myself I was just too nervous to feel anything with Anita—*that's all . . . that's all.*

Another ballad came on and we kept dancing until the music
abruptly cut out, replaced by sirens. "Party's over people," the DJ
announced. That was the way house parties usually ended; sooner
or later, a pissed off neighbor would call the cops to complain about
the music or the dozens of parked cars ruining a lawn or blocking
driveways. Everyone seemed used to it. The crowd began breaking
up calmly. Julio found me and Anita munching on some pizza:
"Blanco, let's get outta here. This party is dead, man," he said. I told
him to hold on a second. "Hey, Anita, can I get your number?" I
asked. "Sure—it's easy—221-3434. You can memorize it." I
touched her shoulder gently and kissed her good-bye on the cheek.
"221-3434—got it," I said, before dashing away with Julio.

"Man, way to go, Studly-Dudly," Julio congratulated me on the ride back home. I tried to act as proud of myself as he was of me, parroting the kinds of things I knew he would say in my position. "Yeah, she's beautiful, man—and what a body. I totally kissed her—it was hot," I said. "I told you, Blanco—I told you. That's awesome—finally! I thought there was something wrong with you," Julio said. "Man, soon we'll be able to ride this baby anywhere, anytime—and pick up all the chicks we want," he said before dropping me off at home. But I didn't feel like going inside. I sat on the front porch. Misu jumped on my lap. I listened to his purring and the rustle of the mango tree whispering into the night. I watched the Morse code of the *cocuyos* twinkling like the stars above me, like so many questions I couldn't answer yet. I wondered why I had lied to Julio, why I couldn't feel what I was supposed to feel with Anita.

The following week, Anita and I talked on the phone almost every night. She loved Tom Cruise, Tootsie Rolls, and the show *Dallas;* I loved Linda Carter, Blow Pops, and *The Brady Bunch*. We both loved Barbra Streisand, dancing, and croissants. Our conversations grew more intimate every time we spoke. She had two younger sisters she hated; I had one brother away at college who wrote me every week. I missed him. Her favorite subjects were English and history—she wanted to be an elementary school teacher, maybe. My favorite classes were math and art—I was definitely going to be an architect, even though my *abuela* disapproved. Anita loved Miami, wanted to live on Biscayne Bay someday, and have three children— all boys; I dreamed of moving to Paris. She had kissed only one guy; I said I had kissed three girls before. She confessed that she missed her father, who had died—she never told him she loved him. I told her that my *abuela* was an awful and mean person. I had never been able to say that to anyone before Anita, even though I didn't tell her exactly why Abuela was so cruel to me.

One night Anita and I made plans to meet up at the movie theater in Güecheste Mall the next Saturday. She was going to bring her friend Monica, and I was to bring Julio. She wanted to set them up and I agreed. Soon as we hung up, I called Julio. Right away he asked, "Hey man—how's your foxy new girlfriend?" "Awesome, man. She's totally cool. We've been talking every night this week. I can't wait to kiss her again," I said. "So listen, we're going to the movies on Saturday. You wanna come? I wanna set you up with one of her girlfriends—Monica." "Sure, Blanco—as long as she's hot. That's cool of you, bro," he said. "Yeah—now I'm getting chicks for you!" I said, proud to be in Julio's favor.

But on Thursday, while my family was eating dinner, the phone rang. Abuela answered. Dinnertime was when her last-minute bets came in. But the call was for me. It was Eric Caraballo: "Hey, you know Julio?" he said. What a dumb question, I thought, everyone knew Julio, and besides, we were best friends. "Yeah, man. Why— what's up?" I replied, thinking it was just gossip about Julio. Maybe he got caught driving illegally or was in trouble again at school— perhaps expelled. "Do you remember his Corvette?" Eric continued. "Well, he was in an accident last night, man. He died—man. He's dead," Eric said. His voice cracked as he went on explaining the de-tails, how Julio had wrapped the car around a utility pole on Forty-eighth Street and Miller Road. It was late at night and his parents had been out of town.

I hung up the phone. My face must've gone noticeably pale, prompting Mamá to ask me, "¿Qué pasó, mi'jo? Are you okay?" I sat back down at the table. All I could answer was, "Nothing, I'm fine," and then a few seconds later: "Julio se mató. He's dead,

Mamá." "*¿Cómo puede ser? Imposible* . . . He was just here last week. I made him . . ." Mamá couldn't complete her sentences; she pushed her plate away and sobbed. None of us finished dinner; we just sat there in silence. Abuela cleared the table—tears falling on the half-full plates as she bused them to the sink. Mamá ushered me to my room, where I fell into bed. I stayed there the rest of that night, then all day Friday, in a daze, cuddling with Misu and watching reruns of *Bewitched*. I knew I should cry, I tried to cry, but I couldn't. It all felt like a bad dream, a prank, a trick, a spell that could be reversed to erase the Corvette from Julio's life.

The funeral was that Saturday, the day Julio and Monica and me and Anita were supposed to have had our double date. Papá drove the family to Rivero Funeral Home. When we arrived, I told Mamá I wanted to be alone; she said she understood, but followed me with her eyes as I drifted into a corner of the salon. I didn't want to see Julio's body or talk to his parents, or anyone, for that matter. Then Anita found me. She sat down next to me and rubbed my back. I let her. Hunched over in my seat with my head bowed, the tears finally came. Hand in hand we approached the casket, but I insisted on seeing Julio alone. I knelt before him: the boy who played guitar and taught me how to talk to girls; the boy who loved Jimi Hendrix and fast cars; the boy with wiry hair and a thin mustache; the boy I had loved like a brother, not how I wanted to love Francisco Hernandez; the boy I would never see again: his mouth closed, his hands still, his eyes shut.

I spent the next day in bed, going over memories of Julio—laughing and crying, loving and hating him. Mamá comforted me, and assured me that going back to school would be the best thing for me. And so I did on Monday morning. Those of us who knew Julio read the disbelief and sorrow in each other's eyes as we passed one another in the halls, but we did not speak of it. We were too young, too naive, too full of life to understand death. An unanswerable *why* haunted my mind, trapped in a different dimension than my body trudging through the motions of each day. Anita was the only thing that seemed real and constant. She and I continued calling each other and seeing each other during the weeks following Julio's death. We'd talk about him and try to make sense of the senseless, reminiscing over all his crazy antics. Tried. Sometimes we'd go out for ice cream at Swenson's or stroll Güecheste Mall holding hands. Sometimes she'd visit me at El Cocuyito on Saturdays and I'd get my *tío* Pipo to give her mother a discount, or I'd round up some fresh produce for her from the cold storage room.

After school I'd walk over to her school—our sister Catholic high school next door to mine. We'd sit on a bench under an enormous banyan tree, enjoy the breeze, and talk about our day: good grades, bad grades, who'd asked whom to go steady, who was having a party. Our friendship—the stories, the laughter, the gossip—filled part of my emptiness, soothed me, and strengthened my trust in her, in *us*. Yet, after nearly two months of us seeing each other, I still hadn't kissed her. Why? She obviously liked me—and I liked her. But it never felt like the right time or place for a kiss—at least that's what I'd tell myself. I didn't want to admit that Anita felt more like a friend than a girlfriend to me. Still, I feared that if I didn't make a move soon, she'd start thinking I was weird. When the homecoming dance was announced at my school, I thought it would be the perfect opportunity. We both loved to dance; we'd have a great time, and I'd think up something romantic to set the mood—to make it feel right. One afternoon I asked her to the dance. She said no at first, and then laughed: "Of course I'll go with you. I was wondering when you were going to ask me."

For weeks I saved all my tip money from my Saturday shifts at El Cocuyito to rent a tuxedo and buy a corsage. But it wasn't enough. Knowing Abuela would help me out, I told her about Anita, and then asked her for a loan. "*¿Qué?* You have a girlfriend? *Ay, gracias a San Lázaro, mi'jo.* I've been praying for a nice girl for you. *Pero* why didn't you tell me?" she said, then darted to her *guaquita*. She returned with a wad of cash and counted out the thirty dollars I needed—and an extra ten bucks. "*Coje,* take a little more," she said. "You don't have to pay me back, but I want to meet her. When is the dance?"

Mamá—and Abuela—drove me to Anita's house the night of the dance. When we arrived Anita was still getting ready. Her mother chitchatted with my mother and Abuela in the living room. Anita's two younger sisters pranced around me, asking dumb questions: *How old are you? Are you on the football team? Do you like our sister?* Finally, Anita stepped into the room. "Wow—beautiful," I said. Anita no longer looked like a girl; she was a woman in her antique lace gown and satin pumps, clutching a purse inlaid with mother-of-pearl. Her hair was in wild ringlets, her eyelashes were thick with mascara, her lips red and glossy. But her beauty and sexiness also made me feel oddly uneasy. I giggled as I pinned the corsage on her, and moved clumsily trying to get into the right pose. While our mothers snapped photos, Abuela badgered us: "*Ay, Dios*—those eyes! You'll have beautiful children. You know, *mi'ja,* I wasn't much older than you when I got married." Anita's mother interrupted Abuela and ushered us to the car; she drove us to the dance at the downtown Hyatt.

For hours, we danced to almost every song: rock, New Wave, punk rock, or ballad. Exhausted, I suggested we take a stroll along the riverside promenade to relax and cool off. Earlier that day, I had snuck a bottle of Moët & Chandon out of El Cocuyito, took a bus downtown to the Hyatt, and stashed the bottle, together with two plastic cups, in one of the planters along the promenade. When we reached the planter, I turned to Anita. "Oh, what's this?" I said coyly and pulled out the bottle of champagne. "Ricky! Oh my God— you're so sweet! How romantic," she said. I popped the cork; we made a wish and tossed the cork into the river. With cups in hand and arms wrapped around each other, we took a sip and sat down on a bench. The moment was perfect; it was time: I looked into her eyes, then kissed her softly. I caressed her back, smelled the perfume on her neck, and ran my fingers through her hair—imitating kisses I'd seen in movies. I felt like I *was* in a movie, like I was acting. I was there and yet I wasn't. I felt the tenderness and intimacy, but not the passion that Julio had described. I knew it should be one of the most beautiful, unforgettable moments in my life—my first kiss—but I also knew in that moment that I wasn't, and never would be, like other boys.

After that night, my relationship with Anita changed. I recognized I could never be who I had thought I could be with her; and I sensed she felt the same way. Surely she could tell I was different, even if she did like me. I drifted away from her slowly, and she let me, though we never officially broke up; we simply ended up becoming good friends. But it couldn't be the same as it had been. The nothingness and aloneness returned.

Several weeks later, I walked into my advanced algebra class and our teacher, Mrs. Carrillo, announced, "Today we are going to study imaginary numbers." I sat up at my desk, my curiosity piqued. *How can numbers be imaginary? They are supposed to be con-*

crete, rational, calculable. "Okay, class, what's the square root of negative four? Well?" she asked smugly. Silence. No hands went up. It seemed we were all as perplexed as if she had asked us to define God. She had our undivided attention. After a pause, she let out a little chuckle and said, "Ah—there is no real answer. So we have to imagine one."

I was totally stumped. Mrs. Carrillo explained the concept of imaginary numbers as one of the limitations of math—one of the mysteries that we can't explain, exactly. "The only way to find an answer is to get on a rocket ship and zip to infinity—where all the answers to everything lie. So for now, we have to imagine an answer. And that answer, that number, is what we call an imaginary number." She took to the blackboard, writing as she spoke: "The square root of negative one is i; therefore the square root of negative four is $2i$ . . ."

I was a whiz at math, and had come to trust it as something unquestionably precise, rational, reliable, true. The idea of imaginary numbers made no sense; it made me question the reality of everything else for the rest of the day. Imaginary or real cells dividing in biology? Imaginary or real French fries at lunch? Imaginary or real boys undressing in the locker room? An imaginary or real God speaking to me in Father Octavio's religion class? Was Julio somewhere in that infinity where all the answers to the unanswerable lie?

This lasted right into final period, Honors English. Our teacher was out sick, and the substitute instructed us to take out our textbooks, read something—*anything*—and write about it until the bell rang. I flipped through the pages aimlessly. Perhaps because I was tired and wanted to read something short, or perhaps because I was in an *imaginary* mood, I was drawn to a poem—"The Love Song of

J. Alfred Prufrock"—the moment I scanned its first line: "Let us go then, you and I / when the evening is spread out against the sky . . ." I could hear Prufrock's voice in my ear as if he were sitting right next to me telling me his story. I read the poem three times, each time spiraling more deeply into his world of sadness and longing coming to life word by word, line by line. It was the first time I had ever been moved by a poem the way I had by songs. It became part of me: my breaths, my heartbeats, my blood.

Inspired, I began writing about the mermaids in the poem—*I have heard the mermaids singing, each to each. I do not think that they will sing to me*—how they represented man's most unattainable dreams and desires and how people—like Prufrock—spend their lives afraid to act—*Do I dare . . . Disturb the universe?*—trapped in a delusion and unable to face their true selves. There were still about ten minutes left before the bell. What else could I write about? Mrs. Carrillo's lesson popped back into my mind. I compared Prufrock's life to the world of imaginary numbers—how perhaps there weren't any *real* answers to anything, not even in mathematics; how Prufrock had to make up answers to make sense of his life—and that was just part of being human. I wasn't sure if what I had written was any good, or if it even made sense, but I figured Mr. Peterson wouldn't grade the assignment too harshly—hopefully he wouldn't count it at all.

Regardless, something felt different as I turned in the assignment and stepped out into the bustling breezeway. The textures of the world seemed more imaginary, yet more real than before: the feet shuffling across the gritty terrazzo floor, the locker doors slamming like cymbals, the boys loosening their neckties and giving each other high fives, a sheet of paper afloat in the wind like a giant white butterfly. At home, later that afternoon, I lay in my bed thinking about

Julio again, just as I had done for months. But it was different this time. Julio's life and death started to make a little more sense. Julio wasn't a fearful, doubting man like Prufrock. Julio dared to disturb the universe—and I began to take comfort in that. He had lived every moment to the fullest, chasing his rock 'n' roll dreams in his Corvette. He had heard the mermaids speak to him. If there was no *real* answer for his death, then I'd just have to make one up for now, or spend the rest of my life waiting to reach infinity. The square root of negative 9 is $3i$—and there had to be a reason why Julio died—I just had to accept that. Words and numbers began healing me that day, but they also began to haunt me: Could I hear the mermaids? Would I ever dare to disturb the universe? Could I not imagine any answers to the questions I had begun to ask myself?

MY SOPHOMORE YEAR ENDED AND I GLADLY RE-turned to full-time work at El Cocuyito for the summer, hoping for grounding in my village of *cubanos*. So much had changed in me, as well as with my body. I had been lifting weights at the school gym, and doing sit-ups and push-ups at home before dinnertime. My baby fat had completely leaned into thick muscle, my biceps had grown a few inches, and I had stretched into the tallest Blanco ever at five feet nine, towering over my five-foot-four father. As I'd been given such obviously poor genes, Don Gustavo attributed my height to *los jambergues*—McDonald's hamburgers—and to hard work, of course. "*Viste*, what an *hombre* I've made of him," he would brag to the customers, slapping me on the back as I'd whisk by carrying a twenty-pound bag of rice under each arm or pushing a cart loaded with boxes of plantains stacked four tiers high. Abuela praised me too—her little *machito,* she called me, claiming it was all her doing, not Don Gustavo's.

Tía Gloria also took notice of my emerging manliness and maturity. She began relying more on me and giving me more responsibilities. Eventually she unofficially made me her assistant manager in charge of all the items that needed constant restocking or rotating: sodas, baby foods, dairy products. And I was the only one she trusted with the restocking of the wines. But my favorite new duty was baking; it was like playing with my cousin Marlene's Easy-Bake Oven. Twice a week the truck from La Estrella Panadería would deliver boxes of raw, frozen loaves of Cuban bread, thin and stiff as broomsticks. I'd pry the loaves apart one by one, placing them on wax paper, five to a tray, and then brush them delicately with drawn butter until their pallid white flesh blushed yellow. They went into the steamer for almost the entire day, where the dough would rise into clammy snakes. Then I'd peel them off the trays and slide them into the fiery mouth of the gas oven. Within a few minutes, the irresistible scent would spread through the store, luring customers to the back door of the storeroom, where they waited, watching me pull the loaves from the oven one by one with my mitt, then sliding each into a yard-long paper bag printed with the Cuban flag.

One morning I walked into the storeroom to find a man about twice my age whistling and listening to music on a Walkman while he sifted through a box of *my* frozen loaves. He returned my peeved look with a warm smile and removed his headphones. "*Hola, tú eres* Riqui, right? My name is Victor," he said, and then extended his hand to me. "Yes, I'm Ricky. Who are you? What are you doing here?" I asked, thinking he was a customer snooping around the storeroom. "*Ah, sí,* I'm new, *compañero.* Here to help you," he replied, and patted my back. *Tía* Gloria came out of the store office to explain that she expected business to pick up that summer. "*Enséñale* how to make the bread. And then show him around," she said.

I said nothing as we arranged the frozen loaves on the trays. I resented his intrusion into *my* store; the threat he posed to my status as *tía* Gloria's favorite. I listened to him answer questions about his life that I wasn't asking: he'd been in the United States only a few years; he loved *our* beer, but hated *our* filtered cigarettes; he was from Camagüey, the most beautiful province in all of Cuba, he claimed, where he had done time in prison, though he didn't say what for, and I didn't ask. He sure looked like an inmate, I thought—a sexy one, though I couldn't admit it to myself. He wore a skintight tank top, a thick belt, and a red bandanna half tucked into the back pocket of his Levi's. As he spoke, I eyed him: his scruffy beard and slicked-back hair; his thick, hairy forearms; his brawny chest.

After we finished the first batch of Cuban bread, he asked me if I wanted to have a cigarette out back with him. I told him I didn't smoke, but he insisted I join him anyway—and I agreed, I wanted to learn more about him: What was he up to and why had he been in prison? He rolled a cigarette, which I'd never seen anyone do. "This is how we did it in Cuba," he said in response to my bewildered look, then lit the cigarette and offered me a toke. "I don't smoke," I told him again. "Well, it's time you started, *compañero*," he said. The authority in his voice, together with the contrasting kindness in his light-brown eyes, let me trust him. I took a puff and began coughing violently; my eyes watered. He laughed, but said tenderly, "*Papo, coño. Tranquilo, tranquilo.*" He ran into the store and returned with a beer. Not what I was expecting, but I took two good swigs. When my coughing eased up, we both laughed, as if we'd been friends for years. "*Compañero*, you've got a lot to learn," he said. "And so do you," I bantered. "Come on—I'm supposed to show you around the store. I'm your boss—remember that."

As *tía* Gloria had done with me years before, I walked slowly down each aisle, pointing out how the store was organized and stressing the importance of presentation and cleanliness to Victor: "Pull all the stock forward. Align everything in neat rows—labels always face out. Remove damaged goods. Wipe the shelves down every time." After every instruction he'd reply with, *Sí, Papo. Está bien, Papo. Como no, Papo.* I figured that would be his nickname for me—Papo; I liked it—it sounded manly yet affectionate. Finally I warned him: "I'm in charge of the wines—don't touch those or I'll fire you," I joked. "*Sí, sí, sí, Señor Jefe.* Whatever you say, *Capitán,*" he came back at me with sarcasm, giving me a soldier's salute. We laughed again—the way I used to laugh with Julio.

I then gave Victor the rundown of the stockroom and took him up to the second-story loft where *tía* Gloria stored the *americano* foods that hardly sold, like canned cranberry jelly and broccoli soup; and also the bulkier but lighter boxes of toilet paper and cereals. "*Oye,* does Gloria come up here?" Victor asked. "Usually on Mondays—when she checks inventory," I explained. "*Ay, qué bien.* We can *hanguear* up here," he said, and started rolling another cigarette. He lit it and passed it to me, and that time I didn't cough at all. We sat on some boxes, and he began divulging more details about his life, blowing out smoke with his words: "*Sabes,* I had to leave everyone *en* Cuba. I can never go back—*nunca,*" he said with a certain vulnerability in his voice. I expected to hear the same nostalgic story I'd heard before from other Cubans like Don Gustavo and Raquel, but then Victor added, "Cuba was hell anyway—it was *de pinga.*" I found that odd—I'd never heard anyone compare Cuba to hell, unless they were referring to Castro. But before I could ask him more, Victor looked away into the distance: "*Bueno,* that's a story for another day," he said, then put out his cigarette on the floor. "There's a lot you don't know, Papo. *Vámonos,* I need to get to work before you fire me, *Señor Jefe.*"

Throughout the week that followed, Victor and I fell naturally into a daily routine. We'd ease into each morning by sharing a *colada* of Cuban coffee while chitchatting with Migdalia at the *cafetería* counter. She would ask Victor if he liked her perfume, or her new blouse, or the color of her lipstick. Victor always answered coldly: yes or no. I found it odd that he'd never return her flirtations, like men usually did. Some mornings Don Gustavo would march by us and make a snide remark like, *Are you señoritas going to work today?* Most mornings, loudmouth Nuñez would join us at the counter and entertain us with his Cuban sayings. I could tell he'd been itching to come up with a nickname for Victor, but I beat him to it. To ease cravings between cigarettes breaks, Victor would suck on lollipops all day long. One morning while he was sucking on one, I dubbed him *"El nenecito,"* or *"Nene"* for short, meaning "little darling boy," an ironic contrast to Victor's buff shoulders and chiseled jaw.

After coffee, we'd walk up and down the aisles and check which items needed to be restocked. I'd jot everything down in a composition book, and then we'd head back to the stockroom, go over the list, and divvy it up. Making our way through the maze of boxes, we'd help each other locate the ones we needed, and then load them on our carts. Victor would clip on his Walkman, put on his earphones, unwrap a lollipop, and head to the aisles.

He was a tough guy, yet helpless when it came to reading English. He'd have to open a box and look at the logo and pictures on the label to figure out what was what and which aisle it belonged in. But sometimes he'd still have no idea and ask for my help. Day by day, box by box, I taught him how to read and translate bizarre consonant blends that had no equivalent sound in Spanish: the *sp* in *spaghetti*, the *ckl* in *pickles*, the *str* in *string beans;* how to decipher the chameleon sounds of vowels in English: the difference between the *a* in *cake* and the *a* in *jam;* and why some letters are silent for no reason: "Just like the *h* in Spanish, Nene," I'd try to explain. Sometimes he'd understand, but sometimes—with words like *ketchup* and *cracker*—he'd stomp away frustrated, cussing at English in Spanish, *"Pa'la pinga, Papo. No hay chino que entienda esta mierda"*—*Fuck this, Papo! There isn't a Chinaman who could understand this shit.*

Victor was a hard worker, yet fun-loving; manly yet childish; predictable yet volatile—just like Julio, I thought—someone who dared to disturb the universe, a rebel with a sense of humor. Perhaps that had gotten him into trouble and thrown in prison; maybe that's why Cuba had been hell for him. After another week working together, one day he called me up to the loft to have a cigarette and kvetch about Don Gustavo and *tía* Gloria, I thought, like we did many afternoons. But that time he had prepared a surprise. He had fashioned a makeshift table and chairs out of boxes, and laid out *pan con bistec* and *medianoche* sandwiches for us. "Nene, what's this?" I asked. *"Nada,* Papo, I just wanted to show you my *gracias* for helping me— for being a good *amigo,"* he explained. "Sit—sit." I was completely charmed by his gesture, but also felt a bit uncomfortable—no man had ever shown me such affection. I wasn't sure how to respond. He also had two frosty bottles of *Muñequitas*—Little Dolls—the name he'd given St. Pauli Girl beer for the German bombshell pictured on the label. We toasted to friendship and good fortune and began eating in the loft—our own little hideaway.

"Hey, Nene, why was Cuba hell? Why were you in prison?" I finally felt I could ask him. "*Ay*, Papo, you have to understand that my Cuba was *muy diferente* than the Cuba all these people talk about here. I grew up after *la Revolución*. No one had anything—no big *casas* or *botes*, no big farms. *Sí*, we had what we needed, *más o menos*, that much was true. *Pero* no one could say what they wanted, live how they wanted, or be who they wanted to be. Come, let me show you . . ." he said. I followed him to the back of the loft, where he showed me a small mural drawn in black and red marker across a row of paper towel boxes three tiers high. "You drew this?" I said, fascinated by the mural's Picasso-like shapes and abstracted figures. "Of course, I was an artist *en* Cuba. I've been working on this a few days," he said proudly, and began explaining the mural: "This is my *tío* Nilo, who is a big *pincho* in the Communist Party— he turned on his own *familia*, so I drew him drowning in his own relatives' blood. The eyes all over are the eyes of the neighborhood *comité* that spies on everyone. *El hombre* in this corner in a black dress is my best friend Omar. He was a painter and a dissident like me—persona non grata in our own country. We got thrown in jail together."

There seemed to be more to the story. "What happened?" I pried. Without taking his eyes off the figure of his friend, Victor explained: "*Bueno*, I got out after three months, but not Omar. I never saw him again." I told Victor about Julio and that I understood what it was like to lose a friend. "*Coño*, Papo, *lo siento*—how terrible," Victor replied. "I still miss Omar too. I hope somehow he's alive. *Quién sabe*, maybe he's here—like me—in Miami, where I can do what I want, love who I want, and no one puts me in jail for it. Maybe I'll run into that *maricón* one day." In *Cubichi*, *maricón*— faggot—was sometimes used playfully, not disparagingly with contempt. I couldn't quite tell how Victor meant it. Was Omar simply his buddy or *un maricón*, for real? Was Victor? I had assumed he was simply a bachelor, but maybe I had it all wrong. "How come you're not married?" I asked. Victor glanced at me awkwardly, "*¿Por qué? What does that have to do with anything?*" he replied. "I don't know," I said nervously, "I was just wondering—that's all." He took one last swig of his Muñequita and said, "There's a lot you don't know, Papo, a story for another day. *Vámonos*—back to work before Gloria catches us up here *jodiendo*."

In the weeks after our lunch in the loft, I began thinking of Victor not only as a coworker, but as a friend, like Julio had been—but different. What I felt for Victor was something more than just a brotherly kind of love. Our routine started feeling more intimate, like rituals; and I became more connected to him. While sharing our morning *colada*, we'd complain about the snobby customers who acted as if they were still as wealthy as they had been in Cuba, gossip about the trampy ladies who would swoon over *tío* Pipo, and laugh over Sonia's conspicuous attempts to match me up with Deycita. During smoking breaks, he taught me how to roll cigarettes, and I'd tutor him in grocery-store English—and cuss words. He'd describe the Cuba I would have grown up in had my parents decided to stay. One Friday I took him to Felipe's house so he could see the cardboard Cuba neither of us had really known—the Cuba of my parents' day. Some afternoons we'd sneak two cold Muñequitas up to the loft and he'd show me more of his drawings, opening my eyes to the beauty of line, color, and form. He'd speak about great Cuban painters like Wifredo Lam, and I'd tell him about my dream of becoming a great American architect like Frank Lloyd

Wright. One day, while we were arranging the frozen loaves of Cuban bread together, Victor told me he had been married once, but that it wasn't for him; he was all alone in the world—and he was fine with it. I told him I had only kissed one girl, once—and that I was fine without a girlfriend.

Indeed, I hadn't seen Anita since the summer had begun, and I didn't miss her as much as I thought I would. My friendship with Victor was more satisfying, somehow; I could be myself around him in a way I could never be around Anita. We began giving one another smiles and playful salutes down the aisles. From a distance, I observed everything about Victor: he'd walk slowly and deliberately as if each step was rehearsed; he'd only eat lime or orange lollipops; he'd wet his hair and comb it two or three times every day. But what intrigued me most was how he'd half close his eyes and bob his head to the rhythm of whatever music he was listening to on his Walkman.

One afternoon, when he was dusting off some shelves, I tapped him on the shoulder. He took off his headphones and I asked him, "*Caramba*, what are you listening to?" "*Coje*—you listen—pure beauty," he said, and put the headphones on me. I was expecting the same old Cuban songs my parents played, but instead I heard a woman singing in a beautiful language I didn't know; she had an ethereal voice that sounded like an angel—no—like a mermaid, like Prufrock's mermaids. While I listened, Victor and I studied each other's eyes for a moment. I handed the headphones back to him. "Weird," I said, "but beautiful. She sounds like a mermaid." "Mermaid? Where did you get an idea like that?" He chuckled. "It's from a poem . . ." I began, but realized it would be too complicated to explain; I'd simply show him the poem someday. "*Bueno*, if you hear mermaids then you hear mermaids," he said, "but this is opera. The lady singing is Tosca—she dies for love at the end."

Victor and I kept our routine and rituals every day except Wednesdays, my day to restock the wines with *tía* Gloria. Occasionally, after we were done she'd let me uncork a bottle of my choice, as long as it was under ten dollars: a pinot noir, a fumé blanc, a Chardonnay. Regardless of vintage, I'd invite Victor up to the loft to share the bottle with me—another ritual. Sometimes, he'd talk to me about *Aida* and *Carmen* and *La Traviata;* sometimes I'd talk about Jimi Hendrix and Duran Duran and Alphaville. One time, I brought him a copy of "The Love Song of J. Alfred Prufrock" and read it to him slowly. He closed his eyes and listened, tapping his foot as he did when he'd listen to opera. "Do you get it?" I asked, wondering if he understood the poem the same way I had. *"Más o menos,"* he said. "It's hard for me to understand all of it, *pero* the man in the poem is sad. Do you feel sad?" His question caught me by surprise. "Sometimes, I guess," I replied. "What does a *muchacho* like you have to be sad about? Are you sad about Julio?" Victor asked. I paused for a moment: "No, not really. Not so much anymore. But sometimes I feel like something is missing. Like nobody understands me. I can't explain it," I said. *"Bueno,* you have your whole *vida* ahead of you. *No te preocupes,* you have time to figure things out," Victor assured me.

Thursdays were also different than the other days of the week. Thursdays were dubbed the day of *la rastra,* the Spanish name for the gargantuan eighteen-wheeler that would arrive from the distributor at 8:30 A.M. sharp. With three blasts of the horn, the driver would announce the delivery. Victor and I would open up the rear gate and guide the truck driver as he backed up to the storeroom. *Tía* Gloria would keep a tally of the boxes, marking each one with a number as it whizzed down the steel rollers out of the dark mouth of the truck and into our hands. Victor and I were unstoppable: moving, sorting, and stacking boxes as fast as *tía* Gloria could count them. Working in perfect synchronicity, we'd unload more than two hundred boxes in a couple hours.

Tía Gloria would never allow us to take off our shirts—a matter of decorum—no matter how much we'd sweat. But one unbearably hot and humid Thursday in mid-August, she must've felt our exhaustion and made an exception. Victor and I peeled off our sweat-soaked T-shirts in relief. *"Ay, papi, qué rico . . . qué caliente,"* Victor joshed in a girly voice. "You too, *machote,*" I teased him. We laughed, but we weren't just kidding. I could feel his eyes on me; the more he looked at me, the more I flaunted my body. I was eyeing him too. The sweat dripping down his hairy chest and his muscular back excited me the same way Francisco Hernandez's body had excited me in the locker room at school.

When we were done, Victor and I headed into the small restroom in the storeroom to cool off and clean up. We wrung out our T-shirts and patted the sweat off our bodies with paper towels. "Can you dry my back?" I asked him. He took the red bandanna from his back pocket and slowly wiped me down. Then I turned around, took his bandanna, and did the same to him. My body tingled—nothing like when I had kissed Anita. I knew without knowing. Then Victor turned around: *"Bueno,* now what?" he said with his eyes frozen on me. *Do I dare disturb the universe?* "Nada, let's get back to work," I said, grabbed my shirt, and darted for the door.

The rest of that afternoon, there were no smiles between us or playful salutes down the aisles. But near the day's end, Victor approached me while I was checking expiration dates on the baby food jars and rotating them—oldest to the front, newest to the back. "*Oye*, it's my birthday on Saturday. You want to come over to my house after work *para celebrar*? Maybe we can have a few Muñequitas?" he said, as if trying to appear casual. "*Pues claro*—I'd love to, Nene. But I'll have to ask my dad if I can keep his car until late. I hope it will be okay," I said. I was supposed to bring home *el Malibú* right after work on Saturdays. To lighten the mood, I joked with him, "*Y qué*, how old are you gonna be, fifteen? Are we celebrating your *Quinces*?" He chuckled and came back at me, "*Las señoritas* never tell their age. *Pero*, I tell you I can almost be your *papá*—almost. Anyway, come over on Saturday—I have something special planned."

The rest of the day and into that night at home I kept wondering what Victor's surprise might be. *What if he . . . what if he . . .* I kept thinking, not daring to complete my thoughts. Regardless, I wanted to get him a present, and I had the perfect gift in mind. I borrowed Mamá's car that evening and went to Diamond's. I had just enough cash to buy him the biggest sketchbook they had, a set of drawing pencils, and a box of oil pastels. Back at home, while I was wrapping the gifts in my bedroom, Abuela came in and asked: "*Eh*, whose *cumpleaños* is it? Who are those sissy art things for?" "They're for Victor at work, Abuela. It's his birthday." I said. "*Pero*, those aren't gifts for *un hombre* like him," she continued prying. "Only *un maricón* would . . ." I knew Abuela would continue pestering me and perhaps even dare to snatch the gifts away. I had to be firm: "He's my friend,

Abuela—he's an artist. So what? Just leave me alone!" I yelled at her. She turned and walked down the hall, muttering something I chose to ignore.

"*Feliz cumpleaños*, Nene," I told Victor first thing Saturday morning at El Cocuyito. "*Gracias*, Papo," he said. "Where's my cake, *cabrón*?" he joked, then asked me to help him out so that he could get through all his work and leave an hour earlier. He had to get home to "prepare," he told me. At four o'clock, with a six-pack of Muñequitas in each hand, he headed to his apartment, which was three blocks down the street from El Cocuyito. After he left, I got *tía* Gloria's permission to take a bottle of sparkling cava—the poor man's champagne, as she called it—to bring to Victor's. In the bathroom at El Cocuyito, I washed up, changed into my favorite long-sleeve polo shirt, which I had brought from home, and splashed some of my father's orange-blossom cologne over my neck and chest. As I combed my hair, I couldn't meet my eyes in the mirror. I felt guilty about being so excited by the thought of spending a night alone with Victor. I had never been to his place, but he had given me directions. I arrived at a detached garage turned into an efficiency, with exterior walls he had painted sage green, just as he had described to me. The contrasting magenta blooms of his bougainvillea vines transformed the otherwise plain façade into a work of art. You could tell an artist lived there.

I heard opera—the mermaids singing—through the door before he opened it. "Papo!" he greeted me, seeming as surprised to see me all gussied up as I was to see him wearing a long-sleeve linen guayabera—freshly ironed—and shiny penny loafers. "Here, Nene—*felicidades*," I said, handing him the bottle of cava and the other gifts. "*Pero* why all this? *Gracias, coño,* I haven't had a birthday present since I left Cuba," he said as he ushered me to the dinette; it was a bit shabby, but adorned with a vase of colored daisies. He set the presents down on the table and asked me to take a seat, then stepped into the kitchenette. The efficiency was one open room: in one corner a twin mattress rested on the floor, neatly made up with an embroidered bedspread. Lit candles adorned every flat surface, it seemed. On one of the walls he had drawn a mural like the one he had drawn in the loft—a collage of distorted figures and shapes.

He returned from the kitchenette with a bowl of mixed nuts, sliced chorizo, and two ice-cold Muñequitas. He handed me one, and then sat on his bed across from me. "*Bueno,* here's to my *Quinces,*" he said, lifting his beer up in a toast. "If you're fifteen, I'm not even born yet," I quipped. We laughed, but there was something different about our laughter—we weren't at work anymore, no longer employees, but two men alone in a room by ourselves. Even so, our evening began with a bit of the usual small talk: how hot and unbearable August had become, the size of Sonia's butt, Don Gustavo's senility and his goof-ups at the bodega. After a second round of Muñequitas, I began to loosen up, and asked him to tell me about the mural he'd drawn on the wall. "It's called *Los Cocuyitos,*" he explained. "Here are all the women that flirt your *tío* Pipo—he's wrapping them in butcher paper; that's your *tía* Gloria dressed as a beauty queen to represent all the beauty inside her; all these people are the customers tossing flowers at her; this is me, finding my way through a maze of boxes; and that's you with a halo of fireflies, floating above everything, on your way to see your friend Julio in the other world."

It was beautiful—like the poem, like the mermaids, like imaginary numbers—and yet I couldn't explain to him what I felt exactly. All I could say was, "Is this the surprise you had for me?" "No, no.

Not yet, Papo," he said, and brought us another round of Muñequi-tas. "Well, open your presents, then," I said, and handed them to him. One by one he opened the gifts somewhat bashfully, but making a fuss. "*Gracias*, Papo, you're *tremendo*! I can sure use these. And this is perfect for what I had in mind," he said. I wasn't sure what he meant. But then he sat on the floor, opened up the sketchbook, and fingered through the pencils I had just given him. He picked one up and said: "Hold still, Papo. I'm going to draw a portrait of you—that's my surprise." "Make sure I come out good," I joked, speaking like a ventriloquist, trying not to move my lips. "You could never come out ugly, even if I tried, Papo," he said and winked at me. The silence as he drew was awkward, yet gorgeous. Victor and I had never had such a moment without words—a moment of pure being in each other's company.

After about fifteen minutes, he got up off the floor and showed me his sketch. "*Mira*. It's not done yet, but I'll finish it. *¿Te gusta?*" he asked. "Yes, yes, Nene. *Coño*, it looks just like me. I wish I could draw like that," I said. The portrait was lifelike, not abstract like most of his drawings that I'd seen; I could see myself—the long line of my nose, my bushy eyebrows. We gazed at the sketch, then looked at each other. He leaned into me and gave me a tender kiss on my cheek. "*Te adoro*—I adore you," he said. I could see my reflection in his eyes: *Do I dare disturb the universe? Dare to kiss him, feel his stubble against my palm, the fine hairs of his chest through my fingers? Feel his strong hands on my body?*

"Me too—I adore you too," I blurted out nervously, then changed the subject. "Let's open the bottle of cava I brought." I expected him to become peeved or even angry with me, but he didn't. Instead he said, "*Está bien*, Papo, *te quiero* anyway. One day you'll be ready." I didn't respond, pretending I didn't know what he was talking about, even though I did—and he knew I did. He knew I was petrified—incapable—of acknowledging the truth that I had always known: I was a gay man, *un maricón*, just as Abuela had feared. But I couldn't disturb the universe—not yet, anyway.

Victor stepped to the kitchenette and returned with cava served in two mugs; we clinked them, but toasted to nothing. Without my asking, he began sharing details about his life: "I knew I was different since I was *un niño*, but I was too scared most of my life to admit who I really was. I even got married, but she felt more like a friend. *Al fin*, I met someone very special—Omar, the man I drew in the mural. I fell in love with him and I couldn't deny who I was anymore. So I got divorced, and went on about my life with him." I had never heard a man speak about another man that way. I avoided his eyes, yet his honesty made me feel closer to him. Though I couldn't be honest with him in the same way, I felt I should say something: "So everything's okay now?" I asked.

Victor paused, took in what I had said, but didn't answer my question. Instead he offered me some advice: "You know who you are, Papo—that's never going to change—*nunca*. I know it isn't easy, but one day you'll know when the time is right and everything will be okay. Until then, you just need to be yourself as much as you can. You'll lose your fear *poquito a poco*. Now, you better get home before you get in trouble. And anyway, I have to work tomorrow—I don't get Sundays off like you, *Señor Jefe*."

We slowly made our way to the front door. Our *adiós* turned into an awkward but genuine hug. I felt his heartbeats, smelled the musk of his neck, heard his breaths, then let go of him and walked away. On the drive back home, I thought about all I hadn't dared to say to Victor: my shame over wanting Francisco Hernandez, how Anita felt like a friend, just like his ex-wife felt to him, what a terrible fake I was around Julio, and how much my *abuela* had ridiculed and hurt me.

On Monday I returned to El Cocuyito, hoping Victor and I could fall back into our same routine and rituals, and our friendship would continue just as before, despite all he had shared with me. But when I arrived that morning, Victor was not there. I asked *tía* Gloria for him. "He called. He's got a fever. You're on your own today, Riqui," she said. I didn't think anything of it until I went up to the loft to fetch some boxes of paper towels. There, pinned to one of the boxes, was the finished portrait of me, but less realistic than the one he'd started on Saturday: a halo over my head—the same one he had drawn on the mural; one of my eyes shut, the other wide open; half my face blurred; my shirt made of fish scales. I knew it was his way of saying good-bye. I thought about going to his house to talk things over, but knew things would never be the same. His friendship—his love for me—would challenge me to face myself and admit what I wasn't ready to admit. It was easier, though painful, to let him go and be alone again: my own face staring back at me from the portrait in my hands, and the words he had written on the back: Adiós, *Papo. Keep listening to the mermaids. You'll know when you know.*

SEVEN

EL FARITO

*T*hat seafood paella *tía* Susana made last Sunday was the best I've tasted since Cuba. *¡Qué rico!*" Papá dared to say that Friday at the dinner table. "It was good . . ." Mamá conceded, "but *un poquito* salty. Don't you think?" she asked Papá, clearing his plate before he had finished or could answer her loaded question. They were talking about the big family picnic last Sunday at El Farito, the state beach park at the end of Key Biscayne. The Sunday picnic had become a tradition that summer, and the responsibility of preparing the feast every week rotated from woman to woman. The coming Sunday was Mamá's turn—and she wasn't about to be outdone or out-cooked by *tía* Susana. "*Bueno,* I think you'll love what I going to make better than any paella," she announced. "I spoke to Ariel yesterday. He's going to bring me *un lechón* from his friend who has a farm in Homestead. We're going to have a real pig roast, just like Nochebuena." "*Qué bien,*" Abuela said, uninterested, not offering to help; her turn had already passed and she had proven herself with a delicious pot of *ropa vieja*. "Ariel?" I asked. "*Sí,* Ariel Jimenez, Margarita's son. *¿No* *te acuerdas?* They came on the same boat with your *tía* Nena," Mamá said, refreshing my memory.

Ariel and his parents were refugees who fled Cuba as part of the Mariel boatlift. I'd first met them at an *almuerzo* at our house just days after they had arrived. Ariel must have been about twelve years old, the same age as I had been, and just as fat—or *hoosky,* as Mamá would say. She had asked me to be friendly and make Ariel feel welcomed. I tried, but he was weird: couldn't speak a word of English, didn't know how to play Monopoly, had never seen any of the *Star Wars* movies. With nothing to talk about, we politely ignored each other the rest of the afternoon. I hadn't seen Ariel or his family since. They weren't blood relatives, and besides, Cubans who had been in Miami since the sixties didn't typically socialize with refugees from *El Mariel.* Miami Cubans had adopted a "we were here first" attitude toward the Marielitos, whom they generally regarded as bumpkins and riffraff tainted by exposure to Castro's socialist regime.

Though I had always thought of Mamá as the *comandante* in our family, as I grew older, I began noticing she also had a fairy godmother side—a soft spot for those in need. She had kept in touch with Ariel's family over the years, helping them fill out job applications and collecting hand-me-downs for them sometimes. I imagined Ariel must've been more than eager to help Mamá when she called on him to find her a pig.

Certainly more than I was that Saturday morning, when she handed me a list of items to bring home from El Cocuyito: ten bags of ice, fourteen heads of garlic, a two-liter bottle of Coke, eight bitter oranges, and six limes. She phoned me at the store midafternoon to remind me, and asked me to be home by six to help her and Ariel, who would be dropping off the pig. *"Ay,* I hope it's gutted," she said, nervous with excitement. "I forgot to ask him. Tell your *tío* Pipo to lend you his big butcher knives, *por si las moscas.*" I arrived home with Mamá's groceries, the cleaver, and an assortment of carving knives I had stowed under the driver's seat of Papá's *Malibú*, which was still in mint condition, he claimed. Parked in our driveway was a late-model Honda Civic halfway through a new metallic-gold paint job, and pimped out with chrome mags and a cracked rear spoiler. *What a bro car,* I thought. *That's gotta be Ariel's Cuban Cadillac.* Topping it all off: a Cuban flag ornament hanging from the rearview mirror.

I opened the door on Mamá and Ariel chatting at the kitchen table over *un cafecito.* I hardly recognized him as she reintroduced us: "Riqui, you remember Ariel, *¿verdad? ¡Mira qué grande y flaco!* He's six inches taller than you. When are you going to catch up?" she teased me. Indeed, he was over six feet tall, nearly hitting the lamp above the dining table as he stood to greet me. "Hey," I said, uninterested as I put out my hand, which he took, pulling me toward him into a bear hug. *"¡Coño, el primo gringo!"* he greeted me, calling me his cousin, though I wasn't; calling me a gringo, though I wasn't. *"¿Qué pasa consorte?* How you been, bro?" he asked. *"Bien, bien,"* I answered in Spanish, thinking he still couldn't speak English, which of course he could, much better than my parents in fact, though intermingled with Spanish and some Spanglish, just like them.

"You looking good, *compai.* Lost all that baby fat, just like me," he said, smacking his rock-hard stomach. Indeed, his T-shirt fit loosely around his waistline, but tight across his chest, the short sleeves hugging his massive biceps. He certainly wasn't the *hoosky* boy I remembered. *"¿Bueno y qué?* I hear you're a genius, man—*y un tremendo* playboy," he continued, dishing out compliment after compliment, surely gleaned from Mamá's bragging. *"Bueno,* I don't know about that, *pero si eso es lo que dice la gente*—so be it," I said, mimicking (or mocking) his mix of English and Spanish. He was loud. He was fresh. He was *very* Cuban. But he had sea-green eyes fringed with thick, dark eyelashes that seemed to slow down time with every blink. "*Vamos,* gringo, let's get *el lechón* out of the trunk—wait till you see it," he said. "No—first *el hielo,*" Mamá intervened, ordering us to fetch the ten bags of ice and empty them into *my* bathtub. "For what?" I asked—a dumb question. "*Ay, niño, para el lechón*—what else? You think I can fit a whole pig *en el frigeraide? Qué bobo,*" Mamá quipped.

Ariel chuckled and patted my back: "That's what *madres* are for. Come on, let's go." We went out to *el Malibú* and carried in all ten bags at once—three on each of his superman shoulders, two on each of mine. I didn't trust Ariel at first, but his chumminess slowly disarmed me. As we filled the bathtub with ice, he went on and on about his dog, a pug named Yakson, whose picture he kept on his acrylic photo key chain. With pride, he explained how he was working a full-time job at Burger King that summer so he could pay for the rest of the paint job on the car. He boasted that he had souped up the engine himself, but wanted to be an architect. "Really? Me too," I said, surprised we had that in common. He liked baseball—*Los Yanquis*—and New Wave music. He asked me if I liked Alphaville. I said yes. When we returned to the Honda, he cranked up their song "Forever Young" on the car stereo as we eased the roasting pan with the pig out of the trunk, which vibrated with the music. "*Qué lindo, eh?* Twenty-five pounds. I helped kill it myself," he bragged. "Wow—nice," I feigned, thankful it was already gutted. New Wave music and slaughtered pigs—something about Ariel didn't quite add up.

With Mamá guiding the way, we carried the piglet inside and laid it to rest atop the bed of ice. "*¡Vengan! ¡Vengan!*" she called throughout the house. Abuela, Abuelo, and Papá crammed into my beach-themed bathroom. Mamá parted the seashell-print shower curtain, unveiling the piglet in the baby-blue bathtub. *"Ahora sí—* what a feast," she proclaimed as everyone eyed and complimented the piglet's buttery pink skin, its fleshy rump, and its ears, which, according to my *abuela*, were the best part—nice and crispy. "But the most important thing is *el mojo*. If not, it will taste like straw," Ariel said with authority. Mamá agreed and said the pig was going to marinate all night long in her special *mojo* that she was going to prepare. "I'll help you," Ariel offered. "I'm known for my *mojo*." I questioned why I didn't know how to make *mojo*, surprised that I even cared, not wanting to admit to myself that I was jealous of my mother's fussing over Ariel. Nevertheless I followed them to the kitchen. I had to figure out how a guy who listened to Alphaville and wanted to be an architect could also know how to make perfect *mojo*.

Mamá served herself and Ariel some Coke without offering me any, then poured the rest of the two-liter bottle into a pitcher. Using a funnel, she filled the empty bottle with the juice of the bitter oranges and limes as Ariel squeezed them. Next they added cumin and minced garlic, pepper and olive oil. They didn't use measuring cups or spoons; instead they shook the marinade vigorously every few minutes, then tasted it. Between debates over whether to add a little more of this or that, Ariel thanked my mother for helping him and his family since they had arrived from Cuba. *"Gracias a ti,* we've been able to get ahead. *Eres un ángel,"* he confessed, choking up before giving her a kiss on the cheek. *"Ay, mi'jo,"* Mamá said humbly, "God is the only one you have to thank—*gracias a Dios* you made it here alive. I wish *mi familia* would have gotten out when they had the chance. Now it's too late." She wiped her eyes with the back of her hand. Ariel gently stroked her back. Was Mamá really *that* special? I wondered. For a moment, it felt as if I were watching a movie in which my mother was not my mother, but simply a *her*, full of loss and fear, love and charity—a complex woman, not just the family overlord. I wanted to kiss her too, and thank her—but I didn't.

Adding one last pinch of salt, Ariel declared, *"Perfecto."* Mamá took a taste before agreeing, *"Sí, perfecto."* Shaking the *mojo* bottle as if it were a maraca, she did a rumba step down the hall, leading the way into my bathroom. She doused the piglet with the *mojo*, working it into the skin as if she were giving it a massage. "Let me help," I said, reaching for the bottle in her hand. *"Tú no sabes, mi'jo,"* she protested. "Let *el gringo* try it," Ariel said, laughing as he turned the pig on its back. *"Arriba,* pour some out—like this—*mira,"* he instructed. Our hands touched and slid over one another as we rubbed the last of *el mojo* through the piglet's ribs. The smell of garlic and cumin rose into the air, carried on notes of citrus that blended with his orange-blossom cologne. I recognized the scent. It was Colonia No. 4711, the same cologne my father dabbed every morning on his freshly shaven face and the handkerchief he carried in his back pocket.

"Bueno, sleep with *los angelitos,"* Ariel joked, bidding the pig a good night. Mamá thanked him over and over again at the doorway and invited him to the family gathering the following day. "You're coming *mañana,* no? We'll be at El Farito. *Tú sabes,* at the end of Key Biscayne with all the pine trees." Ariel fidgeted with his car keys. He seemed nervous, perhaps surprised that he'd been invited. *"Bueno,* okay, if I can get off work." He hugged Mamá good-bye, then turned his sea-green eyes on me. I stretched out my hand for a handshake, and again he pulled me into a hug, his stubbly chin brushing my ear, sending goose bumps down my neck. *"Bueno,* I'll see you *mañana, primo,"* he said, then crouched into his homely

Honda. He blasted another Alphaville song, then honked his horn, which bleated out the notes to "La Cucaracha" as he drove off, waving good-bye.

Overnight, the piglet marinated in its icy bathtub coffin. I could feel the presence of its body as if I were at a funeral wake. Every time I went to the bathroom, there it was. I tried not to look, but couldn't help staring back at its wide-open eyes, the same look my chickens had had in their eyes, frozen with life and death, terror and peace, the day years ago when Abuela slaughtered them in the backyard. Thoughts of Ariel haunted and perplexed me as I lay in bed, trying to fall asleep: he slaughtered pigs but loved his pug; painted his car gold but listened to New Wave music; wore a medallion of San Lázaro around his neck but also a puka shell bracelet. Ariel didn't make sense to me: his skin neither black nor white; his eyes neither blue nor green but a color I couldn't name. I dozed off to echoes of his voice: *Sleep with* los angelitos, primo. *Sleep with* los angelitos.

On Sunday morning I rolled out of bed into my daily routine: one hundred sit-ups followed by one hundred push-ups—plus a few extra to look good for the day at the beach. Was I as muscular and ripped as Ariel? I flexed my biceps and sweaty abs in front of the bathroom mirror. Contorting my body, I inspected the skinny calves I had inherited from my *abuelo*, and my big Cuban butt, inherited from my mother. I imagined myself a few inches taller and questioned if I had *really* lost all my baby fat like Ariel had said. I wasn't completely used to the lean body of the *man* I saw before me in the mirror: the whorls of hair below *his* navel, the veins on *his* arms, the slit down *his* chest, and the jut of *his* collarbones. Preoccupied, I had forgotten all about the piglet in the bathtub until I flung open the shower curtain to the sight of it still marinating, still staring at me, still dead.

"*¡Apúrate!* I need to check on *el puerco*." Mamá rapped on the bathroom door. I had to skip my shower, and sat right down to breakfast. Above the crunch of my Corn Flakes, I could hear Mamá in her beach sandals flopping and squeaking as she scuttled frantically through the house making final preparations. She finished up the black beans and rice she had whipped up that morning in a pot the size of a tire. She pulled out the beach chairs from the hall closet, then stuffed her *por si las moscas* tote with items she'd laid out the night before: sunscreen, mosquito repellent, magazines, moist towelettes, an emergency roll of toilet paper. And the not-so-usual: Band-Aids, Mercurochrome, a mini machete, an extra bottle of *mojo*, and the cruet of holy water that *tía* Elisa had brought back for her from Lourdes.

She commanded Papá and Abuelo to load the pig into *el Malibú* without spilling a single drop of *mojo*; she put Abuela in charge of plastic plates, cups, and utensils. Caco was taking summer classes away at college, so I was stuck with double duty: she ordered me to carry out the beach chairs and the bags of charcoal briquettes; fill the ice chest with sodas; cut down as many fronds as I could from the plantain trees in our backyard; and grab the shovel from the shed. "What for?" I asked—another dumb question. "To cook *el lechón*, what else?" she said dismissively, as if I should've known. I didn't. I was embarrassed and defensive and had to stop myself from mouthing off to her: *Why don't you get your precious Ariel to help you?* But I knew better than to provoke her in the midst of her frenzy.

Returning to *el Malibú* with my hands full, I found Papá cussing, hopelessly trying to ease the trunk closed. As usual, Mamá had overprepared and overpacked. Dismissing Papá's rules about *el Malibú*, she made an executive decision: "*El lechón* will have to go in the car. Go on, get in the backseat," she told my grandparents and me. Papá slid the roasting pan with the pig onto our laps and then Mamá covered it with a towel to keep it cool. "*Qué* cute—looks like a little *bebé*," she joked before ordering, "*Vámonos*, we can't be late." Papá and I both put on our sunglasses and we drove off.

With the windows rolled down, the morning air rushing in was still relatively cool and crisp for a Miami August. The city felt strangely peaceful at that early hour, empty without peddlers trolling the intersections selling one-dollar bags of peeled oranges; without its senate of cigar-smoking men gathered for coffee at La Carreta, debating how Cuba was lost, again; and without its ladies in curlers and old men in straw hats leaning on canes at the lonely bus stops. This empty Miami felt like an unfinished canvas. There was no honking as we sped down U.S. 1. No line at the Rickenbacker tollbooth. No windsurfers gliding on the bay. No cyclists pedaling through the thicket of sea grape trees lining the causeway. No traffic through the business district of Key Biscayne ending at the beach park entrance. The park ranger in his starchy uniform peered into the car and noticed the swaddled pig in the backseat. "No baby—*es un* pig," my ever-so-frugal Abuela told the ranger, making sure he wouldn't mistakenly charge us for six people instead of five. "Yes, ma'am—sure is," the ranger said, cracking a smile under the shadow of his Stetson hat.

As we passed the WELCOME TO BILL BAGGS STATE PARK sign, I thought, just who was Bill Baggs: A general? A U.S. president I'd never heard of? Had he owned this land once? I wondered, the way I often wondered about José Martí and Máximo Gómez—and all the other names from Cuban history that were just as vague to me as the American ones. I always seemed lost between the two, Cuba and

America, unlike my parents and grandparents, who were grounded in Cuba, their beloved *patria*. To them Bill Baggs was just something else in *Inglish* that had nothing to do with them, two words they could at best only mispronounce. *"Bil-Bá, Bil-Bá, Bil-Bá,"* Abuelo repeated incessantly, just like he did every Sunday as we passed the sign, to amuse himself and us. That summer he had started calling the park *El Farito—The Little Lighthouse—*after the not-so-small lighthouse that stood, towering above the Australian pines, at the end of the cape. And the name stuck. El Farito became *our* family's park. The beach became *our* beach, and the sun, *our* sun, beginning to stream through the tasseled pines flickering shadows over *our* road as we drove into *our* lot, and parked in *our* usual spot by the rusty bicycle rack.

Mamá was the first one out of the car. From her tote, she pulled out several strips of an old yellow towel she had torn up, and tied one of them around the car antenna. That was the rule: Whichever family arrived at El Farito first had to leave a trail of markers to the campsite so that the other families could follow. She tied a few strips on branches as we made our way through the sandy paths in search of a place to set up camp for the day. We schlepped around for twenty minutes, Mamá hacking away stray branches with her mini machete to clear the way. Finally she stopped and declared: *"¡Aquí—perfecto!* You see, *gracias a Dios* I got us here early." She thanked God and commended herself for finding a clearing that met the other rule: plenty of shade and at least two picnic tables, which she sprinkled with the holy water from her tote, mumbling a few prayerful words.

After blessing the picnic tables, she unpacked the paper plates, cups, and plastic utensils; laid out all the covered dishes; and then ordered us to arrange the beach chairs in a circle and find a good spot for the hammock. I had to slip away. "Ricardo? Ricardo! Ricardo de

Jesús!" she called after me. I kept on walking through the labyrinth of sea grape trees, until I reached the beach, still empty and quiet at that hour. As I strolled along the shore, the seconds between the waves felt like the sluggish heartbeats of the sea slowly coming to life. I became conscious of my feet stamping the sand—step, step, step—as I walked around the big bend where the lighthouse came into view—step, step—each step a question: Who was Ariel Jimenez? Would he show up today? Who was Ricardo Blanco? Would I be an architect? Would I be a husband and father, or would I grow up to love men as Abuela feared? I dove into the ocean, swam eyes-open underwater, fast and hard until I had to come up for air. Heart thumping, I floated on my back and stared straight up at the clouds as they changed their shapes, continuously becoming something new.

The sound of salsa—congas, trumpets, flutes—grew louder and louder as I left the beach and headed toward my family. The party was in full swing when I arrived. My cousin Danita was stepping side to side and back and forth, swaying her wide hips like a cabaret girl at El Tropicana, as she claimed she had *almost* been once, when she was "a little less heavy." But judging from the sight of her corpulent torso stuffed into a one-piece swimsuit, it was hard to imagine her ever being svelte enough to be a dancer. Regardless, she *did* catch every beat. She grabbed my wrist and tried to pull me in to dance with her, but I squirmed away, complaining I was tired from swimming. Salsa just wasn't cool—that was what all *los viejos* danced. And besides, despite dancing at Deycita's *Quinces*, and all the times I'd danced with my *tías*, I still hadn't learned how to salsa very well.

I spotted *tío* Pepé setting up the domino table and went over to help him. Ten in the morning, and he was probably on his fifth

Schlitz, cussing like a madman because he couldn't keep the table from wobbling. I found a couple bottle caps and wedged them under one of the legs to steady the table. He called me a genius, and to show his appreciation he handed me one of his *butifarras*, homemade Cuban sausages that he was grilling on a hibachi. "*Ay*, Pepé, your sausage is so big and juicy," Cousin Danita teased him, the first of many sexual double entendres to follow throughout the day, from women and men alike.

"*Mira, al fin*—he came!" Mamá shouted when she spotted Ariel walking toward us through the pine trees. I thought about running up to him and greeting him with a bear hug, but I played it cool, eyeing him cautiously from a distance. Dressed like an old Cuban man from the waist up, he wore a V-neck T-shirt that showed off the San Lázaro medallion nestled in his hairy chest. But his cutoff jean shorts, tight around his thighs, were certainly not old-school Cuban. Neither was Yakson, trotting and panting off-leash alongside him. They were an odd couple: the bug-eyed pug seemed even homelier and pudgier beside Ariel's statuesque build and machoness, though both had a peculiar gait. Ariel was slightly bowlegged, which I found oddly attractive—his thick, stout calves helped disguise the fact. And both were affectionate: Yakson licking everyone's sandal-exposed toes as Ariel shook hands enthusiastically with all the men as if they were *his* relatives. The women giggled as he charmed them with hello kisses and compliments, addressing even the fifty-something ladies as *señoritas*.

Yakson dashed toward me, and Ariel came after him. I wondered if Ariel had shown up just because of his affection for Mamá, or if he also wanted to see me again. "*¡Primo!* Good to see you, *broder*," he said warmly. His teeth reminded me of Chiclets—perfectly white and square and glossy. Knowing what to expect, I didn't resist his hug. I hugged him right back, felt his ribs and chest against mine. "Man, you look like a movie star! Those must have cost you *un ojo*," he said, referring to my Ray-Ban sunglasses that he playfully pulled off my head and put on himself. "No, you're the movie star, *primo*," I teased back. "No way, *'mano*, Yakson here is the real star." Ariel laughed as he tried to put the sunglasses on the dog, speaking to him in baby talk: "You love me, don't you? *Sí-sí-sí*. You love me, *¿verdad?* I know Yakson, I know." I asked about Yakson as the dog licked Ariel's strong, fleshy hands. They were also delicate, with perfectly kept fingernails, each lunule like a crescent moon in a fairy tale. "He was a stray . . ." Ariel explained, " . . . ran right up to me at third base in the middle of baseball practice at school. Can you believe that, *primo? Así fue.* So I named him Yakson—you know, like Reggie Yakson—you know—from *los* New York *Yanquis*."

The mystery of the dog's name was solved, though I didn't follow baseball, or any sport for that matter. "So what school do you go to?" I asked. "Hialeah High—it's killer there, *primo*, I love it," he said. I had never heard anyone use "killer" and *"primo"* in the same sentence. As if reading each other's minds, we both sat down at the same time, face-to-face at a picnic table crowded with platters of *pastelitos*, *butifarras*, and *tía* Gloria's famous pimiento *bocaditos*, which I nibbled at as we talked. "But Hialeah High is *so* Cuban. How could you like it there?" I asked, knowing that Hialeah was known as a school full of Marielito refugees. "Yeah, *primo*, that's *why* I love it— feels like I never left Cuba. You know it's not easy fitting in when you come over like I did, *broder*. I am a *cubanaso*, man—those are *mi gente*," he said, striking his fist against his heart.

"So how come you like Alphaville so much? That's not very *cubanaso*," I said. "What do you mean, *primo*? I like what I like, bro— and I love *el* New Wave. Don't you?" "Yeah, that's cool. I'm into

New Wave too, bro," I said. We spent a good hour comparing our favorite bands—Adam Ant, Bronski Beat, Blondie. It was obvious that he loved music, and he seemed to know more about it than I did. I supposed there was nothing *wrong* with a *cubanaso* liking New Wave, or wearing puka shells, or loving a pug. I had never met anyone quite like him, but maybe there was nothing to figure out. If I had been born and raised in Cuba, maybe I'd be a lot like Ariel, I thought, as he went on quoting album titles and band members' names, lyrics, and chart ratings. "We should go to a concert sometime," I suggested. "I think Depeche Mode is coming to town soon." "Yeah, I can take us anytime, *primo*," he said. "Anytime."

"You got a girlfriend?" I asked, feeling I had to change the subject again. "No. I just broke up with my girl," he explained, "*Tremenda mujerona*, but man what a pain. Wouldn't let me do nothing, *broder*, wanted me to call her like every five seconds. I had to let that shit go, you know what I mean?" "Yeah, *broder*," I played along, answering in his Spanglish. He asked me the same question: "No—no girlfriend," I told him, and left it at that. "*Mentira*," he said, "all these *cubanitas* in Miami must be crazy for you, *primo;* they love gringos like you." I never thought of myself as a gringo, though sometimes I wished I were. Feeling a bit taunted, I asked him what he meant, and he explained: "Nothing, *primo, te estoy jodiendo*. It's just that—you know—you grew up here. Cuban girls like that. You know good English, you go to a nice private school—you're different, man. You're not a New Wave *cubanaso*, like me." He laughed, but there was a certain mellowness in his eyes, his face. Unlike the rest of my family, Ariel seemed to admire me, my gringoness.

"Close your eyes, *primo*," Ariel said. "What? No way!" I protested, but he insisted. "Come on. *Anda*, what are you afraid of, *primo*? I'm not going to do anything—don't be a chicken." He egged me on until I closed my eyes—against my better judgment. In a flash I felt something creamy all over my lips and chin. I opened my eyes to realize he had smeared one of *tía* Gloria's *bocaditos* all over my face. "*¡Cabrón!*" I shouted, and reached for a *bocadito* to get my revenge. But before I could, he took off laughing and shouting, "No! No, *primo*! No!" I chased him through the camp, onto the beach, and lunged into the water after him. He was fast, but I caught up, jumped on his back, and crammed the *bocadito* in his mouth. "How do you like it, *cubanaso*?," I teased him, both of us laughing and panting and splashing each other.

We took off our soaked T-shirts and rinsed our faces. "Keep on eating those *bocaditos* and you'll lose that beautiful body of yours," he said, wiping my chin clean with his thumb, standing inches away from me, his eyes the exact blue-green of the sea, the fine hairs on his chest matted against his wet skin. No man's touch had ever felt like that; no man had called me beautiful like that. I tried not to feel what I knew I was feeling, or want what I knew I was wanting. "*Gracias*. You too, *broder*," I said, lowering my eyes, not knowing what else to say or do. Ariel didn't respond. He stared off into the ocean for a moment, his eyes as frozen and lifeless as *el lechón's* had been. His playful mood had changed. He became agitated and nervous, repeating, "*Vamos. Vamos.* Let's go. I don't like being in the water too much. We need to get back." I wondered if it was something I had said, or hadn't said, as we plodded through the water toward the shore.

We made our way back to the camp where the men had crowded into a clearing a few yards away from the picnic tables. They were downing Budweisers and shouting playful insults at each other while arguing about how to cook the piglet in something called a *caja china*, which literally meant "Chinese box." Why not a *caja cubana?*

I thought. The closest anyone in my family had been to China was Kim's Palace in Güecheste. I asked Ariel what it was. "You really don't know? *Primo,* you don't know anything," he said. I shook my head. "It's the old Cuban way of roasting pigs in a pit in the ground. You'll see," he said.

Mamá called the men a bunch of useless drunks. "*Esos borrachos* won't listen to me," she said, and asked Ariel to intervene. "Maybe they'll listen to you." Ariel broke into the crowd, raising his voice above the other men: "*¿Eh, qué pasa aquí, cojones?* You *viejos* have been away from Cuba so long you forgot how to cook *un lechón? Qué pena,*" he teased them. The men admitted it had been a while since any of them had roasted a pig, and complained that the sandy soil kept caving in around the edges. They had to keep digging and digging. By the time Ariel stepped in, the pit had grown to over five feet wide. "Are you going to roast an elephant or a pig?" Ariel continued the banter. The guy who moments ago had touched my face and called me beautiful was suddenly an old-school Cuban just like my father and my *tíos,* the men bantering back at him. "*Mira, mojoncito,* why don't you go help the women?," *tío* Mauricio told him, but Ariel remained cool and confident. He grabbed the shovel out of *tío* Pepé's hands. "Be careful, *señorito,* you might break a sweat," Pepé said, and took a swig from his beer.

"Come on, *primo,* let's show these *viejos* how it's done," Ariel said. "No way—I don't know what to do," I objected, but he assured me it was no big deal. Following his lead, we snapped a few branches and gathered some stones. I placed them around the edges of the pit, working on my hands and knees while he shoveled and shoveled. Drops of his sweat rolled down his spine and shoulders, falling on the ground and on me. As the pit took shape, the remarks from the old men turned into praise: *Mira qué bien. ¡Eres un bárbaro! La verdad que sabe*. After we lined the pit with banana tree leaves, Papá and *tío* Mauricio carried the pig over in the roasting pan, removed the blanket, and set it down in the pit. We slid another, larger pan over the top of the pit, filled it with briquettes, and lit them up. Applause and pats on Ariel's back—and mine—followed as we wiped our hands on our shorts, taking it all in. Ariel dared to pull two Budweisers out of the cooler and handed me one. "Now that's a *caja china, primo. Salud*," he cheered and we clinked our cans together. "You mean a *Cuban box*, right?" I joked, and he laughed with his whole body, though not with his eyes, which he kept sternly fixed on mine.

Papá gave us a sidelong glance, but I supposed he figured we had earned a break and said nothing about us drinking beer, or anything else he might have noticed. Instead, he called us over to join the rest of the men: *tío* Pepé, who had worn the same pair of Groucho Marx glasses since I was a kid; *tío* Regino with his thick yellow toenails and ear hair; Abuelo in swim trunks and the oxfords he wore even to the beach; my oldest cousin, Pablo, still a single *solterón* at age forty-something; and *tío* Pipo from the bodega, stuck in the fifties with his Elvis hairdo and a paunch spilling over his spandex shorts. Papá planted his bottle of Pinch whiskey in the sand and they gathered in a ring of lawn chairs around the roasting pig, taking turns engaging in their usual conversation: *Cuba was* un paraíso; *I had to leave everything to Castro* ese hijo de puta. La Revolución *ruined everything—I heard they can't even make enough sugar anymore! I won't visit* mi familia—qué va—*not until that bastard Castro is good and dead.*

As usual, I had nothing to add on the topic of Cuba, but Ariel did. He broke into the conversation: "*Bueno, Cuba siempre será Cuba,* Cuba will always be Cuba, and Cubans will always be Cuban," he said boldly, taking a swig of his second beer. There was a pause as the roundtable of men assessed the boy who had showed them how to build a *caja china*. "*¡Coño, verdad!* You were raised in Cuba," Papá acknowledged Ariel, then asked him, "Where are you from?" "*Bueno,* I was born in Cienfuegos but we moved to Palmira, and then to Hormiguero when I was nine," he answered. The focus and tone of the conversation changed immediately. "*¿Mentira?* I was the book-keeper at the sugar mill in Hormiguero," Papá said. "Does *el viejo* Antonio still work there? Is he still alive?" Ariel paused before an-swering, "*Sí, sí, claro,* I remember him. He used to play *dominó* with my father all the time. He was alive when I left." Then Abuelo asked, "What about my old *casita*? The one on the road to *la loma,* with the white brick and Spanish tile? Is it still there?" "Yes, *la casa* right across from the old Ramirez farm. *Mi primo* Elio and his *familia* live there now," Ariel said, a bit surprised himself: "*¡Qué cosa!* I didn't know that was your house."

One by one, the men asked Ariel what he knew of their homes and the places they had left behind: the old schoolhouse with the leaky tin roof, Chilo's Bakery next to the sugar mill, the *club juvenil* where many of them had met their wives as teenagers dancing *danzón* under the stars. They asked about old friends with whom they had drunk and sung *décimas,* about neighbors who watched their children, schoolteachers who had spanked them, grocers who had let them buy on credit when times got tough. They asked if the sugarcane fields still looked the same, if the mangos still tasted as sweet, if the palm trees were still as beautiful. But mostly, they asked about family they hadn't seen in years, and would perhaps never see again. "Do you know *mi madre*, Conchita Vazquez? She lives in Palmira, on the street where the old train station was?" *tío* Pepé asked. "I haven't seen her in fifteen years. She says she's fine in her letters, but I don't know." He took off his Groucho Marx glasses and pinched his eyes to keep from crying. Ariel said, "*¡Sí!* She used to trade her homemade *dulces* for rice with my mother. I'd see her once or twice a week. She looked fine, just fine."

For years I had heard of these people and places, but they had never seemed quite as real as they did that afternoon. Listening to Ariel made everything and everyone come to life. Through him, they weren't simply vague stories told by old, weepy men. "*Oye,* Ariel, what about my parents' old house by the reservoir? Is it still there?" I asked him, as if I had lived there and remembered it, as if it were me dressed in a cowboy outfit, sitting on a porch swing, and not my brother, in the old photo on our coffee table. Ariel knew the house, but said he thought it had been torn down. Papá's eyes grew heavy: "*¿De verdad? No . . .*" I grew jealous of Ariel. He knew—saw, touched, smelled—so much that I never had; he could love and understand my family and their country in a way that I probably never could. I didn't know where Hormiguero or Palmira were, what sugarcane fields looked like, or my other grandmother's name—and I had never bothered to ask. Why?

"*Oye, el lechón,*" Ariel said, calling us back from Cuba to the pines of El Farito and the pig roasting in the *caja china*. It took six of us to slide off the top pan, full of red-hot coals. The women watched the spectacle, everyone oohing and aahing, praising Ariel as *un bárbaro,* and the pig as *beautiful*. Everyone except me. The pig looked even more ghastly than it had before: seared holes were all that was left of its eyes; and its charred face was fixed in an expression of agony as if it had been burned alive. How could *this* be *beautiful*? But I thought about *tío* Mauricio's stories about his farm in Cuba, and how Abuelo once wanted to raise a pig in our backyard. Suddenly it made sense, and it was so obvious. They didn't mean *beautiful* as in *pretty* or *gorgeous,* or in the way Ariel was beautiful. The pig was *beautiful* not because of how it looked, but because of what it meant.

It reminded them of who they were—*cubanos, siempre*, always, as Ariel had said, no matter where they lived, no matter how many years had passed or how old they had become.

After we checked on the pig, cousin Danita pranced over, her boom box blaring. *"¡A bailar!"* she shouted, and grabbed *tío* Mauricio by the hips, giving him a quick slap across his butt. Like a whipped horse, he knew exactly what to do and stepped right into rhythm, starting a conga line: one-two-three—four, one-two-three—four, one-two-three—four. One by one, everyone joined in, even Yakson barking as he followed Ariel around. Everyone, that is, except *tía* Mirta, who'd had bunion surgery a week before, and me, embarrassed that I wouldn't be able to follow the steps. *Tía* Susana, Cousin Danita, Mamá, even Abuela tried to pull me out of my chair and into the dance, but I squirmed away each time. Then Ariel circled around, yelling above the music, "Come on, *primo*!" He cuffed his hand around my wrist, flinging me into the line, sandwiching me between him and *tía* Susana, breaking the order of boy-girl, boy-girl, boy-girl. I stumbled at first, distracted by the warm, strong hold of Ariel's hands on my hips, nudging me left one-two-three—four, and right one-two-three—four. But I picked up the rhythm and then, Ricardo Blanco was one with them—kicking up sand, dancing barefoot under the pines of El Farito, one-two-three—four, while *el lechón* roasted to perfection.

After everyone got congaed out, Cousin Danita switched to salsa, and the crowd revived. Danita was as good a dancer as Ariel— and together they became a sensation. We formed a dance circle around them, their bodies moving in perfect synchronicity, shadows of one another. They twirled and twisted, swayed and swept, each move recorded in the sand, an abstract drawing of the dance. Watching Ariel shimmy his shoulders and gyrate his hips, I couldn't imagine him dancing to *el* New Wave. He still didn't quite make sense to me, but what he had said earlier in the day did make sense: *I like what I like . . . I like what I like.* Possessed by those words and the music, I lunged into the circle and cut in on him and Danita, taking her into my arms as if I knew exactly what to do. I must've looked like a fool, but *I like what I like . . . I like what I like.* Good thing Danita took the male lead, placing one hand on my hip, the other on the center of my back, guiding my every move.

Ariel, pretending he was mad with jealousy, playfully tried to cut back in. I wouldn't let him. But when I finally did, instead of whisking Cousin Danita away, he took me and began twirling me around. "*Así mismo,* Ariel. Show Riqui how it's done. You make a beautiful couple," Danita said, and the crowd roared, so amused by his antics that I had to play along. Exaggerating our steps and pretending to fight over who should lead, we clowned around inside the dance circle. "Look, I've turned *el gringo* into *un cubanaso!*" Ariel shouted.

Slowly the dance floor thinned out. The women, who seemed to never drink or sleep much, sat at the picnic tables to chat. But the men, who'd had one too many beers, were ready for a late-afternoon nap. Ariel collapsed into a lounge chair, and I nested in a hammock. Peeking through the hammock's netting, I spied on him—his eyes closed, his mouth slightly open, his chest rising and falling. I watched squirrels scurry over the gnarled branches of the sea grape trees. I listened to the faint sound of the distant waves and my own close breaths until I fell asleep.

Everyone woke up to the sound of *tío* Pepé yelling: "*¡El lechón! ¡Coño, el lechón!*" Papá rushed over and poured a beer over the coals. Ariel and I helped him slide off the top pan as everyone looked on. I was no expert, but judging from the charred tips of its ears and snout, the pig was overdone. Still, no one said a word about the *beautiful* pig as we carried it over to the picnic table. *Tío* Mauricio took off his straw hat and placed it on the pig's head. *"Mira,* he looks like *un guajiro* from Pinar del Río," he joked. Ariel asked for a puff of my *abuelo's* cigar and instead stuck it in the pig's charred snout. *Tío* Pepé took off his Groucho Marx glasses and put them on the pig with no eyes. *"Mira*—it looks just like you, Pepé—when you were younger and better looking," *tío* Mauricio teased. The pig did bear an eerie resemblance to Pepé, but more so it reminded me of one of the bizarre Santería deities that *tía* Irma kept in her bedroom. *"San Lechón del Farito,"* I blurted out, and to my surprise the crowd laughed, taken by my unwittingly witty remark. Maybe I *was* one of them—a *cubanaso!*

Mamá, however, was not as amused: *"Qué come bola.* Now stop fooling around," she interrupted the blasphemy, holding an eight-inch knife. She handed it to me and ordered me to carve the pig. "I don't know what to do," I complained, but she insisted. "I'll help the little gringo," Ariel said, but really it was I who ended up helping him. I couldn't look at the pig's face when Ariel cut off its ears and handed them to Mamá so she could raffle them. She had everyone guess a number from one to twenty she'd written on a scrap of paper. Abuela's guess was right on at sixteen; she got one ear, and *tío* Pepé got the other for guessing fourteen. Next we broke through the bones; the warm pig still felt alive in my hands as I helped Ariel crack off the ribs. He then carved thick slices of pork, which I served on loaves of Cuban bread loaded with raw onions and doused with more *mojo.* Before we dug in, Mamá asked everyone to bow their heads in prayer: *"El Señor es mi pastor . . ."* she began, then asked God to keep watch over those still in Cuba, and gave thanks for keeping all of us safe, able to share another Sunday together. Then she finished with, "But most of all, *gracias* to *San Lechón del Farito,"* as she sprinkled the pig carcass with holy water.

Cousin Danita cranked her boom box back up and the party continued. The consensus was that the pork was absolutely perfect: not too dry, not too soggy; not overdone or undercooked. Mamá glowed. Even Yakson couldn't get enough of the scraps Ariel and I fed him under the table. "Looks like *San Lechón* couldn't save himself," Ariel said, shooing away the flies that buzzed around the carcass as we finished our sandwiches. "*Oye*, why do they call this place El Farito anyway?" he asked me. I explained how no one could pronounce "Bill Baggs" and how my *abuelo* had started calling it El Farito after the lighthouse. Ariel's eyes suddenly grew wide: "*¿De verdad?* A lighthouse? Where? Let's go, take me!" he pleaded, turning into a little boy despite the five o'clock shadow sprouting over his chiseled jaw and square, dimpled chin. "Yeah, sure, no problem," I said, unsure why he was so excited. We put on our sandals, and he whistled for Yakson. "*Eh*, where are you two going? *Necesitan* toilet paper?" Mamá offered, reaching for her tote.

We headed down the trail, the branches of the Australian pines waltzing in the wind, their needles falling as softly as feathers through the air. Walking side by side, we chatted about high school again, and concerts we had or hadn't been to. But I wanted to know more about his life and Cuba, and asked him how he had learned to dance so well. "*Coño, primo*, remember that I grew up in Cuba," he answered, and so I asked him what that was like. "*Bueno*," he began, "I didn't know how *difícil* things were there until I came over here. I had nothing to compare it to, you know? There was nothing over there—blackouts all the time and most days all we had to eat was bread and *frijoles*, maybe some rice. We had no television—or even a flushing toilet, *broder*. I don't miss any of that *miseria*, but I do miss *mi gente, mi pueblo*. Miami isn't the same—no way—no matter how many Cubans you can fit in here. I'm still *un cubanaso, compadre*—

always will be," he said proudly, yet with a tinge of resignation in his eyes.

Ariel stopped walking, tilted his head back, took a breath, and contemplated the pine trees for a moment. "This place reminds me of *la playa* in Rancho Luna," he began again. "*Puedes creer,* sometimes I wake up in my bed thinking I'm still in Cuba." Surprised by his sudden openness and the fragility in his voice, I began listening intently as he continued: "Weird, *'mano.* Some days, *como que,* I'm nowhere—not really here or there. It's like I'm still somewhere in the middle of that ocean, *primo,* in that boat with all those people crammed shoulder to shoulder. We had to take turns sleeping on the floor. Most of the night we spent standing up. For three days, man— *¡tres días!*" As he spoke, I recalled the photos in the *Miami Herald* that ran for weeks as the Mariel boats arrived loaded with refugees. Grimy babies in their mothers' arms and frail mothers in the arms of their sons. Teary-eyed men and children waving peace signs. So many faces like bouquets of flowers wilted with exhaustion, yet fresh with hope. "It was *de pinga, primo!*" Ariel cursed. "One night the waves were tossing the boat around. I don't remember what happened really, but—*bueno,* forget it, why talk about that," he stifled himself. That same faraway look took over his eyes again. He kept quiet until we cleared the trail and stood in sight of the lighthouse.

"*Caramba*—beautiful!" he said. As with the piglet, I'd never thought of the old lighthouse as *beautiful,* exactly; its once red brick had turned a mute pink, scoured by years of salt-laden wind and rain. "*Coño,* why can't we go inside?" Ariel complained, his fingers hooked into the chain-link fence that surrounded the lighthouse grounds. A NO TRESPASSING sign was posted on the fence, but Ariel was determined. "*Cojones, broder,* we have to get in. Let's try this way," he said. We walked around to the other side, but the fencing continued. We made our way through the thicket of pines toward the beach, then meandered through a maze of sand dunes and sea oats and found a way through. "*Te lo dije.* Come on," Ariel said.

I followed Ariel as he snooped around, checking every door on the lighthouse keeper's cottage—all of them locked or boarded up. "*Primo,* check this out—do this," he said when we reached the base of the lighthouse. Following his instructions, I stood beside him, leaned my body face-first against the lighthouse, and hugged it, my fingertips almost touching his. "Now look straight up," he said. I tilted my head back. The lighthouse seemed a hundred times taller and more massive than it ever had before, and yet it also felt small and vulnerable in my arms, as if *I* were mightier than it. "*Coolísimo,* no?" he said, "I used to do this with my brother Mayito when we were *muchachos* in Cuba. There was *un farito* kind of like this one near Cienfuegos. We went whenever we could catch a ride on one of the farm trucks. We'd spend hours there playing Superman, pretending we could lift the lighthouse from the ground and toss it into the ocean. Do you remember, Mayito?" Ariel asked solemnly, looking up at the sky as if speaking to his brother. He let go of the lighthouse. We walked over to the jetty and sat down, dangling our feet over the water, our thighs almost touching, and our backs warmed by the sun hanging low in the sky, the lighthouse shadow inching out to sea.

It occurred to me that none of the men had bothered asking Ariel what *he* missed about Cuba, who *he* had left behind. "I didn't know you had a brother. Where is he?" I asked him. He picked up Yakson in his arms: "*Sí,* Mayito—he's older than me. A real *cabrón,* but I love him. He stayed in Cuba because he was draft age. They wouldn't let him out. I haven't seen him since we left. I'll never forget his face that day—he wouldn't cry, holding my dog Chulo that I had to leave behind too. *Pero bueno,* I send him money all the time—and we write, but not all the letters make it through. I hope I can go see him when my papers come. *Increíble*, all that trouble to get out of Cuba, and now I can't wait to go back." He had the same timbre in his voice and faraway look in his eyes as I'd seen in the old men that afternoon when they talked about Cuba. Only Ariel was a boy—a man—my age. Could I have been him, had I been born and raised in Cuba? What if I had to get in a boat and leave everything I knew, not knowing whether I'd see my brother again, or my friends, or this light-house, or Ariel? What would I do?

"*¿Y tú?* Don't you have *familia* in Cuba?" Ariel asked. "No," I said. "I mean yeah—all my *tías* and *tíos* on my mom's side—and all their children and grandchildren, I guess." I explained that I had only seen them in photos and didn't even know their names. "So what, *primo*? They're still *familia*. Don't you want to go see them? Don't you want to know where you're from?" Had he asked me that the day before, I would have said no, but since then, I had learned to make *mojo* and roast a pig in a *caja china;* I had congaed and danced salsa with a man; I had held a lighthouse in my arms. "*Sí, claro*. I would like to go someday," I told him. "*Bueno vamos,* come with me when I go see *mi hermano,*" he said, half in jest. I played along: "*Está bien,* I'll go, if you take me." He said he would show me my grandfa-ther's house, then the sugar mill where my father had worked, and he promised to take me to the best beach in Cienfuegos and to *el farito* where he and his brother played.

"Close your eyes," I said. When he refused, I insisted, remind-ing him that I had done the same when he had asked me. He snick-ered, but yielded and shut his eyes. I locked my arm around his: "*¡Vámonos pa' Cuba!*" I shouted, tossing us both into the water, jok-ing that we could swim all the way there, right then. "I'll race you!" he yelled, and started swimming away. "You're going the wrong way, *come bola*," I teased him and started after him, calling out, "*¡Tiburón! ¡Tiburón!* Shark!" Trying to catch him, I grabbed his feet, then his legs, his thighs, nearly pulling off his shorts. He struggled and struggled, but finally stopped and turned around. I was ready to meet his sea-green eyes the way I had wanted to all day long, ready to take his face in my hands and bring him to my lips, ready to press my whole body against his. *I like what I like . . . I like what I like*. But instead, his eyes had become delirious, frozen on the sea again as they had earlier that afternoon. "*Tiburón . . . Tiburón . . .*" he muttered to himself, and then swam frantically back toward the lighthouse. In one swift move he pulled himself out of the water and sat on the jetty again, resting his forehead against his knees and covering his ears with his hands as if to keep from hearing something terrible.

I wasn't sure who Ariel Jimenez was anymore. "*¿Qué te pasa?* What's the matter, Ariel?" I asked, bewildered. He lifted his face and looked at me blankly, helplessly. "*Nada, primo, nada.* I can't . . . I can't get it out of my mind," he whimpered, his eyes now a stormy gray. "Can't get what out of your mind? What are you talking about?" I asked. "It was the railing," he began. "My mother says it was the railing. It broke. I don't remember." He stared out to sea, and continued, "I don't remember. The waves were tossing the boat bad and suddenly I was in the water. It was at night. I couldn't see anything. Just everyone yelling, *swim to the boat . . . over here, Ariel . . . swim to the boat*, but I couldn't. I knew how to swim, *primo*, I knew how to swim, but I couldn't. Then someone threw an old tire tube. I clung to it and they pulled me in. It was horrible—horrible."

"It's okay. Take it easy," I said, trying to comfort him as I realized he was reliving the trauma of falling off the boat on his way from Cuba and nearly drowning. I didn't know what else to say or do except drape my arm loosely around his shoulder. We listened to the screech of the seagulls. For a moment, we were the only two people on earth. He turned his eyes back to me: "I'm sorry, *primo*. I get like that sometimes. It's like I'm there again, drowning. I don't understand," he said. "That's all right. *No te preocupes*—you're here now. *Tranquilo, tranquilo*," I told him. "I'm sorry I pushed you in. I can't imagine going through that shit. It must've been terrible. I think I'd rather stay in Cuba," I said, trying to lighten up the mood. "Yeah, right." He chuckled and picked up Yakson, who started licking the salt off his earlobes. Ariel's eyes returned to their usual sea green. "We should get back," I suggested, and he nodded.

When we stood up, he fell against me, his body trembling a little. All six-plus feet of him, tall and vulnerable as the lighthouse in my arms, our wet and cool bodies casting a single shadow. *Ariel Blanco, Ricardo Jimenez*—we were one: one boy who had almost drowned, one man lost at sea without another man. *José Baggs. Bill Martí*: we were *cubanaso* and gringo, one and the same, with one nameless country for a moment, until we slowly loosened our embrace.

Composing himself, he turned around and rested his gaze on the lighthouse: "Do you think someday we'll get to go inside—climb all the way to the top?" he asked. "I don't know," I said. "Maybe—hope so." We made our way back through the sand dunes and headed down the trail again. Neither of us knew what to say, or understood what had happened, exactly, and we were too young to make sense of it. We let the whispers of the pine trees speak for us as we watched the play of sunlight and shadow flickering on the ground like a silent movie over our feet. Back at the camp, most of the men were knocked out, cocooned in hammocks or draped over lawn chairs, while the women bustled around cleaning up. "*Míralos*," Mamá complained to us, "useless. I *know* you two don't grow up to be like *that*." She guilted us into emptying the coolers and backfilling the hole we had dug for the *caja china*. We carved up the rest of the pig—loose meat and leftover bones that Mamá insisted Ariel take home for his family and Yakson. All packed up, she went around whacking the men on their arms and butts with a spatula: "*¡Levántense, dormilones!* It's time to go! Wake up!"

We trekked back to our cars, the haul a bit lighter than when we had arrived that morning. Mamá untied the yellow markers as we went and stuffed them back into her tote. As usual, the family lingered in the parking lot debating next week's feast, until it was agreed that *tía* Mirta would make her famous oxtail stew, despite her recent bunion surgery. "You're coming next week, *verdad?*" Mamá asked Ariel. "*Sí, sí.* Of course," he said. The crowd began to disperse, leaving me and Ariel standing by his half-gold, half-gray Honda. We hugged and I spoke into his ear, "*Nos vemos* next Sunday." He got into his car and rolled down the window to ask me: "*Oye, primo,* who is this *Bil-Bá* guy anyway?" "Bill Baggs," I corrected him, "I don't know—some *americano,* I guess. With so many Cubans here now, they should just call this place Cubanaso Park," I joked. "*Coño,* gringo, you don't know anything." Ariel laughed, winked, and drove away.

I didn't know yet that Sunday after Sunday would come and go with feast after feast, but Ariel would never return with us to El Farito—the summer would end without his sea-green eyes, his voice, his shadow, or Yakson at his side, and we'd never wrap our arms around the lighthouse or each other again. I didn't know yet that we'd never go to Cuba or to a concert, never ride in his Cuban Cadillac with the windows down, blaring "Forever Young," and never dance together again. I didn't know yet that I'd miss Ariel Jimenez, the boy—*the man*—like someone I had known all my life, left behind in a country far, far away. As I watched his car disappear down the colonnade of pine trees, all I knew was that I wanted to see him again and again and again. Maybe I could admit to him what I couldn't admit to Victor. Maybe Ariel was the same as him, and the same as me. Maybe he would be the one.

"Riqui, *dale mi'jo,* finish loading up the car. We need to leave soon," Mamá said, nudging me from my daydream. Indeed, time to leave, time to jump into *el Malibú* or Julio's Corvette, or my *abuelo's* baby-blue Comet, or a Space Mountain rocket ship, or onto my bike, and ride for years down the road toward all my somedays. Someday to my first love, Carlos, as sexy as Ariel, as wild as Julio, as talented as Victor. His skin will smell of oil paints and seashells. He will draw the ghosts of Cuba haunting us both, and I will give voice to them through the poems he will urge me to write. I'll caress him lying in our bed without shame, feeling as alive as the sun bursting out of the sea in our window every morning. Someday to my *abuela* lying in a hospital bed, her eyes gesturing at the apologies that the tubes down her throat won't allow her to speak. She will squeeze my hand— hard—then slip away softly without a word, and I will let her go. Someday to Misu's last meow and the last story of Cuba my *abuelo* will tell me on the porch the day his heart gives up—the last survivors of the farm I'd longed to re-create in every backyard of my life. Someday to the afternoon Caco will call me about his divorce: *I've never been this alone—never. When are you coming home to Miami?* he'll say, his voice withering over the line. And I will understand what has always made us brothers is not blood, but our love.

"*Vámonos*—everything's ready to go," Papá said. Yes, ready to go and keep going until the night I'd see him alive for the last time, in his bed, a book by Nietzsche in Spanish on the night table, my mother and I holding him as he stared blankly at the ceiling, both of us waiting for him to die, waiting for him to say I love you. I love you. Going until the day I'd return to El Cocuyito twenty years a man, the aisles echoing with Victor's arias and the chorus of the village that made me their prince and loved me before I knew how to love anyone, or myself. Going until the April morning on a plane descending into Havana: the flutter of palm trees miming stories, the turquoise sea lacing the island just as I had imagined it, the red clay of the earth begging my hands to dig into it. I will begin to sob. My mother will give me a tissue and ask me what's wrong. I will tell her, *I am all this—I am all that you are.* Going until I'd climb all the way up inside Cinderella's castle, or reach the top of the lighthouse and see forever, or tip it into the sea and dare to disturb the universe. Going until I'd find an answer for the square root of negative nine—an answer as real as the creases in my palm. Going until I'd hear the mermaids not only sing to me, but carry me away with them to the place where my poems would whisper from.

"*Por favor, Riqui,* hurry up. Here," Mamá said, handing me her *por si las moscas* tote. I stuffed it into the trunk. "It's getting dark," she continued, "*los cocuyos* are coming out already. We can't stay here forever, you know." "I know, Mamá," I said, "I know." Time to go, indeed, time to go.

ABOUT THE AUTHOR

RICHARD BLANCO was born in Madrid in 1968 and immigrated as an infant with his Cuban-exile family to Miami, where he was raised and educated, earning a BS in civil engineering and an MFA in creative writing. An accomplished author, engineer, and educator, Blanco is a Woodrow Wilson Visiting Fellow and has received honorary doctorates from Macalester College, Colby College, and the University of Rhode Island. Following in the footsteps of such great writers as Robert Frost and Maya Angelou, in 2013 Blanco was chosen as the fifth inaugural poet of the United States, becoming the youngest, first Latino, first immigrant, and first gay writer to hold the honor. His prizewinning books include *City of a Hundred Fires, Directions to the Beach of the Dead, Looking for The Gulf Motel,* and *For All of Us, One Today: An Inaugural Poet's Journey.* For more, visit richard-blanco.com.